PLAN OF
St JOHN
N.B.

Scale 500 feet to an Inch
By ROE & COLBY
1875

Pioneer Profiles

Saint John City with Portland Point, 1810

Shown in the foreground are the Simonds house, Fort Howe, the Hazen house, and the Chipman place. (From an original water colour painted by a member of the Hazen family.)

Courtesy of The New Brunswick Museum
Photo by William Hart

PIONEER PROFILES
of New Brunswick Settlers

by
Charlotte Gourlay Robinson

Mika Publishing Company
Belleville, Ontario
1980

ISBN 0-919303-44-7
FC2471.1A1R62   971.5'02'0922   C80-094314-7
F1041.8.R62
Printed and bound in Canada

CONTENTS

FOREWORD

Twenty-five years before the Loyalists landed at Saint John, and well before the first rumblings of discontent erupted into the revolt of the Thirteen Colonies, a happy wedding party at the Manor House of Phillipsburg on the Hudson River was momentarily disconcerted by a prophecy.

There, amidst the sumptuous surroundings of that aristocratic household, appeared a mysterious Indian wrapped in a scarlet blanket. He approached the bride, Mary Phillipse, and uttered this solemn warning: "Your possessions shall pass from you when the Eagle shall despoil the Lion of its mane."

Easy to shrug off in 1758, perhaps, but it proved to be all too accurate in 1783. Mary Phillipse Morris did have her estates confiscated. She was just one of thousands of Loyalist women who had to abandon their homes, give up almost everything they had, and work hard — often desperately hard — to build a new life elsewhere.

Sadness is inescapable in telling the stories of Mary Phillipse, her sister Susanna, and nineteen other "Petticoat Pioneers" whose adventures have been so painstakingly researched and presented to us in this book by Charlotte Robinson. Yet throughout the saga of privation and suffering run bright threads of courage, determination and indomitable spirit.

My, they were plucky, these unsung heroines of 200 and more years ago! There was Charity Newton Smith, who foiled a French privateer captain by sewing into her petticoats a small fortune in coins. And Elizabeth Russel, who rescued her small son from Indian target practice. And Elizabeth Innes, who nursed the dying during Saint John's great cholera scourge of 1854. And how about Charlotte Haines, surely one of the youngest ever to choose sides in a political issue. At the age of 10, she ran away from her republican father to join her Loyalist uncle.

They were resourceful, too, these women, like Sara Frost, who on the voyage north to Saint John gathered hailstones "as big as ounce balls" off the deck for potable drinking water.

We are indebted to women like Sara Frost for much of our vivid knowledge of what life was like in Loyalist times, for she was one of many who kept diaries and journals of events. We are also indebted to other "Petticoat Pioneers" who made their mark in Saint John, St. Stephen, Campobello, Darling's Island and other southern New Brunswick communities with action as well as writing. Like Ann Mott, who flouted all convention by taking over her husband's printing business on his death and continuing to publish — most successfully — *The Saint John Gazette* and *New Brunswick Advertiser*. Or Ann Mallard, who ran Saint John's first hotel, the Mallard House on King Street. Or Harriet Hunt, who opened a most unusual "Training School for Young Ladies" at which she taught unheard-of subjects like astronomy and — the scandal of it! — physiology.

Yes, these Loyalist women were courageous enough, and proud enough, and ingenious enough, and tough enough — no fewer than five of the twenty-odd who grace these pages lived into their nineties and even beyond — to gratify the most militant feminist of today.

Did I call them "Unsung heroines" a while back? They are unsung no longer, thanks to the dedicated "detective" work and narrative skill of one of their devoted descendants, Charlotte Robinson.

Geoffrey Crowe
Saint John, N.8.
1978

Betsy Quinton

It was a crisp November day. From the chimney of James Christy's farmhouse smoke dissolved slowly in the frosty air, and the lovely New Hampshire hills circled the furrowed fields of the little settlement of Chester in the year 1761.

Inside the farmhouse there was brisk activity. Mrs. Christy and her daughters bustled around turning the spit and stirring puddings while the aroma of roast duck, spiced ham and savory puddings penetrated every corner of the house. It was Betsy's wedding day.

Excitement ran high as everyone made ready for the ceremony. That is everyone except Betsy, who sat up in her bulky feather-bed that morning gazing at her new clothes strewn about the room. Although Betsy had accepted the man her parents favoured and was ready to give her hand in marriage to this well-off suitor, her heart still belonged to Hugh Quinton, a handsome six-footer with merry dark eyes and curly black hair.

Hugh Quinton was away at the wars, however; at least that's what Betsy thought, for she had not heard from him for months. Letters travelled slowly in those days and news of the troops was even slower.

Hugh Quinton was born on the seventh day of November 1741, near Chester in Rockingham County, New Hampshire, where his father had bought land and settled in 1737. At the age of fifteen Hugh enlisted for the Crown Point Expedition. Even in those days compulsory military service was for home defence only. But Muster Captains drummed their way across the countryside enlisting volunteers for the French Wars.

Husky country lads ogled the smart blue jackets and scarlet breeches of the Captain's company. If they followed the drummers they'd see the world and beat the French, that powerful northern enemy of New England settlers. Adventure crooked an enticing finger, so they signed on the dotted line, or, if they couldn't write, an X with a witness' signature was enough and they were in the army! It was a paying business for the Muster Captains too, as they received from three to six dollars for each recruit, and *they* didn't have to fight. It was a good safe occupation, and New Hampshire alone had furnished a regiment of five hundred men for the Crown Point Expedition.

Hugh Quinton had seen service in three campaigns which usually lasted during the summer season, and then had come home to forget the long marches, the French and the Indians, the mosquitoes and disease; to while away the long winter evenings in neighbourhood frolics and card games, and to pay court to vivacious Betsy Christy. Betsy's parents, however, had little use for this handsome adventurer. They wanted more than a carefree wanderer for a son-in-law, for the Christy's had three daughters and no sons to till their long fields in even furrows.

So, this November day was a milestone in the Christy household. From early morning friends arrived; the women riding on pillions behind their men over the narrow roads. While the men tended their horses and stood about in the dooryard talking about crops and cattle with James Christy, the women hurried into the house agog with curiosity since a wedding such as this was indeed an event! In all the excitement, however, no one noticed that Betsy the bride did not appear.

Alone in her room, Betsy put on one petticoat after another. Reluctantly she stepped into her gown and slowly laced the bodice. All the while she was thinking of Hugh, for although she had not heard from him, she would never be able to forget him. With trembling fingers she tied her bonnet strings and peered into the looking glass on the wall. She looked as if in a trance, for it was not her own face she saw, but Hugh's.

Suddenly Betsy was startled by a shower of pebbles against the window panes. She rushed over, threw the window open and from somewhere below came a familiar beloved whistle. Just as she leaned out to look, however, there was a loud thumping at the door.

"Come, come Betsy!" her father called impatiently.

What was she to do? From the other side of the door her father was saying that the bridegroom, minister and guests were waiting.

"Yes, father!" Betsy answered, and for a moment she stood in a daze. Then snatching up her cloak, she dashed toward the window.

Below stood Hugh Quinton with his arms outstretched! In no time he helped Betsy scramble through the window and up on the pillion behind him on the horse he had waiting. Like young Lochinvar who "came out of the West, through all the wide borders his steed was the best". Off they rode to Chester where they were married. When they signed the register that crisp November day, Betsy Quinton contracted for more than the ordinary in the way of life-time adventure.

Hugh Quinton took his bride to his father's home. He was through with soldiering, he had been discharged as sick. Quite likely he had had smallpox which was very prevalent in the army at that time. He had spent some months at Albany, the rendezvous of the colonial troops. Hugh, however, was *not* through with adventure, for that winter he joined Israel Perley's snowshoe expedition to survey the lands on the Saint John River in preparation for a settlement, and Betsy stayed in New Hampshire with Hugh's parents.

Even before 1761 the New England settlers knew about New Brunswick, or Nova Scotia, as it was then called. Some had visited unwillingly as prisoners of the French or Indians. Others had fought with the English at Louisbourg and knew something of this land. Still others in the more peaceful occupation of trading with the Indians brought tales of the wonderful country.

Spring came again to the hills of New Hampshire and Hugh returned. Although the surveyors reported the country was "dreary, forlorn and forbidding, an almost unbroken howling wilderness covered with snow and ice," Hugh didn't tell Betsy that. Instead, he talked of the lovely land where they could make their home, "as fertile as Egypt" and the beautiful river with green forests stretching back unendingly.

With dreams of a bright future, one fine summer day in 1762 Betsy and Hugh rode off to Newburyport, leaving behind them forever their well beloved New Hampshire hills. Betsy's parents had relented and had sent on all her wedding presents, a desk, spinning wheels, and some household furniture, so they started off in high spirits.

Newburyport was thronged that day. There were six vessels sailing; vessels crowded with six hundred settlers. The Quintons were with the Peabody family and Captain Peabody had charge of the fleet.

They were not paupers, those settlers, for they had sold or rented their farms. The decks were piled high with furniture, spinning wheels and farm implements. Captain Peabody even brought the oak frame for his new house, bricks for the chimney, glass for the windows and hinges for the doors. (This house, built at Portland Point on the Saint John River, was the first to be constructed by an Englishman.)

The August heat was intense when the ship's jolly-boats scraped the gravelled shore near the mouth of the river. Betsy Quinton and the Peabody girls were among the first to come ashore. With their wide skirts swinging and swaying they clambered over fallen trees and boulders and struggled through the underbrush making their way towards the ruins of old Fort Frederick, the only cleared spot around the harbour.

They had great difficulty in reaching the ruins of the old Fort for the tidal wave of 1759 had destroyed all the dykes and part of the fort buildings. The Fort itself had been partly burned by raiders in the previous year. In 1760, the soldiers, tired of the monotony of garrison life, had deserted and sailed back to their homes in New England. This left only a handful of men to guard the ancient stronghold.

John Burrel, a sergeant at Fort Frederick, kept a diary from August 3, 1758 to July 23, 1760. He tells it took from July 15, 1759 to January 16, 1760 to get a letter to his wife in New England. "Sunday ye 8th June", he writes, "Rote a letter home," which he sent with "Captain Moses Curtis and one Doble Loon for to convy ye same to my wife at Abington."

To pass the time the soldiers made thousands of pine shingles, and earned extra shillings for themselves. According to Burrel "Friday ye 6th June, Captain Hart Cassel come and we finished off 63 thousand of the shingles and ye Col. paid 173 shillings 5 pence." For amusement, on "Thursday August 30, we killed a bare swimming acrost ye river." And "September 8th, a white moos come down on ye point and we fired on it." Such were the activities of the garrison at Fort Frederick. Small wonder the men deserted!

The prospects were bleak for the New England settlers too. Behind them were their comfortable homes and well-ordered farm lands; ahead, nothing but barren coast and deep forest of an unknown land.

Early sketch plan of Fort Frederick in Saint John Harbour, at the mouth of the Saint John River. *Courtesy of The New Brunswick Museum*
Photo by William Hart

Since there was no choice of accommodation, Betsy Quinton and the other women spent that first night at the Fort rather than stay on the crowded ship.

When the mists cleared and dawn's silver light framed the red cliffs of the opposite shore on the morning of August 28, 1762, Betsy Quinton cradled her newborn son, James, in her arms. He was the first English child to be born at Saint John.

For days pounding and sawing and chopping echoed across Saint John Harbour. Men cut a pathway through the brush and fallen trees. Settlers collected their belongings, piled them in the jolly-boats and brought them ashore. Captain Peabody's New England adventurers took only three days to build his house.

The Quintons, along with the rest of the settlers, started off for Maugerville, some sixty miles up the Saint John River.

Life was hard for these people, but the women were as courageous as the men. The forest fell before the men's axes. Skilled craftsmen built log houses along the river's edge, as much for protection against the Indians and wild animals as for companionship for the settlers. That first winter at Maugerville was terror to the stoutest heart.

The settlers had to travel on foot down the frozen river to the Trading Post for supplies. Sixty miles between sun-up and dusk on a short winter's day was a long journey for even the strongest. Often a man became so exhausted he'd sit down to rest on the hand-sled he was using to haul provisions. Time and again the rest of the party would go on, thinking their companion would follow, but when he didn't, they'd cut switches from bushes along the shore, go back and whip up the exhausted laggard, and finally their half-frozen companion would reach home. A curious entry in David Burpee's account book tells a story in itself. Charged to his brother Edward, November 1776 is "For rum we drank coming up the river, 6 pence". Why was Edward charged for the rum "we" drank? Perhaps it was Edward's turn to treat.

But Maugerville grew as the forest was pushed back, and Betsy Quinton, fearless and high-spirited, was never out of temper. She was too busy. Year by year as her eight children came along, Betsy inscribed each name in the family Bible, brought from New York by Captain James Beatty in his sloop THE MESSENGER. That Bible was a messenger indeed for from it Betsy found time to teach her children as well as the neighbours' how to read and write.

All this time Betsy, like the rest of the Maugerville settlers, had no life of security in her new home. They lived in fear of the Indians and bands of roving soldiers who pillaged the country and destroyed homes. To add to these dangers, privateers who had visited the Saint

John River previously and knew the country, often raided the settlement.

One stormy night in November 1779, Betsy and her family (with the exception of James who was away at sea) had just sat down to supper when there was a frantic knocking at the door. Before Betsy cold open it an excited neighbour dashed in. Breathlessly he told how he had seen a flight of duck rise from the marsh at the river's edge. He went down to see what had disturbed them, and there in the river was a boat-load of men towing a large vessel inshore behind a point of land.

Hugh Quinton calmly laid down his fork and reached for the gun over the fireplace. He didn't wait for supper that night. Hurriedly he gave Betsy instructions, then dashed out into the night followed by his son John.

No sooner had Hugh Quinton and his son John gone, than Betsy and her daughters began dragging out furniture and bedding to hide it in the woods. They couldn't hide it all, however, without arousing suspicion. Back in the house, fearful of what might happen, Betsy snuffed out the candles, then prayerfully waited in the dark.

Shortly soldiers crashed through the door, dashed in and looted the place. By the flickering firelight Betsy and her children were forced to watch their prized possessions tossed into the sacks the soldiers carried.

They tore the brass handles from the desk that Betsy's parents had given her as a wedding gift. They pried mountings from the andirons and fire shovels. They snatched brass candlesticks and clothing. They forced open and ransacked chests of drawers.

When they found Janey's silver teapot (a gift from her brother James, then in London) Janey could stand it no longer. She rushed out screaming at the top of her voice and snatched at the teapot. Back and forth across the room they struggled. Janey hanging on to the spout of her precious teapot, the soldier to the handle.

Janey and her sisters screamed so loudly that they attracted the attention of an officer who came running into the house demanding, "What's this all about?"

Seeing Janey so distressed, he rapped the soldier over the head with his sword. "Let the girl have her teapot," he ordered with a laugh. Janey kept her teapot.

With their sacks full of loot, the raiders left the house. Soon the rattle of rifle shots could be heard from farther down the river where the men of the settlement had gathered. Betsy was afraid they would run out of ammunition, so she dragged out a heavy leather jacket that Hugh had hid under a pile of logs, and filled it with cartridges that had been stowed in the attic. Then she wrapped up some food for the men, and with a stout stick in her hand she set off in the darkness. Running and stumbling over roots and trees, while twigs lashed and cut her face, she reached her husband. Then, with that extra ammunition, the men drove off the invaders.

When Betsy would tell the story of that night she always talked of "Janey's pluck". There was no reference to her struggle through the woods. That was all in a day's work!

The Quinton home was larger than others in Maugerville and was often the centre of community interests. In an old document, Hugh is listed as "Inn Holder" for frequently he furnished lodging and refreshment for travellers. On Sunday June 3, 1770, the first church service was held. On that day Mr. Zephaniah Briggs, Congregationalist from New England, preached to "a large congregation".

In those early communities farm implements were shared by the settlers. Deacon Burpee owned "the irons of a cart and half the woodwork". His share was valued at "2 pounds 10 shillings", but roads were "too bad to use wheels".

When the deacon had no further use for his "beaver hat", it was handed on from son to grandson. No doubt that venerable beaver had figured at church services in New England long before Maugerville was ever thought of.

Some time after the Maugerville raid, Betsy and Hugh moved from their Maugerville home and took up land at Conway, another English settlement then being established across the harbour from Saint John. Here the Quintons carried on their community effort, for the first school in that district was held in their home. The teacher was Solomon Stevens, an old soldier from New Hampshire.

At Conway, one bright spring morning, a handsome soldier in scarlet rode up to the house. He was thirsty, and seeing the women churning, asked for a drink of buttermilk. He decided the buttermilk was good, and the girl who gave it to him very pretty. Back he came the following day for more buttermilk, and the day after that. The sequence lies in a notice in an old newspaper, "March 7, 1788, married, Henry Nase to Jane Quinton". It was Janey of the teapot incident.

But there was always constant fear of Indians. Indians on the warpath are very different from those we see today selling their baskets and mayflowers in our country markets. The Malacites were fierce fighters. Their hunting grounds comprised all of the Saint John River valley from what is now Maine up to the Province of Quebec. Led by their chief, Pierre Tomah, a wiley old warrior and a keen bargainer, they streamed in from the forest ready to drive the white settlers from their homes.

Since the last of the British troops at Fort Frederick had been withdrawn, leaving only one corporal and four men to guard the Fort, the Indians were bolder than ever. In the spring of 1780, six hundred warriors descended on the undefended settlers. They took prisoner the chief traders at Portland Point, Mr. Hazen and Mr. White, but finally the settlers managed to send to Halifax for aid. As a result of this Michael Franklin, Indian Commissioner for Nova Scotia, arranged a pow-wow at Saint John.

In a letter to Chief Tomah he promised gifts from the "Great White Father George", so the Indians settled down to the greatest pow-wow ever held, while they waited for the gifts to arrive.

Hugh Quinton with the other men of the district met the Indians, while Betsy and her daughters waited anxiously at their Conway home.

The long night echoed with the throbbing tomtoms as the Indians danced and howled around their campfires. All night long Betsy and her daughters waited with fear in their faces as the Indian camp fires reddened the skies and reflected far down in the waters of Fundy Bay.

In the morning Betsy saw two vessels sail by. One was the ALBANY, a sloop-of-war from Halifax, bristling with guns. The other was the MENAQUASHA, laden with the promised gifts for the Indians.

Chief Tomah and his braves watched the ships too, then decided perhaps it would be better to talk things over and see what gifts the Great White Father had sent before going to war. The Indians were finally appeased and they wound up the proceedings by going on board the ALBANY and drinking King George's good health in rum.

Each brave was presented with a pound of gunpowder and promised more presents. It was a costly business. Presents and hunting supplies amounted to nearly two thousand dollars. The invoice of that cargo reads like a trading post stock sheet. There were: "50 pairs of blankets, 40 shirts, 1 piece of Blue Stroud, 54 yards Ribbon, 6¾ yards Blue and Scarlet cloth, 100 rings, 200 Flints, 3 Pieces Blue Stroud, 3 pieces White Kersey, 60 milled caps, 40 worsted caps, 50 Castor hats, 2¾ cwt. Shot, 100 yards Embost Serge, 1 barrel Gun Powder, 100 Hoes, 1 cask of wine, sent by Mr. Franklin for the squaws and such men as do not drink Rum". Along with these gifts were axes, pots, kettles and knives thrown in for good measure. One more expensive gift was "A large silver Cross with the figure of our Savior on it".

Then there was Dr. Shannon's account for attending the Indians who had feasted too well, and payment for three beaver traps supposed to have been stolen by the settlers. One Indian, Charles Nocout, was paid ten dollars "to make up for an Englishman's beating of him". Never before or since had there been such a pow-wow! Satisfied, the Indians agreed that now "White man, Indian all one brother". Small wonder that even Indians of today still have a traditionary knowledge of that treaty!

Years afterward, old Chief Tomah met Jesse, Betsy's youngest son, "You Quinton papoose sartin," he said, looking up at the tall dark lad who resembled his father. "Father good man," continued Tomah, "Much me like him."

This, then is the story of Betsy Quinton, the gallant little bride of that band of courageous pioneer women who came to Maugerville with the first English settlers.

Gay little Betsy, eloping with the man she loved. Patient Betsy, teaching the children from her Bible in the farmhouse on the banks of the Saint John River. Brave Betsy, running through the woods to carry ammunition to her husband, doing the hundred and one daily tasks required of a pioneer woman.

And Betsy Quinton lived to be ninety-four years of age.

BIBLIOGRAPHY

From the *Quinton Diary* — Archives Dept., New Brunswick Museum
John Burrel's Diary (A sergeant at Fort Frederick) 1760 — Archives Dept., New Brunswick Museum
Letters by James Simonds, New Brunswick Historical Society, New Brunswick Museum.

Modern day site of Fort Frederick   *Courtesy of The New Brunswick Museum*
Photo by William Hart

Hannah Simonds

In every generation there are Canadian brides with much the same story as that of Hannah Simonds; girls who leave the comfort of good homes and familiar surroundings to face loneliness and an uncertain future in a strange land. But in one point Hannah's story is different, for she was the first bride to come to the Saint John River when Portland Point was only a little outpost in the wilderness between the forest and the sea.

Hannah first saw Portland Point when she was eleven years old and arrived with her father, Captain Francis Peabody. The old Captain was a born adventurer. He'd fought at the siege of Quebec, sailed ships to England and traded with the Indians all along the Atlantic coast, so Hannah was no stranger to forest and sea.

The Peabody family came along with the other two hundred families to take up land at Maugerville on the Saint John River, and Captain Peabody was the agent for the New England Adventurers who came from places along the New England coast, mainly from Massachusetts.

They were a far-sighted lot, these doughty adventurers. The rumblings of the American Revolution were in their ears; and George the third was on the throne in Britain, knowing little and caring less for the troubles of his loyal New England subjects. But now Canada was under British rule and the Government of Nova Scotia wanted new settlers, so these people decided time was ripe to sell out and make their homes elsewhere.

Israel Perley with his band of New Englanders had returned that spring from his famous "Snowshoe Expedition" of 1761, when lands along the Saint John River had been surveyed in preparation for settlement.

It was August 27th, 1762, when the New England Adventurers, "two hundred families, six hundred souls", arrived in five ships, bringing with them their furniture, spinning wheels, farm implements and building material.

Captain Peabody brought an oak frame for his house all the

way from Newburyport, Massachusetts. He had not overlooked glass for the windows, bricks for the chimney, nor latches for the doors, and those adventurers built the Captain's house in three days; the first framed dwelling ever built by English-speaking settlers in the Saint John River.

Here Captain Peabody with his daughters Hannah, Elizabeth and Heprabeth, and his sons Samuel, Francis and Stephen lived for three years. A very convenient location for Captain Peabody who directed the New England Adventurers, for other groups of settlers were on their way to join the two hundred families already located along the Saint John River.

A "Notice" in the *Boston Gazette and News Letter* of September 20th, 1762, reads: "These are to give notice to the signers under Captain Peabody for a township at the Saint John River in Nova Scotia, that they meet at the house of Mr. Daniel Ingall in Andover on Wednesday the 6th day of October next at 1 o'clock P.M. in order to draw their lots, which are already laid out and to choose an agent to go to Halifax in their behalf and also to do any matters and things that shall be thought proper by them. And whereas it was noted at their meeting April 6th, 1762, that each signer should pay 12 shillings to defray the charge for laying out their land and 6 shillings for building a mill thereon, and as some of the signers have neglected payment they must pay the account at the next meeting, or be excluded and others admitted in their place. Signed James Fry, John Farmer, Henry Ingall. Place, Andover, Sept. 2nd, 1762."

The business of settling the Adventurers required Captain Peabody to move to Maugerville where he built another house and cleared his farm. And when the Captain's wife died, fourteen-year-old Hannah took over the housekeeping.

Her sisters were little trouble, they were old enough to be helpful. But when Francis and Stephen slipped out of her sight a chill crept along Hannah's spine. Unfriendly Indians prowled around and the woods were full of wild animals. Then there was the river running swift and deep with logs floating inshore to tempt adventurous five and nine-year-olds.

And as if housework was not enough, Hannah taught the young Peabodys to read and write from the family Bible and an almanac. Determinedly she set the lessons; equally determined, the youngsters invented excuses to postpone them. There was wood to be cut, water pails to fill, or the cow had got loose. Hannah would smile at the sudden interest in chores, but she persevered and when other devices failed, birch rods were plentiful.

Then Samuel would come home from a day in the woods and Hannah, cooking venison for supper, would watch him cleaning his gun by firelight. How handsome he was, thought Hannah, as the youngsters sat beside him plying him with questions. For Samuel knew the habits of every bird and animal and could run a straight line through dense woods when surveying land for the settlers. His exploits are legendary in New Brunswick. We're told that the white-throated song-sparrow, whose high-pitched call is so often heard in New Brunswick's woods is calling for Sam Peabody, Peabody, Peabody. And how he teased Hannah!

When trading vessels from Portland Point sailed up to Mauger-ville with supplies, Samuel quickly chose leather breeches and fear-naught jackets. But thrifty little Hannah pondered long over the bolts of calico, cashmere and stroud. "Aye, choose the crimson," Samuel would say "t'will catch the eye!" And Hannah, clever with her needle, made gowns for herself and her sisters and left-over scraps were dutifully pieced together for quilts; there would be a suitor some day and it was well to be prepared.

Now down at Portland Point where the cold grey tides of Fundy swept the shores, James Simonds had established a Trading Post. The war between Britain and France was over and keen merchants of New England realized there was their chance to trade with settlements in Nova Scotia. This enterprising young man from Haverhill, Massachusetts, had heard the call "go North, young man, go North". James went, and "having in the course of the years 1759, 1760, 1761, and 1762 been at great expense in viewing the different parts of the province of Nova Scotia in order to ascertain the nature of the soil and the value of the land and advantages attached to them with an intention to make choice of a situation", writes cautious James, "and finding there was a large tract of marshland and lands that afforded great quantities of limestone adjacent to the Harbour of Saint John," and having been promised a grant of "5000 acres in whatever part of the country he might choose" by the Government of Nova Scotia, James decided on the Saint John Harbour location.

So in Halifax, February 8, 1764, Montague Wilmot, Lieutenant Governor of Nova Scotia, signed the document, reading "License is hereby granted to James Simonds to occupy a tract or point of land on the north side of St. John's River opposite Fort Frederick, for carrying on a fishery and for burning limestone, the said tract or point of land containing by estimation ten acres."

Ten acres was only a beginning for ambitious James, for before long he secured for his Company some 2000 additional acres "lying to the eastward" where "The Island in Kennebeckatious in front of the tract is included."

James proceeded to organize a company of friends and relatives to "enter upon and pursue with all speed and faithfulness the business of the Cod Fishery, Seine Fishery, Fur Trade, Burning of lime and every other business that shall be thought advantageous to the Company." William Hazen and Leonard Jarvis handled the business at Newburyport, James Simonds and James White the Portland Point Trading Post. Messrs. Simonds and White sailed from Newburyport with thirty workmen on April 10th, 1764, and reached Passamoquoddy on the 14th and the Saint John River on the 18th.

Page from Simonds-Hazen Account Book, 1769-70

Courtesy of The New Brunswick Museum
Photo by Gordon Anderson

James Simonds did not let grass grow under his feet. From Passamoquoddy Bay he writes on August 18, 1764, "The Sloop Batchellor is now ready to sail with 251 quintals of Cod and Pollock of her crews catching." Lime burning was successful too. "I have been to the King's chief mason [in Halifax] and have shown him a sample of our lime; he likes it well and gives me encouragement that he will take all from me that he wants, either for public or private use (he is the only Dealer in lime in town) at a rate that will net at St. John's three dollars or more per H'hd [hogshead]."

The Trading Post furnished supplies to the British Garrison, then quartered at Fort Frederick. Trade increased and Captain Peabody's house at Portland Point was not large enough to cope with the business. "We must have another house with a cellar", James writes. "The latter is now dug and stoned and will keep apples, potatoes and other things that will not bear the frost for a large trade. This building will serve as a house and store and the old store [a log hut 20 x 30 feet] for a Cooper's Shop." The new house 19 x 35' with an additional building 16 x 40' in rough boards was used as a kitchen and shelter for the workmen. "With respect to the Indians' trade," advises James, "it is absolutely necessary to get a license, both for that and selling liquors." Evidently both licenses were granted for they developed a lucrative trade with the "sons of darkness" as James later referred to them, and with good reason.

But all was not fair sailing at Portland Point. "I have long waited with impatience for the arrival of the Sloop with Goods and Stores", James tells his Newburyport partners, "have now given her over for lost." And the wily Indians with huge debts piled up at the Post knew well that James was short on pots and gunpowder, so they held on to their beaver skins and stayed away from Portland Point.

Down at Passamoquoddy conditions were even worse. "They have little or no provisions", writes James, "no hay for the cow" and "she being exceedingly good, shall endeavor to save her life till you can send hay."

The fishermen had no coffee, no molasses, no rum. (They'd been promised five pounds of coffee and a barrel of molasses to every vessel for the fishermen each year.) "We have not had any of these articles, nor any tea except that of the spruce kind for three months past." And at the Trading Post the men were "in low spirits having nothing to eat but Port and Bread and nothing but water to drink."

From the settlements at Maugerville came news of scarcity there. "The people have but little money, their pay must be in Shingles, Clapboards, Rafters, etc., pray send word whether it will do to take such pay for goods."

At Portland Point the partners had bad luck with burning the lime. "The wood being wet as the snow had just left the ground. The piles of wood and stone are now frozen together. [This on the tenth of May!] The Mill could not go before the middle of April and the ice has been continually breaking the dam ever since." But "the want of hogsheads [for the lime and fish] is the greatest difficulty."

James Simonds didn't wait for his hogsheads from Newburyport that year. Instead he went up to Maugerville to get some white and red oak for boards and staves. And he called on Captain Peabody. He spent an evening or two in the tidy home, comparing its comforts with the scarcities at the Trading Post where, until Mr. Hazen had sent some furniture and linens from Newburyport, "truly none was ever so barely furnished and gentility was out of the question."

Now Hannah was a pretty rosy-cheeked young girl when James came along. And as he talked about barrel staves with the Captain and Samuel in the comfortable kitchen, he kept an eye on Hannah as she bustled about preparing supper. The food was well cooked too, the best he had eaten since he left Newburyport and James cleared his platter with more gusto than usual.

That evening as he sat watching Hannah's nimble fingers making a coat for Stephen he enjoyed her bright chatter. For James was lonesome, and although he did not realize it, the ambitious young trader was falling in love.

He forgot all about his barrel staves and went walking with Hannah along the shore. They went out rowing and took a picnic basket filled with Hannah's good cooking. And James remembered that even the Bible said it was not good for man to live alone. So he mustered up his courage and asked Captain Peabody for permission to marry his daughter.

There were no clergymen in New Brunswick then — in fact there was no New Brunswick, it was then the County of Sunbury in the Province of Nova Scotia. So at the end of the summer Hannah and James sailed back to New England, where, with all traditional ceremony they were married at Haverhill, Massachusetts, on November 9th, 1767. James was thirty-two and Hannah just sixteen.

That winter Hannah and James stayed on at Newburyport while capable James White attended to the lime and fish, gunpowder and rum at the Trading Post on Portland Point.

But James was not idle. From morning till night he worked at the firm's warehouses and between-times he rounded up men for lime burning and coopering and fishing for the Saint John River enterprise.

Hannah, left to her own devices, visited with her friends. But she didn't like the way the young matrons of Newburyport stared at her country clothes. And she hated the stuffy houses all sealed up for the winter, but "aired" every morning by a servant carrying a shovelfull of burning coffee from room to room. Hannah longed for the clean sea breezes of Fundy and the freedom of outdoor life.

That winter everyone in Newburyport talked of the Revolution and the hard times to come, so Hannah and James were heartily glad to sail for Saint John on the first spring trip of the company's schooner.

And Captain James Stickney was indeed a proud man when he docked the fishing schooner "Eunice" at Saint John and disembarked, with his other passengers, the first bride to arrive at Portland Point that April day of 1768.

James had built a fine house on the spot where LaTour's Fort had stood when the French owned all the territory of Nova Scotia. And although the tables, bedsteads and stools were made of rough planks, when Hannah unpacked their goods and arranged the shining pewter porringers, mugs and platters on a shelf, she was content.

There was a fine view across the harbour and down the bay from Hannah's windows, and every morning when James went off to the Post, Hannah could hear the drums and bugles of Fort Frederick across the river, and often she would pause in her work to watch the Red-Coats of the British Garrison marching out to drill on the parade ground.

There was plenty of excitement and work. The huge kitchen where she prepared the family's meals also served as a dining room for the workmen. And when Hannah made a pie she used the "bake kettle", a covered iron pot into which she dropped the pie and then placed the kettle in the hot ashes of the fireplace, just guessing when it would be done crusty and brown. There were no oven thermometers in Hannah's day. And every Saturday night Hannah watched the fishing boats come to anchor along the rocky ledges and the fishermen going off to the Post to settle for their week's work.

Often when James posted his ledger in his office he'd have to stop to sharpen his goose-quill pen, or thaw out the frozen ink. But the old ledger is still good reading. They sold everything from mousetraps to boots and razors and looking-glasses, as well as corn meal, axes, pots and trinkets for the Indians. Bills were made out in two currencies, with one column marked I.M., "lawful money of Massachusetts" to distinguish from the pounds, shillings and pence system used in Nova Scotia.

In James's ledger we read that passage by four persons from Portland Point to Newburyport cost "2 pounds 8 shillings," while the freight of "nine heifers" to the same destination was "5 pounds 8 shillings". As long ago as 1769 James Simonds shipped coal mined at Grand Lake (the present Minto Mines) back to his customers at Newburyport. "You have sold the schooner of coals better than we expected", he writes, quite satisfied with the transaction.

But the firm needed "bottoms" for carrying their trade and they began building a schooner. "As Hodge is here and out of employment is very desirous of building the schooner after the most solemn promises of amendment." (Hodge was too fond of rum.) "We have agreed with him to build her for 23¼ currency pr. tun, measuring to the wales [gunwales] and to lay the Deck a foot higher. Have about half Iron enough to build her that came out of the old sloop and if we find the anchor that was lost [when the old sloop sunk in the harbour] we shall have two suitable anchors."

Business had its slumps at Portland Point. In June 1768 James writes, "It rained almost every day of this month" . . . "The whole of the time of burning and drawing the lime" . . . "which has done some damage to the casks that goes in the Sloop." Then: "We have a smaller collection of Furrs this year than last, occasioned by the large Demands of the Priest for his services and his ordering the Indians to leave their hunting a month sooner than usual to keep certain Festivals."

The Indians used the barter system and while their spring beaver was worth $1.66 apiece and a fox pelt brought $2.00, they often wanted more than they had pelts to pay with. So when the pelts ran out they'd leave their medals, charms and bracelets as pledges. Often these were quite valuable. James tells of one bracelet worth four pounds sterling.

"The inhabitants", James laments, "have paid little or nothing of debts this spring" and "the family of new settlers [whose passage had been advanced by the firm] taken in at the Eastward will never be able to pay a farthing." And he adds sadly, as others before and since have done, "we have ever found that ye business for others is an office the most unthankful and equally unprofitable."

All that summer disaster and adversity seemed to dog every step of the way. For, "Leavitt in the 'Polly' has just arrived from Annapolis; he says he had lost a fare of fish for want of sufficient length of cable to ride, and that he must have one by the middle of August or he shall lose one or two fares more at Grand Manana." "Corn that came in the schooner is totally spoiled for any sale."

He begs the Newburyport partners to hurry on barrels and Hogsheads. Although the Cooper Shop at Portland Point was in full swing, "Abbot and Middleton will both do about one man's work and Stevens tho' an industrious peaceable lad had not the experience to make any dispatch at coopering." Grimly he records, "Old Abbot did not do one day's work for sixty days after his wife arrived" and "Stevens went a fishing in the spring of his own accord."

Then to make matters worse, on July 25, 1768, he writes, "The Troops are withdrawn from all the outposts in the Province and sent to Boston to quell the mob. The charge of Fort Frederick is committed to me, which I accepted to prevent another person being appointed who would be a trader. I don't know but I must reside in the Garrison, but the privilege of the fisheries on that side of the River and the use of the King's boats will be more than an equivalent for that inconvenience."

With the Garrison withdrawn there was no protection for Portland Point and no drums, no bugles were heard — no flag flew over the Fort. But the "flags of increase" fluttered on Hannah Simonds' clothesline. For the first of Hannah's fourteen children had arrived.

And at the same time came the American Privateers.

These vessels, manned by ruthless crews, the scrapings of American gutters, were supposed to have Government licenses to capture enemy ships. But they didn't stop at that. With or without their "letters of marque" they raided settlements up and down the Atlantic coast for years. And they paid particular attention to Trading Posts.

For years Hannah Simonds watched Fundy Bay like a hawk. Every time a sail appeared she would round up the children and with a basket of food in one hand and a string of frightened toddlers in the other she'd run for the woods. There were nights of terror when Hannah and the children scuttled to the cellar to hide behind the barrels till morning. And every time James went out to hoe his potatoes he took his musket along.

James appealed to the Government of Nova Scotia for protection, but they had troubles of their own. Entire communities were being raided right under their noses, and the North Atlantic Squadron based at Halifax had more than they could do to patrol every small bay and inlet, so the Privateers, or Pirates, slipped by.

Once the raiders stole the entire cargo from a ship anchored in the Harbour. It was loaded with supplies from Maugerville consigned to the British Garrison in Boston; but they dumped those pigs and cows and crates of hens into their own vessels and sailed away, while James Simonds and his workmen stood helpless on the shore.

Then "Mr. A. Green Crabtree" sailing his armed vessel paid them a visit. He cleaned out the Trading Post like a cyclone, carrying away everything that wasn't nailed down; twenty-one row-boat loads in all, including the Indian pledges. James Simonds was furious, for he never knew when the Indians would arrive with their pelts demanding their charms and bracelets in exchange, and he had to protect his reputation as an honest trader.

The Indians came, but not to trade. Persuaded by American agents, they descended on the settlers at Saint John Harbour and before the traders could summon aid from Halifax, James Simonds was taken prisoner by the Indians. Small wonder that James Simonds complained later, "we had to combat the sons of darkness alone."

Finally James and Hannah could stand it no longer, so they got a "Gondola", piled in bedding and boxes and children and chairs and sailed up the Saint John River to Loder's Creek.

There wasn't a tree cut in that wild country, but James built a log house on the river bank and for seven years Hannah and the children were safe; as safe as they could be with hostile Indians prowling in the woods and winter's blizzards and spring's freshets. Every fresh snowfall showed tracks of wild animals to their very door. Many a winter morning the blankets on their beds were white with frost, and small fingers stiff with the cold, fumbled with buttons.

There wasn't a neighbour for miles in those woods. Was Hannah lonely? She didn't have time to be, and she was a good organizer. All the children had special tasks, while she sewed leather seats in small boys' britches and made "Mother Hubbard" dresses and woolen petticoats for the girls. Then there was the cooking and the children's education, history repeating itself as she used a Prayer Book to teach the young Simonds to read and write.

And that gallant little woman had seven children to care for.

All the years while the Simonds family lived at Loder's Creek, James persistently urged the Government to do something for the protection of the settlers. Finally in the Autumn of 1777, Major Studholme arrived at the Saint John River with "fifty men and four six-pounders." Fort Howe rose on the gray rocks behind the Trading Post, but it was not until 1784 that Hannah Simonds and her children returned to live at Portland Point.

James White, the partner at the Trading Post had gone up to Maugerville just as Simonds had done. He, too, fell in love with one of the Peabody girls and soon another house was built at the Point. Hannah was delighted to have Betsy nearby, for although some of the workmen's wives lived for a time at Portland Point, many were city women, discontented with the lonely life, nagging their men to return to New England; they were always coming and going, never staying long in one place.

But other settlers came. Far-sighted William Hazen had arranged for his house to be built before he left Newburyport, and the first road in the settlement ran between Hannah's home and the Hazen house. Laid out in 1775, and now named Simonds Street, it is the oldest street in Saint John.

One evening in 1830 Hannah and James stood at the window of their home; though streaks of silver showed in her hair, Hannah's cheeks were still like little rosy apples and her eyes sparkled as she chatted with James.

Together they watched the sun scatter jets of flame in the windows where the houses in neat rows edged the streets of the city built by the Loyalists. Across the river to the west the snug homes of Conway were scattered along the shores. And all along the harbour waterfront vessels with furled sails lay at anchor. That day children, grandchildren and great-grandchildren had gathered to celebrate the sixty-third anniversary of Hannah and James' wedding.

Years had passed lightly over the head of the first bride to come to Portland Point. Neither famine nor Indians, blizzards nor Privateers had dampened Hannah's courage and she lived to the ripe old age of ninety-three years.

Only a green mound marks the spot where Hannah Simonds' house stood and every trace of the Trading Post is gone. There are no Indians bartering soft, glistening pelts for guns and kettles and calico and rum now, but oddly enough, just around the corner from the street that bears her name, over the doorways of small shops are signs "Deer Skins Wanted."

Traces of the old Indian Trail may still be seen winding up from the shore of the Saint John River just above the Reversing Falls. Near the New Brunswick Museum it lies hidden under the pavement, but from there the track worn by thousands of naked feet twists down nearby Bentley Street to the Harbour's edge.

And to courageous little Hannah Simonds we owe a debt of gratitude. For Hannah served in an army without banners in that march of progress of pioneer days.

BIBLIOGRAPHY

Genealogy Peabody Family: courtesy W. Howe, Toronto
Advertisements from Boston Gazette and News Letter, Sept. 20, 1762
The Saint John River, by Rev. W.O. Raymond, L.L.D., F.R.C.S.
Edited by Dr. J.C. Webster, C.M.G.
"Letters Written at Saint John by James Simonds 1764, 1765"
    Compiled by Rev. W.O. Raymond, in Collections of the New Brunswick
    Historical Society

Betsy White

That winter of 1770 was the coldest the settlers had known in their eight years at Maugerville. Huge fires blazed day and night in the little log houses strung along the river front, but windows were thick with ice, and frost crackled like pistol shots in the rafters and pencilled the floor boards with icy fingers. But there was no snow.

The men coming home at night from the woods were grave and anxious. They wanted snow. Enough to swirl in banks against their houses and stop the icy draughts through the floors. Enough to cover the trails so they could get out their winter's cut. Even the stoutest oxen could not haul logs over rutted frozen trails, and without boards, rafters and shingles to trade for supplies at Portland Point it would be another year of scarcity for the Maugerville settlers.

But while Betsy White shared their anxiety she hoped their would be no snow, at least for a while. For Betsy wanted to return to Portland Point and the river was the only means of travel. Each morning she woke fearing the river would be blanketed in white. Each night she went to bed satisfied that another zero day had thickened the ice.

The river was safe for travel now and the settlers would go down to Portland Point with their sleds and toboggans to bring up supplies and Betsy White would go along. She wasn't afraid of the cold or the wolves. Her father, Captain Peabody, objected strenuously, her friends said she was daft. But Betsy was determined, for it would be late April before the ice ran out, and she had been away from home long enough.

Betsy White had come to Maugerville late in the fall to visit her father and see how her fourteen-year-old sister Hepsie was getting on with the housekeeping. Then winter closed down with a snap. The little schooner POLLY dared not attempt a trip from Portland Point with supplies, and Betsy knew it was too late to go by horse-back along the trail.

Perhaps it was just as well. For Dr. Phineas Nevers, the only physician in Sunbury County at the time, lived in Maugerville, and

Betsy's son first saw the light of day in the warm little bedroom off the Peabody kitchen.

Two months later on a dark winter morning before the sun was up, a toboggan heaped with robes and blankets waited at the door of the Peabody home. Betsy with young James wrapped in blankets, settled herself on the toboggan, tucked in her wide skirts, put her feet against the hot stones and said goodbye to the family. Then two of her father's trusted Indians fastened the strap of the toboggan on their shoulders and off they padded over those endless miles of white silence.

It was nothing unusual when the fur-laden toboggan drawn by Indians arrived at the Trading Post. But when Betsy, carrying her baby son, scrambled out from beneath the heaped furs, the settlers' astonishment knew no bounds.

It had been an eventful year for Betsy, for when James White came to Maugerville to arrange for timber for the masting business at Portland Point, he followed the pattern set by his partner James Simonds, and fell in love with another Peabody daughter.

James was a handsome broad-shouldered young man who wore his homespun and long stockings with a military air. He had keen blue eyes and fair hair neatly tied with a black ribbon. It was his own hair; others less fortunate who fought at Ticonderoga had left theirs dangling at some Indian's belt. He had served as an Ensign in a "Regiment of Foot", with a commission signed by Governor Sir Francis Bernard of Massachusetts in the days when Boston was loyal to Britain and young men in blue coats and scarlet breeches marched against the French and Indians in the Seven Years War.

When James retired from service at the age of twenty-one, "William Tailer and Samuel Blodgett", merchants of Boston, needing a commissary agreed "that we the said Tailer and Co. do allow him twenty dollars per month as long as said White is in their service at Crown Point as Clark", and James stayed on from September 1761 to 1763. Then he joined James Simonds as a partner at the Portland Point Trading Post.

There is no record of Betsy and James' marriage, for there were no resident clergy in Sunbury County as New Brunswick was then known. Couples either returned to New England for the ceremony as Hannah and James Simonds had done, had no marriage service at all, or made a public covenant before a group who met to worship at one of the Maugerville homes.

An old document dated "Maugerville, Feb. 23, 1766," reads: "In the presence of Almighty God and this congregation Gervas Say and Anna Russell, inhabitants of the above said Tounship, enter into marriage covenant lawfully to dwell together in the fear of God the remaining part of our lives in order to perform all ye duties necessary betwixt husband and wife as witness our hands.

Gervas Say

Anna Russell

Witnesses,- Daniel Palmer, Francis Peabody, Samuel Whitney, Richard Estey, George Hayward, David Palmer, Edward Coye."

Mary Elizabeth White, ca. 1835, daughter of James and Betsy White. Mary Elizabeth married Nathaniel Hubbard DeVerber who became High Sheriff of Queen's County. *Courtesy of The New Brunswick Museum*

It was not until 1774 when the Reverend Seth Noble was appointed pastor and the Maugerville settlers began the building of their Congregational Church that the first Protestant Church was established on the Saint John River.

Down at Portland Point while James White built his house, Betsy and James shared the Simonds' home.

Betsy White and Hannah Simonds weren't the only women at Portland Point. There were workmen's wives living there too. And in 1773 the third Peabody daughter, Hepsibah, married Jonathan Leavit, a captain who sailed the Trading Post vessels and was also a shareholder in the enterprise, and had come to live at Portland Point.

But the workmen's wives were mostly town-bred women always wanting to go back on the next boat to New England. The men didn't care if the harbour was full of alewives and salmon, and fishing was held up for lack of help. They had their snug little huts, drew supplies from the Post's store and stayed home to enjoy watching a woman running the house again and let Simonds and White do the worrying.

The mills suffered too. For there was a grist mill near the present-day Lily Lake and a sawmill on an inlet below Fort Howe, a "tide mill" with its huge wheel turned by the tides of Fundy. Even the weatherman conspired against the partners, who recorded, "The mill could not go before the middle of April and ice has been continually breaking the dam ever since."

But the march of progress went on at Portland Point. Betsy watched the first wharf in Saint John Harbour being built. Over four hundred tons of stones were hauled on drags by plodding oxen and surely but slowly the little pier took shape. Now ships could be safely moored by stout hawsers instead of riding at anchor in the Harbour.

With the wharf completed, the Portland Point partners turned their attention to ship building and all the summer of 1769 caulkers' mallets rang, as on the strip of cobbled beach below the Trading Post rose a trim seventy-ton vessel, the first of many ships to be built at what is now known as 'Straight Shore'.

Late in August the little schooner was ready for launching. And while the workmen clustered together on the shore to celebrate the event with a keg of rum, it was Betsy White who cracked a bottle of Madeira across the ship's stern as THE BETSY slid down the ways to settle in the harbour waters.

James White was a 'natural' when it came to trading; he had quite a system when the Indians came to the Trading Post with their furs. James would put his hand on the weighing scales and say, "Brother, when my hand is on the scales it weighs one pound." Then he'd put his foot on the scales, look the Indian straight in the eye and announce, "Brother, when my foot is on the scales it weighs two pounds." Evidently they were convinced that all was fair and square and they weren't being cheated, for the Indians called James "Kwafeet, the Beaver" because he worked hard at whatever he was doing.

Fur trading was good. In ten years the partners shipped forty thousand beaver skins back to Newburyport. Then, one beaver skin bought fourteen pounds of pork, thirty pounds of flour, or two gallons of rum. Two beavers traded for one large basket, or two yards of stroud, a coarse woolen fabric used for making jackets or blankets.

But the Indians coveted the scarlet, blue and green plush breeches that lay on the Trading Post shelves. Even at a guinea apiece they proudly bore them off to dazzle their fellow tribesmen. Often an entire winter's hunting was traded for a gorgeous gold-laced jacket worth some £3, which later, when worn by those forest-dwellers, proved a marvelous pasture for lice.

When business was over for the day, James White recorded the transactions in neat script in one of the ledgers. There was one each for the Indian trade, business with the white settlers, the Trading Post employees and Garrison supplies. Even Jonathon Eddy, busy stirring up rebellion amongst the Indians, paused long enough in his forays to purchase "22 grindstones" from the Trading Post. At the beginning of the Revolutionary War the rebels expected support from the former New Englanders who settled at Maugerville and Portland Point. And when it was not forthcoming, both Privateers and Indians plundered the settlement all too frequently.

When Captain Eddy and his cohorts returned from an unsuccessful attempt to capture Fort Cumberland, the Portland Point partners were their unwilling hosts for a time, furnishing supplies to prevent Eddy from plundering the settlement. An unpaid account for "41 Spanish milled dollars for value received", drawn on the "Honorable Council of Massachusetts States", was all the partners received for their generosity.

For years Betsy White watched the Indians file down to the Post, with their squaws trailing along behind carrying bundles of furs and cooking pots and papooses. The Indians brought them along to do all the dirty work, and Betsy felt sorry for the poor creatures. She couldn't understand why they had to wait on their lords and masters and then be content to pick up leftover scraps of food after the Indians had finished their meal.

When the Indian children were sick, kind-hearted Betsy tried to help them. But their sores and their lice terrified her. She couldn't bear to bring them into her home, so they squatted around in the dooryard while she prepared poultices and potions. The squaws were suspicious, however, and preferred the weird ritual of their medicine men who danced around the patient squealing incantations to scare away the disease. Finally, James persuaded Betsy that nursing sick Indians was a thankless job and involved too great a risk for her own family. Besides her son James, four girls had followed in quick succession and the White family with their servants was listed as ten persons in the census of 1775 when Portland Point boasted a total population of seventy persons.

It was then the American rebels tried to induce the Portland Point residents to join their cause and when this failed they used every means to incite the Indians to attack the white settlements. With the ever-haunting nightmare of Indian and Privateer raids, some of the Portland Point settlers moved further inland. But not Besty White. James built another house some three miles away at the head of the marsh that the Indians called Seebaskastaggan and with some six hundred acres of lake-like marsh to discourage raiders, Betsy and the children retired to comparative safety.

One morning, however, an Indian, glistening with war paint, strode into the Trading Post and demanded to speak with James. After a few preliminaries he warned James of a surprise attack. "Many canoes, many warriors" were even now on their way down the river. It was a tense situation with Fort Frederick's garrison disbanded and only a handful of men with a few old muskets to defend Portland Point.

James White had been appointed deputy superintendent of Indian Affairs at the Saint John River because of his ability to handle the Indians, and James acted quickly. Hurriedly sending a message to Betsy, James started up the river with a canoe of trinkets. Unarmed, and at the risk of his life, he met the party of some ninety canoes full of painted warriors at Long Reach.

Whether James or the Indians were the more surprised is not recorded, but James certainly did not expect such a flotilla. Pretending he was on a trading venture, he spread out his wares and cautiously began his bargaining. James had not been named "the Beaver" for nothing. All day long he talked with the Chiefs. Finally the peace pipe was passed around, the trinkets distributed, and thankfully James watched the warriors paddle their canoes up the river, back to their encampments. Later on James was rewarded by a grateful Government the vast sum of a dollar a day for his services.

As if Indian raids were not enough to endure, there came to Portland Point the horror of smallpox. There had been a frightful epidemic in New England — rich and poor had contracted the disease, for smallpox was no respector of persons. The more fashionable young ladies often wore small black silk patches to cover the larger scars, but young people with pitted faces were a common sight.

Portland Point up to now had fortunately escaped, but Betsy

was afraid that some sailor coming with the ships would bring the disease. Preventive medicine was practically unknown, but Betsy had heard of the "inoculations" against "pox" as practised by some Boston doctors, which gave a light case and made the patient immune to further contagion.

It took considerable persuasion, but James finally agreed. One day Doctor Ambrose Sherman, a surgeon stationed with the Fort Howe garrison, arrived at the White house. From his little black bag he took clean rags, a small sharp knife and a bottle of "Kine pock" and the entire White family and their two servants were inoculated. The old account book records that Doctor Sherman received £9 for his services. Betsy White was satisfied. The company's ships could come and go but there would be no fear of contracting smallpox from the sailors of the EUNICE or POLLY or PEGGY AND MOLLY.

THE BETSY, which had been launched so ceremoniously on the beach below the Trading Post, after making several successful trips to New England, was sold for £200, and the partners, well satisfied with their venture, began building another ship. A party of rebels from Maine, however, sneaked up the harbour one night and burned the vessel on the stocks.

The workmen gathered in solemn debate as they viewed the charred ruins, but James White, striding down from his office, called cheerfully, "Don't be discouraged boys! Keep up a good heart. Why, ships from England will come here yet." And come they did; but little did those settlers realize that they were pioneers of an industry that led Saint John to be called "The Liverpool of America," and become the fourth largest Port in the British Empire. Later there were dozens of shipyards in and around Saint John; schooners and brigs, cutters and sloops, barques and snows came sliding down the ways to dip their keels in the seven seas.

Old "Sailor John" tells us:
"They built 'em on the beaches and they built 'em in the creeks
They carved her figurehead themselves and fashioned up her sticks
They didn't have no blueprints when they set her up in frame
For her builders they were sailor men what knew the sailin' games."

And from the time of THE BETSY those sailing ships were beautiful, with white canvas spread like gulls' wings and carved figureheads that were works of art. Frequently the figureheads represented the person for whom the ship was named — often a woman's figure with long carved wooden dresses shaken out in graceful folds as if by the wind. In September 1795, William Jackson, ship's carver, advertised his trade inviting business and promising that "with perfect

determination and unwearied strictness to business and by employment and industry, he trusts will rise him above the Frowns of Fortune
and stop the mouth of calumny, which is his ardent wish." Fast
sailers those ships were too. The MARCO POLO, a three-decker 185
feet long, took only fifteen days from Saint John to Liverpool, an
unheard-of record. The keel was laid down at Marsh Creek in Saint
John in 1850. On the stern were two reclining figures of the Venetian
explorer; one as a youth, the other as a man, gazing east and west.
After a long voyage to Australia, when the MARCO POLO averaged
364 miles a day, she lay in Salthouse Dock, Liverpool, with a huge
banner strung between her masts "The fastest ship in the World".

Marco Polo figurehead
Courtesy of The New Brunswick Museum
Photo by William Hart

After thirty-three years of sailing history she piled up in a gale
on Cape Cavendish, Prince Edward Island, and one of the figures of
Marco Polo, rescued from the wreck, now dominates the Marine
Gallery of the New Brunswick Museum in Saint John.

Ship building had its hazards too. In 1835 a ship crowded with
spectators capsized as soon as she struck the water, but the huge
cloaks worn in those days billowed out like life preservers, so no one
was drowned.

Red-hot spikes, used to bore holes, would be dropped accidentally into a pile of shavings and in a moment the whole yard would be

ablaze, and often the ship burned to cinders.

Another time a heavy gale tossed a ship adrift and all the workmen aboard were drowned. Or a ship's staging would collapse taking the men with it and several were killed.

More often than not, rum was more responsible for unsteady footwork than anything else, as no gathering was complete without the "Little Brown Jug" in those early days.

A Notice was posted at Portland Point warning unlicensed taverns which "Publicly forbid any person at this place selling strong liquors under penalty of law, except those who have licence or permits from Authority for that Purpose. Given under my hand at Fort Howe this third day of July 1781. James White, J.P." For James was now a Justice of the Peace and the following year was appointed Collector of Customs, as Saint John had now become a Port of Entry. Twelve vessels of 165 tons cleared the harbour and eleven ships of 144 tons were on the entry list of that first year.

James was a very busy man examining cargo. Perhaps he let the odd keg marked "Fish" slip by, even if it didn't smell fishy, but did gurgle a bit; for he knew if it was good sherry eventually some of it would come his way.

It was Betsy who fed and clothed the children and provided their education. Reading and writing were learned from Betsy's cherished copy of "Watt's Psalms and Hymns", and literature from the Family Bible; for those were the only books she had.

Then one day excitement ran high; twenty ships crowded the harbour and three thousand exiled Loyalists prepared to take up home-sites in the new county. Betsy and the women and children of Portland Point crowded the little wharf, while James White and his son, James, Junior, walked down the path that skirted the rocks of Fort Howe to meet the newcomers. And the epoch of Portland Point was over. Government authorities gave notice that shares in the Townships on the Saint John River and lands held by non-resident grantees were to be forfeited for the accommodation of the Loyalists.

But Betsy White only saw the beginning of the Port City of Saint John, for she died five years after the Loyalists arrived. In a faded old copy of the *ROYAL GAZETTE and NEW BRUNSWICK ADVERTISER* appears a brief notice under the date December 23, 1788: "Died on Thursday last, the Pious Mrs. White, late amiable consort of James White, after a lingering illness of several years which she bore with great fortitude and Christian resignation. On Sunday last her remains attended by a respectable number of friends were interred in a decent Christian manner. These are they which came out of great tribulation and have washed their robes and made them white in the blood of the Lamb."

View of Main Street, Saint John, below cliff

Photo by William Hart

Gone is the drama of Portland Point with its traders and Indians and Privateers and sailing ships. And of Betsy White's house not a trace remains. But Betsy's descendants, scattered to the four corners of the globe, can still recall the stories of her brave journey by toboggan through that icy wilderness with her baby son; and her kindness to the sick little Indian children who gathered in her door yard. And for those whose imagination is touched by things of the past, there is a street in Saint John named Portland in honour of the first English settlement at Saint John Harbour.

On the site of the old tide-mill, where saws whined their plaintive rhythm as logs were sliced into boards and rafters for the trading partners, the modern Union Station stands on Mill street. That narrow path below the cliffs where Fort Howe once perched like an ancient flagpole sitter, is Main street, a traffic artery connecting west and central Saint John. Where the thriving settlement of Portland Point once stood there are streets and houses and wharves and railroad tracks; but there's always an invigorating tang in the sea air where the bright blue waters of Saint John Harbour sparkle in the sun.

BIBLIOGRAPHY

Genealogy of the White Family; Notes from James White's Commission from Governor Sir Francis Bernard, Courtesy Arthur White Howe, Toronto.

St. John's River Day Book 1764, No. I. Archives Department, New Brunswick Museum.

At Portland Point, Reverend W.O. Raymond, LL.D., F.R.S.C., Collections of the New Brunswick Historical Society.

The River Saint John, Reverend W.O. Raymond LL.D., F.R.S.C.

"Sailor John", quoted from *The History of the Ship Building Industry In New Brunswick* by Donald Ross.

Wooden Ships and Iron Men, by F.W. Wallace.

Elizabeth Innes

A Diary, a sampler, a silhouette and a pair of black lace mittens outline the life story of Elizabeth Innes, pioneer Canadian nurse who cared for civilians, soldiers and sailors long before the world had ever heard of Florence Nightingale.

Elizabeth Innes was born in 1786, the daughter of Sergeant John Innes. Innes came from Edinburgh and was stationed with the Fort Howe Garrison, the first battalion Royal Regiment of Artillery (known as the 'Regulars' of the British Imperial Army), one of the early regiments to carry the banner of British protection in the new country. Elizabeth's mother was a Quaker, and her father was one of those who greeted the Loyalists on their arrival in Saint John, in 1783.

From the rockbound fortress at six o'clock each morning came the shrill call of bugles and Elizabeth began another day. Rain or shine, snow or heat, the red-coats tramped out to drill on the steep promenade. After breakfast for Elizabeth, came school. There they'd sit, those children of the Garrison, on the hard pine benches while an old soldier supervised the lessons. Tiny fingers clutched around quill pens, small heads bent over copy books, and woe betide the youngster caught whispering to a classmate. Strict garrison discipline extended to even the youngest, and those were the days when "children were seen and not heard".

But when the noon gun boomed from the fortress, shut went the books; future captains and belles scurried from the classroom. School was out.

School may have been out, but Elizabeth Innes was not free for the day, for like other girls of that period she had household duties to learn. Evidently her Quaker mother believed that good cooks were trained, not born, and Elizabeth spent some time every day in the kitchen. Then there was needlework, not just plain seams and gathers but fine little stitches in exquisite designs. There was a little stool near the window where Elizabeth sat with her mother beside her guiding the small fingers. Here Elizabeth worked her sampler, and if she made a mistake it was ripped out and done over again. Elizabeth worked the letters of the alphabet in brown, blue and red silk and stitched in large letters at the top of her sampler "Elizabeth James, her work, age 8 years 1794." Then she finished the border with a wavy scroll embroidered in light blue.

Perhaps the gay laughter of her lighthearted playmates romping on the promenade disturbed her. Perhaps some of those neat little stitches of red and blue were blurred with tears; and if one looks closely there are tiny brown dots where Elizabeth pricked her finger with the needle (blood spots remain indefinitely), but as she worked on it patiently and carefully Elizabeth never dreamed that over a hundred years later, visitors to the New Brunswick Museum would be fascinated by her neat little stitches on that sampler.

Perhaps after her needlework lesson Elizabeth would play at nursing the sick doll. It would be a little rag or wooden doll; there were no wonderful bisque creations with eyes rolling shut when little mothers rocked them to sleep then; and anyhow, Garrison Sergeants' pay did not permit expensive playthings for their small daughters. But Elizabeth loved her doll and she sewed little bodices and wide skirts and scoop bonnets for it. She even put it to bed in a long 'chemise'.

Page from Elizabeth Innes' letter, August 2, 1838
Courtesy of The New Brunswick Museum
Photo by Gordon Anderson

But that was before Elizabeth wore the black lace mittens and had her 'profile' taken. "Profile Portraits" they were called, and William King, the "Portrait Maker" was in Saint John at the time. Evidently William found it a lucrative business, for he advertised extensively. In the *Royal Gazette and General Intelligencer* of October 3, 1807, we read: "William King, Profile taker requests Ladies and Gentlemen desirous of having their profiles taken correctly to improve this opportunity at his room in the house of John Pugsley, King Street, Prices for 2 profiles on beautiful wove paper is 2s, 6d., or reduced to a very small size for lockets for 5s."

William King catered to the vanity of the Saint John youth, and those not so youthful too — genteel maiden ladies, hook-nosed and thin-lipped; portly dowagers in frilled bonnets and with wattled chins; beefy, bulbous-nosed, thick-necked gentlemen, all had their portraits done by this persuasive artist. It was the fashion.

But Elizabeth Innes' profile portrait in its black oval frame has a fine outline, a sweet, rather old-fashioned primness. Her hair is brushed up in a high coiffure held by an ornament at the back, possibly a shell comb, which was the fashion then. There's a fluffy bow of ribbons at her throat, evidently supporting a locket with perhaps a miniature or a cherished lock of hair.

Saint John was not a dull place in those days in spite of the hardships those pioneers endured. For gentlemen, who had folded up their expensively tailored coats and put them away while they chopped down trees to clear land for their homes, now took them out of those old brass trunks and put on their fine raiment again.

They joined their friends at entertainments; there were gay little supper parties and dancing assemblies in the new city. Ladies in flounces with flowers in their hair graced those assemblies. And Elizabeth in her best blue sprigged muslin with its dozen frills, her hair brushed up in tantalizing little curls, fluttered a fan in her black lace mittened fingers as she listened to the conversation of some bright young gentlemen. Bright and colourful dandies there were too, with their tight breeches, embroidered waistcoats and high collars. And they had plenty of competition for ladies' favours with the scarlet-tunicked soldiers from the garrison. Lilting strains of a Gossec minuet brought dancers on the floor, stepping gracefully, bowing gallantly, and romance blossomed during the intricacies of quadrilles right under the watchful eyes of the ever present chaperone.

Did a gay romance finish up in tears and heartbreak for Elizabeth? Did some tragedy come into Elizabeth's life? (Many were the ships that sailed away with loved ones never to return again.) Or did Elizabeth set too high a standard and the young bloods of the day didn't quite measure up to it? That is Elizabeth's secret, for when she sat down at her little desk, dipped her quill in the inkpot and began her diary she makes no mention of any affair of the heart.

Elizabeth's diary is quite a large book — its pages ruled in pale red ink. Her fine slanting script proclaims she was a painstaking individual, and the contents of her diary proves she was serious-minded. She tells of the arrival and departure of friends and relatives, of fires and accidents. There are records of sermons and their texts. She lists many deaths and tells of the patients she nursed.

There was no training school when Elizabeth began caring for the sick. Nurses worked according to their own ideas and knowledge was picked up by practice — it was as simple as that. One didn't require a college education to learn how to make beds with nicely squared corners. How could one 'square' a featherbed? There were no materia medica classes; no study of toxicology, but instruction was frequently given by individual surgeons when they had time. There were several physicians in Saint John at the time, and of course surgeons were stationed with the Garrison. And all were ready to do business; they'd extract teeth, set bones or amputate a limb at a moment's notice and without the benefit of washing up or other preliminaries. A kitchen table and a few instruments were all that was required. Sterilizing of instruments was unknown then, so germs had their heyday. A surgeon would hang a leash of waxed thread through the buttonhole of his coat, so he wouldn't have to hunt for sutures during the operation. Then he would rummage through the bottles and boxes in his little black bag and produce a bone-handled knife. Some old surgical instruments folded into a case like an ordinary pocket knife. Some had engraved frames. Often an animal's head, or a lady's figure formed the handle, but all were far from being aseptic. There were no face masks; no caps and gowns to make nurse and operator look like ghosts in a graveyard; and the patients kept on most of their clothes, sometimes even their boots. With no anaesthetic, except a stiff hooker of Jamaica Rum to bolster up intestinal fortitude, patients were heroes all. Those were the good old days — it was survival for the fittest.

Elizabeth Innes took risks and endured hardships, for nursing was a hazardous occupation then. Cholera, typhus and smallpox came with the ships, and many an epidemic got its start when a sailor spread disease amongst the crowds at the docks, or at a "Coffee House Bar".

Elizabeth saw the Harbour white with sails in the days when wooden ships made history in Saint John. And for Elizabeth there was adventure in every new call. In her neat gray gown and cap she stepped quietly about darkened rooms making her patients as comfortable as possible with the slim means at her command. Carefully she supported some grizzled head as she held a glass to the lips of some grim old sufferer. Tenderly she held a feverish hand and spoke kindly words of comfort when she knew the worn-out body could not be mended by medicine or food. Grateful patients smiled up at Elizabeth as she smoothed down the humps in those voluminous featherbeds. Stricken households welcomed her as an angel of mercy.

Night after night while candles burned down to the sockets of old silver candlesticks and the wind howled dismal and cold, Elizabeth kept compassionate vigil.

Patiently she bathed some child's burning face and smoothed damp little curls with her gentle hands; and when pathetic wondering eyes were closed she folded the little wax hands before the rough pine coffin enclosed the tiny body. For cholera scourged the city that year of 1854; young and old succumbed to the dread disease. Carpenters couldn't keep up with the demand for coffins. From June till October the cholera raged; only the cold weather drove it out, but the death rate was enormous. And often as the early morning light spread a glistening sheen over the harbour waters, and cartmen rattled their loads along to the wharves, Elizabeth Innes would wend her way homeward to her little house on the "Shore Road in the Parish of Portland."

From inshore boats came the shouts of fishermen bringing in the early morning catch. From her home Elizabeth could watch the small boats being rowed towards the "Trafalgar" and "Waterloo" steps on either side of the Public Landing. Barefoot boys would drag large baskets of fish up the stairs where casks and salt waited to pack the catch. Shoppers with their baskets were already abroad. Shutters were being taken down from shop windows. A group loitered around the "Coffee House" door. It was not quite seven o'clock, but Saint John's business day had begun.

From the windows of her home Elizabeth watched the flames devour the wooden houses of Saint John in the disastrous fire of June 14, 1837. Flaming paper and faggots were carried nine miles from the city by the high wind and one-third of the commercial section of the city was destroyed.

Many were the accidents in those early days, for sailors were careless, jovial fellows fond of visiting the taverns strung along the waterfront. There were no lights or guards of any sort on the wharves, so often a sailor, whose feet just wouldn't behave, missed the last plank and a cry of "Man, over bo-o-a-rd" rent the stillness of the night.

Elizabeth's diary tells that "The bridge below the Falls fell on the 8th of August 1837 at nine o'clock in the morning. There were seven men killed and seven very much hurt by the fall of it."

"The upper stage of Storm's ship fell with four men upon it. All were more or less hurt, some very much hurt indeed."

"Mr. George Smith Briggs fell into the hold of the ship 'Ann Dashwood' on Friday evening the first of September and lingered in great distress until Sunday the 2nd, when he died in consequence of his fall."

"Captain Cordingly, Master of the Bark 'Lord Mulgrave' was

instantly killed on board that vessel on Wednesday morning the 27th of June 1853 by a barrel of pork falling on him accidentally."

Elizabeth keeps up with other events too. "A balloon went up in Saint John on the 10th day of August 1840 at five o'clock in the afternoon."

"The opening of the 'Crystal Palace' in Saint John on the 9th of September 1851 for the show of articles made in New Brunswick of all descriptions, and closed on the 20th of the same month."

Outside the 'Crystal Palace' apple-women shrilled their wares. Perhaps there would be a trained monkey performing in the dusty roadway, or a tame bear lumbering mournfully around his post with his chains rattling, and excited children keeping a respectful distance away. Inside the Palace there were booths all decorated with leaves and greening. When the Band played, their shrill instruments and throbbing drums drowned any attempt at conversation. Ladies in stiff silk gowns and gentlemen in top hats sauntered around admiring the "New Brunswick" handiwork. There'd be children and dogs underfoot and a clatter of voices.

Elizabeth went visiting too. She packed her little horse-hide trunk, put on her shawl and black mittens and was off for the journey: "I went to Kingston on the 2nd of October to Sheriff Drury's and from Kingston to Norton on the 14th of November. Returned home 18th of December 1844." Perhaps this was a social call; again it may have been a professional visit. Elizabeth may have travelled by stagecoach, which left Saint John daily for Cumberland, "Weather permitting", but we don't envy Elizabeth her journey over those rough roads.

And then there were the visitors. "Cousin Betsy Fish arrived here upon a visit the 18th of September from Maguadavic and went away again on the 22nd of the same month 1845. Ruth went home to see her friends at the same time and returned on the 22nd of October."

There are prescriptions in Elizabeth's diary. One directed to be used as a "plaster for a weak joint" contains "Rosin, Sulphur, Beeswax, Castile soap and Lard boiled in half a pint of good spirits until thick enough for spreading".

For Rheumatism, Elizabeth recommends "Beeves' Galls, Camphor, Oil and Turpentine", and last, but not least, "a pint of Jamaica Rum." She does not include directions however. Was it used internally or externally? One guess is as good as another. Perhaps it depended upon the patient's preference for Beeves' Galls, or Jamaica Rum.

Judging by the records in Elizabeth's diary, the Innes' were a long-lived family. "Grand-mother Elizabeth Pratt", she writes, "was born May 1727 and died in 1817 aged ninety-one years." Her father,

"Sergeant John Innes [who welcomed the Loyalists] died on Wednesday the 6th of October 1841 in the ninety-fifth year of his age." And her mother, "Mrs. Elizabeth Innes departed this life on Monday 21st of October 1850 in the 85th year of her age."

Elizabeth Innes, born at Saint John, N.B., 1785

Courtesy of The New Brunswick Museum

And what did the days of her years bring to Elizabeth? The diary does not tell; but a photograph, taken when she was quite an old lady, shows her wearing a tight-bodiced gown and lace cap. She stands in quiet dignity beside an old carved chair and her face is tranquil and kindly. Her strong, capable hands express much character — hands that soothed and comforted through long dark days and nights.

The sampler with, "Elizabeth Innes her work aged 8 years old 1794", done by nimble fingers, when grown-up land seemed so far away, laid in her trunk for years, and, when nursing sick children, Elizabeth would think of the little girl on the stool near the window stitching patiently with brown, blue and red silks — and that sharp needle.

Silhouette and lace mittens joined the sampler in the darkness of the trunk and memories of spring evenings, dancing assemblies, beaux and music came surging back. But Elizabeth had no time for frivolities, there was work to be done. She had chosen her career, this pioneer nurse, who cared for the sick and injured in those early days in Saint John.

BIBLIOGRAPHY

From the *Diary of Elizabeth Innes*, The New Brunswick Museum.
Newspapers in the Archives Dept. — The New Bruncwick Museum.
Early Records of Medicine and Surgery.

Charity Newton

Before the noisy Revolutionists broke up the peace of the New England Colonies, Charity Newton lived in the comfort and plenty of her father's home in Rhode Island. For her father was a wealthy landowner; fields and flocks flourished under his able management. His big house with its gables and porches towered over well-kept lawns and gardens, and his family lived in the elegant eighteenth century manner.

Though Charity and her sisters helped their mother supervise the work in the house, Charity much preferred to ride over the fields and look over the crops with her father rather than do needlework or cooking. She was venturesome, daring and romantic, this daughter of the Newtons, and she attracted adventure as a magnet picks up pins.

Charity enjoyed travelling too. Many were the journeys she took in the family coach to visit friends and attend balls and receptions. It was a carefree and delightful life; and though her father often scolded about his daughters going out so much to kick up their heels at balls, when they could be more profitably employed at home, secretly he was proud of their popularity. But Charity Newton wasn't altogether content with this sort of life. The Newtons belonged to the same family as the celebrated philosopher, Sir Isaac Newton; he who watched the apples fall and devised the laws of gravitation. Perhaps Charity inherited an analytical mind too. At any rate she wanted to do more than tap her nights away dancing in little satin shoes and swinging wide skirts while she flirted with the bewigged and velved-coated beaux.

Charity was attractive, gay and amusing, but idle days and enchanted nights did not fit into her scheme of things. She may have been capricious, but at least she could make up her own mind, and besides there was Ebenezer Smith, the son of a not-so-well-to-do neighbour.

Often, as Charity cantered across the fields on an errand for her father, she met young Smith, also going on an errand. It was pleasant there in the fields chatting with Ebenezer while their horses grazed around; much more pleasant than when she reached home more flushed and excited than any early morning ride would warrant. For Charity's father scowled and muttered. Ebenezer Smith indeed! Those rascally British and their taxes! Mr. Newton loved his fine linens and tea and good leather boots. And he was having trouble with his farmhands too. Far too many were sneaking off drilling at Freetown far too often. He didn't agree with Ebenezer and his folk on matters concerning the Colonies; for Ebenezer was a Loyalist and Mr. Newton was not. And Charity's mother often declared that Ebenezer could never provide her daughter with her accustomed luxury.

But Charity, gay and charming and thrilled at the thought of adventure, had a mind of her own, so in spite of her parents' disapproval she married Ebenezer Smith and when the Loyalists sought new homes under the old flag Charity and Ebenezer came to New Brunswick. And while Washington was settling the future of Rhode Island, Charity and Ebenezer did a little settling of their own in the wilds of King's County, New Brunswick.

Some of this land in New Brunswick had been settled during the French regime by Pierre Chesnet, Sieur de Breuil, whose grant is dated January 7th, 1689. His territory included land on both sides of the Kennebecasis River, then called Rivière du Bruhl (a corruption of de Breuil). Nearby was the old Indian trail which in French times formed a part of the overland route between Louisbourg and the Saint John River. By this route in 1755 some of the expelled Acadian settlers drifted into the partially cleared land and it became known as French Village.

Here the Robichaud and Thibideau families had lived for generations, possibly descendants from de Breuil's settlers. The French inhabitants cut masts for ships and floated them down the river to the New England Trading Post where Simonds and White (owners of the Post) exported them from Portland Point to New England.

A letter from James White dated December 17, 1781 reads: "This day from the Kennbecashus saith the French people are cutting masts etc.:" Simonds and White paid well for the masts and the 'French people' felt quite prosperous. The French were also engaged to build dykes for Simonds and White, who had undertaken to reclaim the great marshes from the tidal waters of Courtney Bay. There seemed to be no end to the undertakings of these traders, Simonds and White.

But the French people were a simple industrious group, living undisturbed in their village until the Loyalists came; then, because they had no title to their lands and would not take the oath of allegiance to the British Crown, they became wanderers again, and rather than leave their buildings to the newcomers they burned their peaceful village before moving on.

Here to this lonely spot came Charity. Such a contrast to the refinements she had known, tinkle of fine glass; clink of heavy silver; morning horseback rides; servants, balls and receptions. But Charity had no regrets as she cooked the simple fare in the little one-room cabin; she had married Ebenezer for better or worse and she was far too busy. From daybreak till dusk Charity followed the round of household tasks, and she had her babies to care for; five sons and three daughters without benefit of medical aid were born in that little cabin. But children were considered an asset in pioneer days for as soon as they could toddle around they were given chores to do.

Even if Charity was busy, she had her exciting moments too. There in the new land adventure beckoned again, for one day a former settler returned. He carried an old map. The surrounding country was accurately drawn and down in an intervale a spot was marked 'X' where a huge ash tree had stood. The tree had been blazed with an arrow, the Frenchman said, and he told of buried treasure.

In the meantime the energetic Loyalists had cleared the intervale, and no one remembered where the ash tree had stood. The 'X' didn't indicate the spot now, for the river had widened and changed the shore line. Day after day the Frenchman tramped around digging dozens of holes, but nothing was found, and Charity who was so keen for adventure was really sorry for the man.

Perhaps when she wasn't too busy Charity pinned up her petticoats and did a little digging on her own, but she had no better luck and today under some field of waving grain there lies the Frenchman's treasure. Perhaps some day a road-making bulldozer will toss up a strong box in its iron jaws and de Breuil's treasure will again glitter in the sun.

At first, life in the wilderness was a struggle for mere existence, but after years of hard work Charity and her husband became fairly prosperous. Then Charity felt the urge to visit her former home in Rhode Island. So, one year when the tiny green tufts in Charity's vegetable garden showed promise of a bumper harvest, Charity decided this was the time to prove to her family in Rhode Island that she was neither freezing nor starving as they'd predicted. All summer long Charity coaxed and wheedled for Ebenezer's consent to the journey, and finally he agreed, though he fervently hoped that something would turn up to prevent this rash venture.

"La! Mistress Charity", said the wives at the settlement when they dropped in for a dish of tea. "La, but the journey is fraught with danger!" But inwardly they envied Charity's spirit.

"La!" whispered the maiden ladies to themselves, shaking their heads sadly, "Maritime ships are rugged, but the sea takes its toll." Then they peeked in their little oval mirrors. After Charity had gone they'd bake a raisin loaf and take it over when they went to see how the children were getting along, poor wee things! And Ebenezer was such a fine figure of a man. Such fields, such a nice house.

"La, la," sang Charity as she went about the house happy in the thought of seeing her sisters again. There would be a lot of gossip to catch up with, one had to be discreet in letters, no telling into whose hands they might fall.

But it would be no pleasure cruise. England and France were at war and Privateers of every nation swarmed the coast and combed the seas for prize cargoes. There was an embargo on cargoes too. Passengers had to be landed at certain specified points under embarrassing restrictions and at considerable expense. But danger did not daunt Charity.

So, one fine September day Ebenezer filled a barrel with vegetables grown in their own garden. Charity packed her clothes in a basket in lieu of a trunk (baskets had handles, but trunks were awkward to carry). Then she wrapped her baby in a warm shawl and off she started. She managed to get passage on a vessel sailing from Saint John. On the crowded wharf, while anchor chains creaked and gear rattled, Charity bid her husband good-bye. After the vessel swung out to sea Ebenezer bolstered up his courage with a pint of good Jamaica at the nearest Coffee House before riding home. And from the deck Charity watched the houses and shore line disappear.

It was a long and dismal journey in fog and rain. The crew were a dour lot; they looked like ruffians Charity decided. With nothing to do except care for her baby Charity sat in her cabin and listened to the creak of timbers and slap of the waves as the vessel headed south.

One day when the sun broke through the cold gray skies Charity found they had entered Long Island Sound. From the deck she watched the familiar landmarks slip by. Suddenly the wind died down, the ship was becalmed; and just as suddenly Charity recognized a house belonging to a cousin where she had often visited. Its wide white porched beckoned invitingly and brought back sudden memories; nights when she and Ebenezer had danced in the wide parlours; walking under the apple blossoms on starlit nights and the long rides in the early mornings with Ebenezer beside her.

Charity sat on the deck gazing at the still blue water that separated her from the shore. Then she had a bright idea. Up she went to the Captain. Why could he not put her ashore here? It would save her days of travelling back from New York. But the Captain had his orders, no passengers ashore until he reached New York. There would be fines and he couldn't afford to run afoul of the law. Charity smiled and cajoled; laughed at all his excuses and finally the old man had to give in. He would be busy, very busy, in his cabin for an hour or so, he announced; but, he added, with a twinkle in his eye, "if any of the sailors wanted to take her ashore, it would be absolutely without his permission, absolutely!" Charity jumped at the chance. Some wangling and the sight of a silver dollar helped a sailor to make up his mind. Barrel, basket, baby and Charity were soon in the longboat; oars splashed in the water and they crawled away from the ship.

Delighted, Charity found herself on the shore and ran up the path to the house. She sounded the big brass knocker, but there were no answering footsteps, and the house seemed strangely quiet. Then she noticed that the shutters were closed, so around to the back of the house she went and peeked through a broken shutter. For all her courage Charity's heart sank at what she saw: the room was completely empty! It was evening now and growing more chilly every minute. Across the stretch of water a mist was rising, and she could see no trace of the ship. Down in the woods a bird sang its night song and then all went silent again. Dejected she sat on the wide front steps and nursed her baby. She remembered that the nearest neighbour was some six miles away. All Ebenezer's warnings came crowding back vividly while the dark September night closed in.

But life in the New Brunswick woods had taught Charity self-reliance. Down to the barns she went and her spirits rose again when she found some cows there, for she knew that someone had to come in the morning to milk them. So, calmly she made a bed for herself and the baby in the hay. It was warm there with the heat from the cattle and in spite of her loneliness she slept well.

When morning came the farmhand arrived and explained that Charity's cousin had moved to another farm and had sent him to drive the cattle to their new home. Charity couldn't wait until he had returned with a carriage, so she travelled the six miles on foot carrying her baby, and the welcome she received was reward enough for her journey.

Then home she went to her family. Her old room was just as she had left it, her sisters bubbled over with gossip; but her Mother, ill for a long time, now sat in a chair all day long, and to make matters worse she scarcely recognized her daughter. For Charity's dark brown hair was streaked with white, her hands rough and calloused, but her sun-tanned face more resolute. And one day when visitors came for tea Charity heard her mother remark, "It doesn't seem possible she was ever a child of mine, she has grown so coarse-looking, she is not the Charity Newton of days gone by."

But it was good to be at home again and sit around the well filled table watching her father with his sleeve ruffles turned up carve the roast, while the maids passed around the heaped platters.

Her father was proud of his adventurous daughter, who wasn't afraid of Privateers or Atlantic storms and could talk so well about crops and cattle as they rode across the fields again. Charity's barrel of vegetables proved she wasn't starving, despite her father's opinions of the land of ice and snow. Her sisters did their utmost to induce Charity to spend the winter with them but she was remembering the little house in the New Brunswick woods and Ebenezer and her other children waiting for her.

So, off to New York went Charity, where she dashed around visiting and shopping; but the cobblestoned streets hurt her feet; the shops were full of expensive fripperies; her friends seemed changed under the new order and she was glad to be on board ship again homeward bound.

Again adventure lurked around the corner. One day when she watched the Captain searching the seas with his telescope she sensed danger. Soon, she too could see the sails that had appeared mysteriously on the horizon. She heard the Captain's: "Crowd sail and get away!" And word went around that a French Frigate was heading straight towards them. The passengers gathered excitedly around the Captain. Couldn't he do something? The Captain was in despair for he carried a valuable cargo as well as passengers. He had other worries too, for he had a large sum of money on board. And there was no chance to get away, for the Frigate was faster.

Then Charity heard the Captain damning his luck! If he could only save that money he could ransom his ship, otherwise, ship, cargo and money were lost. Charity offered her help. The Captain blustered, 'What could she do'? But resourceful Charity had thought of a plan.

Down to her cabin she sped, collecting the other women as she went. Once inside and the door bolted she took off her petticoats. One by one she tossed them on the floor and explained her plan to the amazed women. Out came the needles and thread and all set to work. Never in their lives did they sew so fast, and the Captain's silver dollars disappeared one by one as they were safely quilted between Charity's petticoats, just far enough apart to prevent clinking. As they finished there was a tramp of feet on the deck. Orders were bellowed back and forth, then came "All hands on deck". Charity climbed back into her petticoats, picked up her baby and followed the frantic women on deck.

The Frigate's commander swaggered around gloating over his prize, while shouting orders to his men. Other women clutched around the railings for support, but not Charity. She just stood there holding her baby and praying that her petticoat fastenings wouldn't give way. But the weight of those petticoats was more than she had bargained for. She could scarcely walk, and she dare not sit down for fear she couldn't get up again! With characteristic politeness the Frenchman didn't bother to search the women passengers, but the men searched the luggage very, very thoroughly.

When they came to Charity's basket all they found were some presents for her children and a new dress for herself. Then they set sail for the nearest port and ordered all ashore. When Charity's turn came to disembark she was nearly frantic. What if she would slip, those silver-lined petticoats would surely drag her under water!

But the Captain was ready for that. He had extra planks placed and as he led her to the railing they made arrangements for the return of the money. Charity reached shore safely and it's doubtful who felt the greater relief, Charity or the Captain. She lost no time reaching the Inn where she got out of those petticoats as fast as she could and ripped out the silver dollars. Soon the Captain recovered his money and ransomed his ship. Again they set sail for New Brunswick, while the Frenchman, pockets jingling with silver dollars went off to look for other victims.

Once home again Charity and Ebenezer talked long into the night before the open fire. "You weren't worried?" she asked, as she related her experiences. "No", he answered, "I knew you would manage, you always do."

Little did Charity Newton imagine when she married Ebenezer Smith what a chequered and adventurous life lay ahead. And though the Newton family chose to remain in Rhode Island, (and their descendants are there to this day) Charity, who put her faith in the new land had no regrets; for she lived to see grandchildren and great-grandchildren inherit the land she had chosen.

It is over one hundred years since Charity went on her last great adventure for she died in 1846. She rests in the family burial place on a little knoll nearby the homestead she loved.

But she has a lasting monument, for in New Brunswick is a prosperous farming community, almost entirely populated by Charity's descendants, and it's named "Smithtown".

BIBLIOGRAPHY

From the story "Silver Dollars" by Rev. W.O. Raymond, in the Collections
     of the New Brunswick Historical Society. New Brunswick Museum.
Court Records, Hammond River, King's County, New Brunswick.

Elizabeth Regan

In a sturdy frame house on King Street in Saint John, New Brunswick, a small girl stood on tiptoe looking out the window; her nose a tiny white button pressed against the pane.

There was so much to watch on this busy street, for early each morning the "Tea-water" man would push his cart with its huge dripping puncheon and ring a little bell while he called out: "Tea-water! Tea-water! Two pails for a penny!" And Elizabeth would watch the housewives scurry out with pitchers and pails for their day's supply. It was much safer to buy tea-water than dip it out of the back-yard well where barns and outhouses crowded the city lots behind the houses.

Elizabeth Regan never tired of watching what went on in the busy street. Often a pig or two would dispute the sidewalk with ladies bent on shopping. Dogs and cats fought for scraps of food thrown carelessly in the gutters. This highly unsavory condition continued until the City Fathers, growing tired of complaints and threats, finally appointed their 'Fence viewers'; and these gentlemen promptly made it their business of insisting that the inhabitants keep their fences mended and their pets at home.

This was Saint John as Elizabeth saw it from the windows of her father's house, for Jeremiah Regan had drawn one of the King Street lots when he came in the LOVELY LASS to this refugee haven. Her father was the son of a London Bishop and had first come to America with Lord de Lancey who had large estates in Virginia. During the long journey from London, Jeremiah fell in love with the beautiful Miss de Lancey and when they reached Virginia they were married.

Amongst the wedding gifts were forty slaves, given by Lord de Lancey. When Jeremiah and his wife moved to New York they had no room for such a staff in their modest home, so Jeremiah gave the slaves their freedom. And when Jeremiah's wife died he married Mary Leggat of New York, who was Elizabeth's mother.

Even after New York, Saint John was a fascinating place, True, there were no cobblestoned streets; nor did the servants scrub the

57

front steps every morning; nor were lanterns hung every seventh house to light the traveller on dark nights. But ships anchored at the Landing Place at the foot of King Street and brought all sorts of cargo, and the little peak-roofed warehouses along the waterfront were stocked to the eaves with furs and wines and silks and groceries.

Just across the street from the Regan home stood Mallard's Inn. Here travellers arrived and departed with a clutter of boxes and trunks, and one cold February day Elizabeth watched preparations for a very important ceremony.

The first Governor for the new Province had arrived. At the door of Mallard House stood gentlemen in velvet coats and three-cornered hats waiting for the distinguished visitor. There was a deafening salute from the guns at Fort Howe and all the ships in the harbour. Crowds lined the streets and Governor Carleton, in his gold-laced coat and plumed hat, stepped out of the carriage to cheers that echoed across the harbour.

Elizabeth's father explained all this ceremony to his thirteen-year-old daughter, for Jeremiah Regan was a cultured gentleman, a clergyman and teacher, and he took and active interest in community affairs. He also insisted that Elizabeth begin her studies at an early age. So, while other girls were lucky if they could read and write, Elizabeth received a classical education.

There were no schools in Saint John. Universities were closed to women, for women weren't supposed to meddle in things thought only proper for the stronger minds of men. Jeremiah Regan encouraged his daughter to study, however, and he taught her the art of fine living too. So, with such a man for her father, Elizabeth couldn't help being a very unusual young woman.

But if there were no schools in Saint John for the Loyalists' children, strange as it may seem, schools were provided for the Indians. Founded and maintained by a 'Benevolent Society', the "New England Company for the Education and Civilization of American Indians" conducted an "Indian College" at Sussex in New Brunswick. Jeremiah Regan, being appointed Chaplain and Commissary of the Indian College, moved his family to Sussex.

Every Autumn the Indians would load their families and cooking pots and furs in canoes and set off for school. Sussex, on the Kennebecasis River, had mostly Malecite pupils, and to keep the children happy during the school term often entire families would make a temporary camp nearby, drawing generous supplies as an inducement to have the children educated. The Indian children were clothed, fed and housed at the school. Their parents received clothing, blankets and provisions and "a pound of tobacco and a pipe each week."

58

In spite of the generous arrangements the Indians were not impressed. While Mr. Regan and his masters saw to it that the grimy little Indians absorbed their A, B, C's with their porridge, they didn't make such headway with the older boys, who were supposed to study farming methods. They had their own ideas and instead of attending classes they'd go off on hunting trips. Often they would earn as much as 20 or 30 guineas in a season for pelts, and just as often they spent most of it for rum.

The older girls too were difficult. One old Indian reported that his daughter was so saucy as not to speak to him when he visited her, and he blamed the masters for teaching them to despise their parents.

Strict discipline at the school was almost impossible. It was a hectic life for Mr. Regan. In one letter he writes: "Tho I have some leisure hours [at the school] there is such a rant of unruly children that I have very little time to write free from complaints, or disturbance of some kind or another and am forc'd to write as fast as I can when alone, for fear of interruption."

Sundays brought release from school, though there were always church services, and Elizabeth Regan, very prim and sedate — as became the Reverend's daughter — sat beside her mother and listened intently while her father preached, even though she had heard most of the sermon before. For Mr. Regan often wrote his sermons in Greek and translated them into English as he preached.

And such crowds of people attended those services. Churches in those days were the centre of social as well as religious activities, and after the services whole families went visiting. Grandfathers would sit out on the shady side of the house and talk of world affairs. The younger men went out to look at the crops, and while the women prepared those famous "hearty meals", their babies all slept together in huge four-poster beds.

After dinner the teenagers went strolling along Sussex's tree-sheltered lanes. It was then Elizabeth Regan met James Fairchild. Hand in hand along her father's road they sauntered. (It's still known as Regan's Road, though Jeremiah and his Greek sermons have long been forgotten.) Down to Fairchild's Gate (which is still a landmark in the community) they strolled — Elizabeth stepping fastidiously in the dusty roadway, careful of her fine kid slippers, James in his Sunday best with his new, tall, grey top hat, the latest fashion for young men. And Elizabeth smiled shyly under her wide-brimmed bonnet while James talked oh so convincingly of their future.

The sequel lies in a faded old marriage certificate. "To whom it may concern. These may certify that on the Fifth day of December One Thousand and Seven Hundred and Ninety James Morgan Fairchild and Elizabeth Regan were joined in the Bonds of Marriage and Pronounced man and wife by me Ozias Ansley, Justice of the Peace."

Back to Saint John came the Fairchilds. Elizabeth brought her linens and quilts with their lovers' knots and roses. Solid silver spoons and the little silver cream jug that had once belonged to Oliver Cromwell were gifts from her parents.

James Fairchild built a lovely home for his bride with the oak frame and heavy beams brought from England. The walls of Elizabeth's bedroom were painted in lovely woodland scenes with birds and brooks and trees and flowers. The ceiling was sky blue and a soft moss green carpet covered the floor. The huge mahogany four-poster was so high that Elizabeth had to use a little stepladder before she slid down into the billowy featherbed.

Two huge chests of drawers stood on either side of the fireplace, and on winter nights the firelight threw dancing shadows on the scenic walls. Winter or summer, a candle burned all night beside Elizabeth's books on the little bed table, and safely stored away under the big bed during the day was a child's trundle bed, which was taken out at night and one by one Elizabeth's children slept comfortably near their mother.

Well mannered and lovely were Elizabeth's four daughters. When their mother entertained on her day "at home" they would politely bob in curtseys and sit fascinated on little stools listening quietly to the visitors chatter: Had Mistress Fairchild seen the new 'Maids, Wives and Widows Magazine'? No? How ravishing were the new styles; their pleats, their flounces, puffs and ribbons: And four new pews were for sale in Trinity Church: even seats in the gallery could be had; three pews had been forfeited for non-payment — and it would be more comfortable since the stoves had been installed, and more convenient. No need to bother with those hot bricks wrapped in shawls to keep one's feet warm during Dr. Byle's long sermons!

And Dr. Josiah Flagg, the first dentist to arrive in Saint John "was doing such wonderful repair to disordered teeth!" One could read his advertisement in the New Brunswick Gazette of March 1805: "Dr. Josiah Flagg continues the safe and salutary practice of his profession as a Surgeon Dentist at Mrs. Hardy's on King Street. Tooth and gum brushes, chewsticks, tinctures and dentifrices adapted to the several ages and complaints and suited for both warm and cold climates. For sale by retail or by quantity with directions for their use."

Here was no ordinary street corner tooth puller! No charlatan on his public stage where shouting and song attracted a crowd! Had not Dr. Flagg whittled down ivory and sheep's teeth and wired them firmly to replace the decayed "foreteeth" for the Ladies and

60

Gentlemen of Boston? And what is more, he guaranteed them to be not only ornamental but of real use in "speaking and eating". Even General Washington wore a set of false teeth — complete with gold wire springs. New teeth, be they ivory or sheep origin, did "give such a youthful appearance". And Dr. Flagg was so dependable! He "recommended an enquiry of his skill of the ablest physicians in town." He "made loose teeth fast and hardened gums with perfect ease. Teeth were reinstated by him that were despaired of by the patient".

And while conversation flowed on, Elizabeth's daughters sat with hands primly clasped and looked up at the visitors' awful front teeth; watched the long chins wagging vigorously and wondered why the visitors did not consult this wonderful Dr. Flagg.

When they heard how "Children's teeth could be arranged in perfect symmetry and if crowded can extend the jaws to receive their due proportion without pain", four roly-poly editions of Elizabeth gave thanks from the bottom of their hearts that their teeth were straight and sound and did not require the service of this Dr. Flagg and his gold wire.

When tea was served Elizabeth's daughters helped the servant carry round the fine gilt cups, and while the guests stirred their tea with the lovely silver spoons and remarked on the delightful quality of the Hyson, Elizabeth sipped her cup of oatmeal water, for she never drank tea or coffee — they corroded the teeth and marred the skin. Even when Elizabeth was an old, old lady she had the most marvellous pink and white complexion.

But life in the Fairchild household was not all "at home" and curtseys and visitors. For, taught by their mother, Elizabeth's children were well schooled in every subject proper for young ladies of their time. And for lighter moments they had their storybook.

And what a book! Only two inches by three and a half, its light blue cloth covers mended by strong linen thread; the letters of the alphabet printed painstakingly in its margins and on its fly leaf in a childish hand "Elizabeth Regan Fairchild, her book." As short story material for children's entertainment it has no equal. There's a grim story about "The Trial and Execution of the Earl of Strafford." Another, about Lady Jane Grey, is equally horrifying. "The dire results of the Power of Conscience" would make even a strong man weep. And the exploits of the female duellist in "An Amazon of Lorraine" would win fame in present-day Hollywood.

When summer came Elizabeth's children visited their grandparents. Trunks were packed. Excitement reigned — dressed in travelling cloaks and plush bonnets they piled into the huge stage coach to rumble along the rough road to Sussex Vale. Evidently Polly, the eldest, was a favorite with the old folk for she prolonged her visits. And Caroline writes to her Grandmother Regan:

Saint John, Oct. 10-1810.

Ever Honored Grandmama, For the first time I take my pen in hand to address my loved Grandmama and feel much ashamed that I have so long neglected what I acknowledge was my duty, but trust Grandmama will answer it. We were happy to learn by Mr. Fairweather our dear Grandparents and Sister enjoy a tolerable state of health as we are at present. May Heaven Bless our aged Grandparents and preserve their health and may the Omnipotent Being preserve our worthy Mama and send His Blessing upon her children.

I cannot forbear mentioning the melancholy accident that happened Friday the 2nd inst. Mr. Venning fell from the Church Steeple (the south side) which immediately put a period to his Existence; his body was carried in the meeting house and Mr. Black preached his funeral sermon Sunday, from the words, "Be ye also ready", a text very applicable as I believe he was a sincere Christian, he has left a Disconsolate Widow and five children to lament his loss.

Whenever my dear Grandmama will do me the honor of writing me a few lines be well assured nothing will come more acceptable to your Dutiful Granddaughter. I feel thankful that I can write tho' it is but poorly, which I should not have known had it not been for my Dear and Ever Honored Grand Papa. Mama and sisters join me in kindest love to our Dear Grandpapa, Grandmama, Sister, Aunt and Uncle Spicer, the Doctor and his Lady and all enquiring friends. I am, Dear Grandmama, Your most Dutiful and affectionate Granddaughter, Caroline Fairchild.

Folded and sealed with red sealing wax, this was sent by Mr. Fairweather for there was no regular mail service.

Elizabeth was only 34 when James Fairchild died. But she did not retire as many widows did. Instead, she turned her learning to good use and opened up a school for boys.

Around the large table in her spacious dining room Elizabeth's pupils wrestled with Arithmetic and English Grammar; and for Geography she used the book her father had taught from, "Guthries Geographical Grammar."

School began early. On dark winter mornings candles flickered in huge candelabra until the sun came streaming in through the many paned windows. Well sharpened quills clutched tightly in small fingers made scrolls and beautifully formed letters in those days of the "fine Italian hand"; for penmanship was highly esteemed as part of a good education. And while Elizabeth's ears rang with the rhythm of young voices in "Bonus, Bona, Bonum", dishes clattered in the kitchen where her daughters prepared dinner.

Noon, and school dismissed for the day, Elizabeth's pupils sorted out cloaks and caps and scarves and set out for home. Always by a roundabout route. Down to Market Square they went, where a huge wicker cage stood under the balcony of City Hall.

Strict authorities had a very successful way of dealing with delinquents. In the cage, locked up for punishment, would stand one or two unfortunate youths, in duress vile for some minor infraction of the law — boys caught abusing animals; or being too boisterous on city streets; or not attending Church services. Here the unfortunate culprit stood, often the target of overripe fruit and vegetables, until his sentence expired.

Elizabeth's pupils would walk around inspecting the occupant of the cage, or if the cage were empty they'd watch ships being unloaded, and sailors in colorful stocking caps and tarred pigtails would toss them nutmegs and raisins and periwinkles. Then with bulging pockets and appetites sharpened they'd finally reach home, free until the six o'clock school bell rang next morning.

Life was not all school and housework for Elizabeth's daughters for Cupid got around in the 1800's. Wedding bells rang for all four, and on a brisk March day in 1812 Caroline married James Wood. Caroline's trousseau was the talk of the town. Forty dresses, flounced and ribboned and pleated and puffed. Seamstresses sewed from sunrise to sunset. Fittings took days. Scraps of brocade and satin and gauze and wool littered the house for months. And for years to come those dresses have been worn at masquerade balls by Caroline's descendants.

Even today one lovely brocaded white satin dress treasured by Caroline's descendant shows those tiny stitches done in fine silk thread. The wide skirt flares from a slim waistline. The low-cut bodice is trimmed with a dozen tiny gauze ruffles, each edged with narrow bands of cerise satin, and the wide topped sleeves narrow down to a V-shaped wrist.

In 1814 Ann Fairchild writes to her grandparents:

"My Dear and Ever Honored Grand Papa,- With inexpressible pleasure we received your kind letter by Mr. Pittfield. With pleasure we hear that my dear Grandparents and friends are well. The English Fleet has not yet arrived. As soon as it does, Mary will get the things you mentioned in the best manner she can. I have only one moment to write. Polly was to have wrote but had not time, we have a great deal of work at present. Little Mary Ann Wood grows finely. Mr. Wood and Caroline send their best love to my Dear Grand Papa and Mama. Mama and sisters join in the kindest love to my Dear Grandparents, to Aunt Spicer, Mrs. Guimarin, the Doctor and all friends. In Haste, I am, Dear Grand Papa your ever affectionate Grand Daughter, Ann Fairchild."

For years Elizabeth taught her school. Sons of former pupils came for instruction. And long after her teaching days were done Elizabeth lived in her comfortable home surrounded by her beautiful pictures and books and furniture. Day after day her former pupils came to visit her and it warmed her heart to know they still thought kindly of her.

Elizabeth Regan Fairchild died in 1849 and on the day of her funeral all the stores in Saint John were closed that afternoon while former pupils, businessmen and clergy walked in a long procession.

Her devoted daughter Caroline could not bear to change the arrangement of Elizabeth's lovely bedroom, so she kept it as it was — even to the open book on the table in memory of her mother — for over 28 years.

There is nothing left of Elizabeth's home today, for the disastrous fire of June 20th 1877 reduced it to ashes. But of Jeremiah Regan's house on King Street, where the small Elizabeth watched history in the making, there still remains a portion of the cellar. And we're told that after the great fire some old wine bottles were found, but the heat from the fire had blown out the corks and Jeremiah's fine wines evaporated. From a manhole in the present sidewalk one can still see the old stone steps that led down to the cellar.

Down through the years have come the Guthries Geographical Grammar and the little Storybook with the alphabet printed in its margins. Caroline's wedding gowns are still lovely to look at. The little silver cream jug that once belonged to Oliver Cromwell and the lovely silver spoons still grace a present-day tea table.

But Elizabeth Regan Fairchild, pioneer teacher, left a greater legacy, for her influence reached far into the unknown future through the lives of those pupils who studied around her dining room table in Saint John so long ago.

BIBLIOGRAPHY

Letters, Documents and Family History by kind permission of Nina Fairchild Simon, Rothesay, New Brunswick.

Advertisements from Newspapers in Archives Department, New Brunswick Museum.

Indian Schools, From Dr. W.F. Ganong's Notes, and Patrick Campbell's *Travels in North America 1791-1792.*

Ann Ludlow

The spacious Verplanck plantation buzzed with more than the ordinary activity that September day in 1760; for it was Ann Verplanck's wedding day and the guests had come from far and near to attend the ceremony.

Groups of gaily dressed young people gathered on the lawns under wide shade trees in the warm afternoon. Laughter and gay voices echoed in the wide hallways where the scent of boxwood and frost-felled fern mingled with the perfume of hair powder and dress sachets. And from the out-kitchens came delicious odors of roasting chicken, spiced hams and savory pies; for Verplanck hospitality was noted throughout the length and breadth of the colony.

Upstairs in a high-ceilinged room Ann Verplanck stood before a tall mirrow while girlfriends crowded around putting last minute touches to the bride's flowers and ribbons. Then down the broad staircase came the seventeen-year-old bride and a hush descended on the throng when she stood in the flower-decked drawing room beside Gabriel Ludlow, and the ceremony began.

Afterwards there was feasting and toasts: then Gabriel and his new bride rode off to their Long Island Home. And Ann brought her husband a dowry of seventeen thousand acres of land to add to his already broad acres.

Ann Ludlow was a descendant of Abraham Verplanck, who came to New Amsterdam about 1635. These sturdy settlers had prospered and the Verplanck family were prominent in New York for generations. Their names are found among the lists of judges, congressmen, educators and writers, and they served their adopted country well in cultural, political and charitable pursuits.

Gabriel Ludlow was descended from good British stock; the first Gabriel at the age of thirty-five had landed in New York on November 24th, 1694, to try his luck in the new land.

But time changed the fortunes of Ann and her husband, for the Ludlows were strong supporters of the Loyalist cause; and when the American Revolution came, Gabriel Ludlow raised a troop of soldiers and joined Oliver DeLancey's brigade in 1776.

From the wide porches of her home on Long Island, Ann Ludlow watched her husband ride away down the tree-shaded avenue until his bright red coat, with its blue facings, blurred in the gathering dusk. Then she walked slowly through the wide doorway into the house, the house where she was needed everywhere; for Ann carried the entire responsibility of the great plantation. She cared for her three children, one son and two daughters, and all the plantation workers as well. Sickness and suffering found her ready with sympathy and help; quarrels needed her guiding hand, for the panic-stricken slaves looked to her for protection.

The Landing of the Loyalists

Courtesy of The New Brunswick Museum
Photo by William Hart

Heartbreaking days and terror-ridden nights lengthened into years of anxiety — and when the bitter struggle was over and the Peace signed, Ann had lost all her acres at Hyde Park, and Gabriel his estate on Long Island.

So, when the drums beat that May morning and boatloads of refugees were brought ashore from the vessels in Saint John Harbour, Ann and Gabriel and their children sat patiently on their luggage, gazing at the unfriendly wilderness and waiting a chance to draw a "Location Ticket", which entitled them to land for their new home.

Soon tents were put up and what had been a dense forest, with only small clearings around Fort Howe and the Trading Post, soon became a lively spot.

The engineers, led by Paul Bedell, laid out plans for a city. They staked out straight streets; there are no converted cowpaths in Saint John, as one often finds in other old cities. King Street, in the main shopping district, is one hundred feet wide and has often been noted as the widest, shortest, steepest main street in Canada.

Bedell's engineers planned large open spaces right in the centre of the city; today in the public squares children play about in the walks and feed the pigeons that flutter around in calm disregard of traffic. Old folk doze comfortably in the shade of ancient trees and a fountain provides safe sailing for tiny yachtsmen; for Saint John is a city of sailors and the murmur of the sea is ever near.

Saint John has been called "the City built in a day", for as soon as lots were drawn — 1454 of them — axes bit into the forest and houses were built. Men, who had never before lifted anything heavier than a goose quill pen, took off their expensive coats, rolled up their lace-frilled shirt sleeves, swung picks and axes and trundled wheelbarrows with the most hardened laborers.

Soft hands were blistered; stately backs ached with unaccustomed toil, but these people had not left their comfortable homes for a mere whim.

Gabriel Ludlow drew lots 196, 197 and 198 in Carleton, now called West Saint John, just across the river from the main city, on the site formerly occupied by Fort Frederick.

Rocky, forbidding and partly burned over, portions of Fort Frederick had been carried away by a huge tidal wave which destroyed the surrounding dykes. According to John Burrel, a sergeant stationed at Fort Frederick with Brigadier General Monckton's forces, "Sunday ye 4th Nov. Ye wind blue a hye tide that washed ye shores or Blue it to Peaces that some of ye Provisions fell out into ye Tide this Day."

Previous to British occupation the French had built a Fort on this site and called it 'Menogoeche', or 'Forte la Rivière de St. Jean'.

Here, Villebon, Brouillon, Charinsay and other French worthies carried on a successful fur trade with the Indians.

Governor Villebon's term of occupation was not without complaints; for the Fort, being separated from the mainland by water, even at low tide, was a great inconvenience and a greater one was the lack of good drinking water. One of Villebon's officers in a letter dated June 23rd, 1699, writes, "The Governor keeps all the water within the fort for the exclusive use of his kitchens and his mare, others being obliged to use snow water, often very dirty."

But with their usual industry the French cleared land on the hillside and planted gardens for food supplies. When the British took over in 1758 the old French Fort was in ruins. Logs and huge timbers collected for its reconstruction lay rotting on the ground, but the fruit trees planted by the French blossomed in the hillside garden for many a year.

The British rebuilt Fort de la Rivière St. Jean and renamed it Fort Frederick in honour of one of the Princes of the House of Brunswick. Never before, nor since, had there been such activity on those rocky hills. Six hundred men wielded picks, axes and shovels, and the winter of 1758 saw an army of two thousand encamped back of the Fort, while a fleet of a dozen or more vessels lay at anchor in the Harbour.

For ten years the British had an uneasy time of it, keeping one eye on the French and the other on the Indians. Then with the surrender of the French and submission of the Indians, duty at Fort Frederick became monotonous.

The soldiers had too much time on their hands — time to reminisce about the comforts of their New England homes, and they deserted quite openly. Burrel writes, "Monday ye 5th May, a number of Capt. Garashes men with some others Desarted on Bord of a Schouner." "Tuesday ye 13th, 30 of our Company went home in a Schouner to England." Though the men had enlisted for the great struggle with France, with the surrender of Louisbourg they decided the war for them was over.

Even Sergeant Burrel could stand it no longer. "Tuesday, ye 9th, We left Saint John and sat out for Anapoles. Monday, ye 21st, left Cap Ann & put away for Boston had a south east wind & we gott into Boston at night. Son setting Tuesday ye 22nd, & came to Abingan & went as far as Grandfather Humphres at night. Wednesday ye 23rd, went home & found my family well as I left them."

Here on the site of old Fort Frederick, Ann Ludlow watched the joists and timbers raised in her new home. It was a pretentious house, two and a half stories high with a sloping roof and dormer windows. Including the ell, which was used as servants quarters, the

Ludlow home was nearly one hundred feet long. A massive doorway and wide front steps were shaded with elm trees. With great beams in the high ceilings, wide hallways opened into large rooms. And all through the winter Ann's servants were kept busy feeding logs to the huge fireplaces. Often there were ten fires burning in the house; for even with half a dozen woollen petticoats the draughts blew chill and women accustomed to milder climates found it difficult to keep warm.

Every Spring brought a froth of blossoms on the trees in the old French gardens just behind the house, and year after year Ann Ludlow added apple and plum trees that survived for generations. Recently, one spry old gentleman admitted that when he was a boy he used to steal apples from that orchard. It was over eighty years ago, but he can still remember how bitter and sour those apples were.

And while Ann Ludlow was busy supervising the work in her new home Gabriel had his responsibilities also. For in 1785, when Saint John became the first Incorporated City in Canada, Gabriel Ludlow was appointed Mayor of the City. He held this post for ten years nd his name is engraved on the first link of the 'chain of office' that all Mayors of Saint John wear on official occasions.

Saint John's first City Hall was in Market Square near the Public Landing Place. It was a large two-storey brick building, whose first floor was used as a Market and the second floor for the City Council offices. After every civic election the old and new council members dined at McPherson's Coffee House just across the Square at the foot of King Street.

Genial Charles McPherson had come to New York with a Scots Regiment, and being a loyal British subject, arrived in Saint John with the Loyalists. He drew the lot at the corner of King Street, but was not overly pleased with the location, so he tried to persuade some of his fellow refugees to take it off his hands. He offered it for "one gallon of Jamaica Rum and one Spanish Doubloon", but Mr. McPherson had no bidders; so he set about to make the most of what he considered a poor bargain and built a substantial Inn, a sort of Shakespearean tavern where the leading merchants of the day met and discussed business, and old men sat and sipped their toddy and gossiped and smoked their pipes.

In the Long Room used as an Assembly Hall, Societies held their Celebrations, and travelling entertainers played to appreciative audiences. Here Don Pedro Clorioso performed "the most surprising feats on wires and ropes" one hot August day in 1796. Small boys gazed pop-eyed at the agile Spaniard. They could hardly wait till they got home where the family clothesline and Grandmother's precious linen sheets provided equipment for balancing acts and many an embryo Don Pedro did a little less exciting but more distressing balancing act on Father's knee afterwards.

The Ludlow's old Georgian house became a gathering place for the leaders of the Province. Celebrities visiting Saint John were entertained there; for hospitality did not permit important visitors to stop overnight at an Inn.

Governor Carleton dined frequently at the Ludlows' table; and when Prince Edward, the Duke of Kent, visited Saint John in 1794 there was a gay dinner party in his honor. Representatives of militia, church and state and their ladies were there. Down to the Landing Place rumbled the Ludlow coach for the distinguished visitor. Prince Edward, with as many of his suite as could crowd into the vehicle, rode in state up the hill, while crowds lined the streets for Royalty's first visit to Saint John.

In the wide hallway Ann and the ladies swept graceful curtseys with a discreet rustle of silk as guests were presented to Prince Edward, and on the arm of their guest Ann led the way to the well set table.

The afternoon sun flooded Ann's dining room and glistened on Ann's silver and crystal. Good talk flowed with good wine. But the jovial young Prince could scarcely keep his eyes of the attractive young ladies. And the tale of his exciting escape from capture by a French frigate, while on his way to Martinique, added a dramatic note to sober conversation.

Years afterwards, when the Prince's daughter Victoria was born, Ann recalled that dinner party and wondered who would have been on the throne of England if the French had captured that choice prize, the Duke of Kent.

Ann Ludlow was a good manager as well as a gracious hostess. It took no small effort to cope with unexpected and famous guests. Ann couldn't send around to the corner grocery store for extra goods, but she kept a well-stocked cellar.

As in her Long Island home, there were bins of vegetables and kegs of beef and pork salted down. Smoked fish and hams hung ready for use and preserved fruits were always at hand. Each morning, with her housekeeper carrying a basket. Ann went from cellar to storehouse, checking supplies and bringing up provisions for the day.

And when she entertained at afternoon gatherings for the ladies (those fashionable teas and gay conversation parties), Ann expected her guests to arrive by three o'clock and leave before six, so the servants could have everything cleared away before evening prayers at seven.

But Ann didn't spend all her days entertaining guests and tending household affairs. She had wider interests. And when the need for public schools was recognized by the City Council, Ann helped with many constructive ideas. For with her family grown up and in homes of their own, Ann had more time to devote to community interests. So, night after night Ann and Gabriel sat before the fire discussing the school problem. Gabriel's huge desk was crammed with papers dealing with school matters. (Today the old desk may be found in the Provincial Gallery at the New Brunswick Museum.)

Perhaps next morning Ann would go walking up the hill to the big rock where two seats like little armchairs are hollowed out of the solid rock by rains and frosts. Here she would sit, quiet and undisturbed, thinking and planning while she watched the river rush swiftly between Navy Island and the Carleton shore, where the water foamed so white it was called "Buttermilk Channel".

Desk of Gabriel Ludlow, first Mayor of Saint John

Courtesy of The New Brunswick Museum
Photo by William Hart

Ann would look across to Saint John where the neat rows of new houses edged the straight streets — but Ann could see farther than that: she pictured lonely farmhouses scattered abut the Province where children had no opportunity for an education. There was no compulsory education in New Brunswick at that time. Private schools catered to those who could afford to pay fees, and in country districts usually the best educated person in the community taught the youngsters for a few weeks in one of the homes. Books were scarce; often families only had a Bible, or an ancient History Book, or perhaps an Almanac. So, teachers concentrated on the three R's and for that reason letters of by-gone days are so beautifully written.

In Saint John the hit-and-miss method prevailed. There was a school for boys located on the King Square next door to a pioneer bakery. Often the pupils would slip out from classes to buy fresh gingerbread in large squares at a penny apiece. If it happened to be a day when the fish were biting, well, the youngsters conveniently forgot to return to the classroom. Small wonder that the teacher often had to persuade the would-be Waltons with a touch of the tawse!

In 1803 when Governor Carleton returned to England, Gabriel Ludlow was made Administrator of the Province, and Ann Ludlow's fine home became the first Government House in Saint John. While Gabriel held that position Grammar Schools were provided for the City and every County in the Province as well. Ann Ludlow's influence aided more than a little in planning these schools, although women did not get the spotlight in those days.

The new schools opened at six o'clock in the summer months. October and November were holiday months and there was no 'end-of-vacation' getting ready for school preparations. They didn't make trips to the dentist, nor get new shoes and clothes, or last minute haircuts. They simply went back to classes.

Often before the sun was up tidy little girls in pigtails and bonnets and frilled pantalettes peeking from beneath wide skirts would trip dutifully to the schoolroom. Small boys loitered in the dusty streets for a last-minute game of 'shinny' before the school bell rang. But they managed to get an education, and from those early settlement schools in New Brunswick came men and women who have made us proud of our Canadian Heritage.

Ann Ludlow's house is still standing, but Ann herself would never recognize it. The long ell, where servants lived, and the coach houses have disappeared. A mansard roof covers the dormer windows; and in their zeal for improvement, the builders replaced the massive doorway and its graceful fan lights with no less than three entrances. The high-ceilinged rooms, where the Ludlows entertained the Duke of Kent and other celebrities have been divided into small apartments. The cellar is still cool and dark under its heavy oak beams, now black with age, and the stout walls of granite and red sandstone are still standing. The beautiful shady elm trees are gone, and where the French gardens stood and Ann's apple trees blossomed on the hill behind her house, there is now a street of houses.

The Ludlow House (Old Government House) on Ludlow Street, Saint John
Courtesy of The New Brunswick Museum   Photo by William Hart

A short distance up the hill there is a modern brick school and youngsters for generations have raced across the street at recess time to sit in those little armchairs in the rock, where Ann used to sit and think and plan.

Further up the street on what was called Courtney Hill, stands an old grey Church and in the adjoining cemetery Ann and Gabriel Ludlow rest under green sod. Old trees make pools of shadow on the grass and little 'Stars of Bethlehem' cluster around pioneer headstones; for many of the early settlers were buried there.

Down towards the river in the old French burial ground, now obliterated by modern pavements, is the grave of Villebon, the first Governor of Acadia, who died at Saint John July 5th, 1700.

Villebon, whose "Fort de la Rivière de St. Jean", with its

73

barracks and Chapel and prison and well of good spring water, held sway over all Acadia, is now only a page from the storied past. All that is left is an old French cannon, hooped with iron to give additional strength, unearthed by workmen when the present King Street, in West Saint John was graded some sixty years ago.

On the same site British redcoats from 'Fort Frederick' marched out with their bugles and drums in the cool of the morning.

But Ann Ludlow's house, "Old Government House", still stands on the slope of the hill.

Perhaps on some moonlit night, when the gray mist gathers over the river, the ghost of Ann Ludlow returns to curtsey to phantom Royalty in that high-ceilinged room, or haunts that cool cellar searching for supplies.

Perhaps she comes quietly to the little armchair on the rock and sits again looking across "Ludlow Street" and the River to the old City of Saint John.

BIBLIOGRAPHY

Ludlow and Verplanck family history, courtesy of J. Clarence Webster Library, New Brunswick Museum.

Story of "Fort de la Rivière de St. Jean" and "Fort Frederick" from the W.O. Raymond papers in collections of the New Brunswick Historical Society, loaned by courtesy of Mr. Fred J. Nisbet, Renforth, N.B.

Story of "Old Government House" and "Pioneer Cemetery", courtesy of Miss Bessie Wilson, West Saint John.

"First Grammar Schools in New Brunswick", Archives Department, New Brunswick Museum.

Susanna Phillipse Robinson

In the rolling hills on the bank of the Hudson River at Yonkers stands the Manor House of Phillipsburg, and here in 1727 Susanna Phillipse, daughter of the Honourable Frederick Phillipse, Speaker of the House of Assembly, was born.

Susanna's grandfather, Frederick Phillipse, had built Manor House in 1682 and it was held by the Phillipse family for three generations. The first Lord of the Manor, Frederick Phillipse, or Vereryk Philipsen as he was then known, was born in Bolswaert, Holland, in 1626. Coming to New Amsterdam (New York) when he was a young man, he was employed by the Dutch West India Company as master carpenter to supervise and appraise their various enterprises.

He was also "Church master" in charge of repairs for the old Dutch Church erected in 1642 at Fort Amsterdam. The guardhouses at Fort Esopus (Kingston, New York) were built under Frederick's direction and Governor Stuyvesant frequently "referred the carpenter's work to the opinion of my carpenter Frederick Philipsen" when building.

Frederick Phillipse became a Burgher of New York in 1657 and was granted a lot at the corner of Whitehall and Stone streets. Prospering as an architect-builder, he became a merchant-trader but still retained his connection with the Dutch West India Company as consultant.

He was a genius in trading and much of his income came from speculation in wampum, the Indian money which was part of the currency of the colonists. Were he alive today he would be a Wall Street tycoon, for he not only bought the shell beads in bulk from the Indians, but he had them strung as "wampum" which greatly increased their value.

After the English conquest of New Amsterdam when the supply of wampum was at its lowest and its value advanced some 400 percent, it was recorded that "one Frederick Phillipse the richest Miin Heer in that place was said to have whole hogsheads of Indian money or wampum." 'My Carpenter' of 1658 had become 'Sieur Frederick' in 1666 and 'De Heer Frederick Phillipse' in 1686. Frederick had used his wealth and influential connections to secure a "patroonage", for in 1685 he bought from the Indians a large property on the Pocantico.

In the meantime Frederick Phillipse had married Margaret, the widow of rich Peter de Vries. She was beautiful, well educated and also an excellent business woman. It was a business as well as a matrimonial partnership, for Margaret managed her own estates, purchased her own ships and made trips to Holland to the extent that one voyage recorded, ". . . in small flute-ship called the CHARLES of which Thomas Singleton was master but the superior authority over both ship and cargo was in Margaret Phillipse who was owner of both".

After Margaret's death Frederick married Catherine Van Cortlandt. Each marriage brought him large inherited fortunes.

Phillipse built a house on the Pocantico that was a veritable fortress. Castle Phillipse had thick stone walls with gun ports facing the river. Its seven-foot muzzle loaders could blast away at any marauders that dared attack.

Phillipse spent more time at New York, however, than at Castle Phillipse. When he received a grant of land at Yonkers, he erected there the Manor Hall of Phillipse Manor. In 1693 a Charter in the name of William and Mary granted Frederick the title "Lord of Phillipsburg". He also received the right to construct the toll bridge across Spuyten-Duyvil Creek to be called "Knightsbridge". Even today it is known by this name. Everyone travelling to New York paid "three pence current money of New York" into Frederick's contribution box.

The Manor House was built of Dutch brick. Its immense windows could be secured with solid wooden shutters. In the south porch under a fine colonial transom stands a ponderous Dutch door with its great iron hinges and heavy lock brought from Holland in 1681.

On either side of the south entrance hall stretch the East and West Parlours. Wainscotted walls of the East room reach to a ceiling decorated with floral borders and portrait medallions. In the elaborate centrepiece a girl with a mandolin, a man with bagpipes, another with a hautboy, a dancing girl and cupids complete the arabesque. Colonial woodwork carved with roses and oak leaf designs frames the mantle over the huge fireplace where an interesting eighteenth century fireback bears the Royal Coat of Arms. Beside the massive chimney a creepy secret passage extended underground to the river. Tradition has it that Captain William Kidd, the pirate chief, then living in New York, sailed up the river with his contraband goods to store them in the subterranean chamber of the Manor House. Privateering, as it was called, was a popular addition to legitimate trading then, and merchants often took little side ventures, an issue which did not trouble the authorities very much.

From the south entrance the broad stairway with its beautifully spiralled balusters leads to the second floor. In the spacious West Chamber the open fireplace, lined with blue and white Delft tiles, shows Biblical scenes; Zacchaeus in a tree with Christ and His disciples passing by; Joseph fleeing into Egypt with the young Child and Mother riding on an ass; the miracle of the Loaves and Fishes, and others. Here the stove-plate depicts in relief Elijah being fed by the ravens and below an inscription reads:

Ich habe den raben befolen dich zu vers.

At the bottom of the plate are the ironmaster's initials B.S.D.W. and the date 1760.

In the attic were the slaves' quarters with rude plank floors and hand-hewn timbers. The doors there swung on wooden hinges edged with leather to prevent squeaking. This section of the house was much used for when Susanna lived at Manor House they had over fifty slaves.

Slaves tilled the soil in thrifty Dutch manner and the entire estate was self-supporting. There were carpenter shops, a smithy, a cooperage, a dairy and even a saddlery to make harnesses when horses succeeded the oxen for work in the fields.

Shrubbery edged the velvet lawns and formal gardens reached far down to the banks of the Hudson where the Albany Post Road skirted the river. Along this road came the Indians, and traders with their bolts of calico and pins and buttons. Along this road came the missionaries and soldiers, and French prisoners trickling down from Montreal and Quebec, for New York was a British Colony then.

Along this road came Beverly Robinson of Virginia. Very handsome was this tall young man with his London tailored coat fitting well on broad shoulders, and as his horse's hoofs clattered down the road, Susanna's bright eyes watched from the Manor windows. Young Robinson fell in love with the beautiful daughter of the Manor House. It was a happy romance and in 1747 Susanna became the bride of the handsome young Virginian.

For a wedding present her father gave them a large estate at Tarrytown near Castle Phillipse on the Hudson river. Here the Robinsons built a long two-storied house with comfortable low-raftered rooms in the style of the country seats of England. Gardens and lawns surrounded the house and there were fruit orchards and deer parks. Up the Hudson to Beverly Robinson's landing place came ships from England bringing beautiful mahogany furniture, good shoes and elegant dresses, farm implements and books.

Susanna was a very busy woman, for besides being mistress of Beverly Manor on the Hudson there was a city home in New York on Robinson Street (in the neighbourhood of the present Barclay Street) that required her attention. Susanna, however, had had some experience in managing large houses, for she was Chatelaine of Manor House at an early age.

Beverly House must have taxed Susanna's talents as hostess, for we're told that "under no roof were so many strangers of distinction sheltered than at Beverly House on the Hudson."

When a midshipman on one of the frigates, Prince William Henry, afterwards William the Fourth of England, enjoyed the Robinson's hospitality. He was the first person of Royal birth to visit the New World. General Knox, George Washington and other illustrious guests feasted in the long-remembered dining room. In tribute to such generous hospitality gifts frequently arrived at Beverly House.

One day a servant reported that a keg had been put off a sailing vessel and was down on the wharf. Beverly Robinson strolled down to have a look at it and then had it brought up to the house. There was no letter, no card. No one knew where it came from. When the keg was opened, however, out of the sawdust packing came an elaborate silver tea urn, the first of its kind to be seen in America. Who sent it remained a mystery. After it had been in use for some time, a servant, while cleaning it one day, happened to unscrew the ornamental top and in the bottom of the tapering ball was engraved "Hunter to Robinson 1750". It was a gift from a former visitor to Beverly House.

One day in February 1756 while George Washington was travelling on an errand to Governor Shirley in Boston, he decided to call on his old friend Beverly Robinson. As youngsters they had been neighbours, for Augustine Washington, George's father, had an estate adjoining the Robinson home in Virginia. Someone else was on the way to Beverly House that day. It was lovely Mary Phillipse, coming to visit her sister Susanna.

"Polly" as Mary was called, was a very attractive young lady and an accomplished one as well, for since her sister's marriage she had taken over the management of Manor House and she saw to it that every asset on the estate continued to be used to advantage. She even had a log house built near Lake Mahopac, where she lived each summer during her annual visit to the tenants of Phillipse Castle. Here she checked supplies, listed requirements and collected rent. If the pence were not forthcoming, she'd accept a couple of fat hens instead.

When Mary's coach clattered down the Albany road that day, George Washington was also riding to Beverly House. Over his buff and blue uniform he wore a gay white and scarlet cloak. His sword was knotted with red and gold and his horses' fittings glittered with the Washington crest. His aides rode beside him and his servants followed at the rear of the party.

Washington was an excellent horseman and he spared no expense in the matter of clothes. In his carefully kept expense accounts there are immense outlays for his tailors, hatters, jewelers and saddlers.

Washington's glittering cavalcade had just arrived at Beverly House when Mary's coach with its jet-black horses drew up. He was accustomed to meeting beautiful women and he never lost his head. As he watched Mary Phillipse alight from her coach, however, he lost his heart instead. It was love at first sight. He forgot all about his errand to Governor Shirley. He forgot everything except the charms of beautiful Mary Phillipse. Together they strolled about Susanna's gardens. Together they rode the bridle paths through the park. Susanna smiled to herself as she watched the courtship, for well she knew that Washington loved land, and her sister Mary owned some fifty thousand acres.

One evening after dinner Mary and Washington were together in Susanna's "little parlour". It was candle-lighting time and small flames flickered in silver sconces. The glow of sunset spread across the river, and the sweet scent of applewood burning in the open fireplace filled the room.

Washington's glance was a caress, his voice low and persuasive as he spoke of love. But Mary? Well, for some reason she did not return his affection. (She was a belle of society enjoying balls and entertainments and she had hosts of admirers.) There was plenty of time to think of marriage, she explained.

Then gay voices and snatches of laughter drifted from the drawing rooms where other guests were settling down to an evening at cards. Courteously the handsome figure in blue velvet bowed and followed Mary to the drawing room, the guests and the cards.

Though he liked her candor, Washington was disappointed. Nevertheless, he was not entirely discouraged. He stayed on for another five ardent days and invited Mary Phillipse and her sister to visit New York (such a gay city then with its ten thousand three hundred inhabitants) and view the wonders of the "Microcosm". This entertainment was advertised as the "Elaborate and Celebrated piece or mechanism of the World in Miniature. Built in the form of a Roman Temple after 22 years of close study and application by the late ingenious Mr. Henry Bridges of London. It will be shown every day from six in the morning till six at night to any select company (not less than six persons) at six shillings each."

The Microcosm was so exciting that they saw it twice. Later

that evening while his servant carefully folded away his fine raiment, Washington sat at his desk and entered in his expense book "treat ye ladies to ye Microcosm 18 shill." The following day ye Colonel treated himself to a horse sale in New York, where he bought three mares. Then he tipped the Robinson servants "five pounds eight shillings", not too generously, and went on to Boston and Governor Shirley.

Governor Shirley had already planned the summer attack on Crown Point and Ticonderoga, then held by the French. He had ordered that "drums beat anywhere within the Province [Massachusetts] for enlisting volunteers for His Majesty's service in a regiment of foot to be forthwith raised for the expedition against Crown Point." As Colonel Washington was in full command for the Virginia forces, the Governor wanted to discuss what support he could expect from Virginia.

Even in Boston, with serious matters harassing him, Washington could not forget the torment of his heart. For over a year and a half he wrote to his friend Joseph Chew in New York, asking him to keep an eye on Mary Phillipse.

Chew's replies were not too encouraging. Dated New London, March 4, 1756, a postscript reads:

I have this moment a letter from our worthy friend B. Robinson, The agreeable Miss Polly and all his family are Very Well.

Again from New London on July 13, 1757, Joseph Chew writes:

As to the Latter part of your letter, what shall I say. I often had the Pleasure of Breakfast with the Charming Polly, Roger Morris was there (don't be startled) but not always, you know him he is a Lady's man always something to say, the Town talk't of it as a sure and settled affair, I can't say I think so and that I much doubt it but assure you had Little Acquaintance with Mr. Morris and only slightly hinted it to Miss Polly: but how can you be Excused to Continue so long at Phila? I think I should have made a kind of Flying march of it if it had been only to have seen whether the Works were sufficient to withstand a Vigorous Attack, you a Soldier and a Lover, mind I have been arguing for my own interest now for had you taken this method then I should have had the Pleasure of seeing you. My Paper is almost full and I am convinced you will be heartily tyred in Reading it — however will just add that I intend to set out to morrow for New York Where I will not be wanting to let Miss Polly Know the sincere Regard a Friend of mine has for her and I am sure if she had my Eyes to see thro she would Prefer him to all others, if my Brother is in your way let him know I am well, now my Dear Friend I wish you Eternall

Happiness and Content and assure you that I am with sincere Esteem

Your most Obed't Serv't
Jos. Chew.

Again Joseph proves a good friend, for on August 8th he writes from New York:

I arrived here a few days agoe Mrs. Robinson and her Dear little Family are well. Miss Polly has had a pain in her Face but is on the mend and I pray Heaven to Protect you and Assure that I am my Dear Sir, Your Obed Servt, Jos. Chew.

Washington, however, was a very busy man arranging for "drum beating up" the Volunteers, and seeing that they were supplied with "a lamp, kettle, a Bowl and Platter and the officers of each Company two, and every man a spoon," so he did not get back to Beverly House for some time. Later he found that lovely Mary Phillipse was already promised to Roger Morris.

It was a winter wedding, January the 28th, 1758. The sleighing was good and with bells jingling, guests drove up from New York to crowd the Manor House. Under a crimson canopy stood Mary and her three bridesmaids. Since her father had died in 1751 while in Barbados, the bride was given away by her brother, Lord Phillipse.

Lord Frederick was elegantly attired and wore the gold chain and jewelled badge of the Master Ranger of the Royal Deer Forests of Bohemia, inherited from Viscount Phillipse of Friesland.

The wedding banquet was a sumptuous affair, but it was marred by a strange incident. During the feasting a tall Indian, wrapped in a scarlet blanket, appeared unannounced at the door of the banquet room. He raised his arms in salutation and a hush fell on the assembly. Speaking directly to Mary, he said, "Your possessions shall pass from you when the Eagle shall despoil the Lion of its mane." Then he vanished as suddenly as he came. Years afterwards Lord Phillipse's old coloured valet would roll his eyes and shiver with terror as he repeated the story, for the Indian was real enough; so was the prophecy.

In the summer of 1758 Roger Morris left their town house on Stone Street to go to Fort Frederick on the Saint John River. Later he took part in the famous 'seven minutes' fighting' of the shortest battle in history — the Battle of the Plains of Abraham.

By 1765 Roger and Mary decided to retire to a country home. They built on "the most desirable and commanding site on the Island of Manhattan". Today the old house stands on the top of a hill at Harlem Heights. Behind wrought iron fences spacious lawns and sunken gardens provide an oasis of quiet in a desert of din.

Roger and Mary did not enjoy their new home for long. Soon

the Revolution started and with it came the years that tried men's souls. Beverly Robinson raised a regiment from tenants on his own estates and Susanna watched with a sad and anxious heart as her four sons joined their father and rode away. During the struggle the rich landowners on the Hudson were plundered and robbed by bands of marauders in the name of either the British Crown or the Colonial Government. Many descendants of the original Dutch patroons became ardent British supporters.

Silver Helmet Creamer, 5½ inches high. Typical of the Loyalist era.

Courtesy of The New Brunswick Museum
Photo by William Hart

Susanna's brother, Colonel Frederick Phillipse, the last Lord of the Manor of Phillipsburg, also declined to join the Americans. After being taken prisoner, he escaped and took refuge in New York. Later he went to England where he died in Chester in April 1785.

At length the day came when Susanna went about the rooms in Beverly House picking up valuables to pass on to her family. Silverware, jewellery, pictures, and the massive silver tea urn that had been a gift from the English visitor. Susanna took one last long look at her favourite 'little parlour', so crowded with memories of herself and Mary; her cherished furnishings — the house she loved. Then she walked down through the garden paths for the last time. The coach stood ready to take her to New York from where she sailed for England. Her husband joined her later and they never saw Beverly House again.

Susanna Phillipse Robinson; her sister Mary Morris; and Margaret Inglis, wife of the Rt. Rev. Charles Inglis, Rector of Trinity Church New York, were the only women in all America to be banished forever and forbidden to return under penalty of death, for "adhering to the enemies of the State." Their crime? Was it treason to be loyal and follow one's husband? But their huge estates were confiscated.

Mary Morris with her children sailed for England also, where after the War they were joined by Roger Morris.

As fate would have it, General Washington and his officers took over the Morris home in New York as Military Headquarters. He used the library as Council Room, and for his bedroom the General chose the southwest room on the second story. From the portico floated the Continental Flag, the British Union Jack with thirteen red and white stripes. How could he keep his mind on the campaign with so many reminders of his former sweetheart around him? But we are told that he chose this house in order to protect Mary's possessions.

The Indian prophecy came true. The Phillipse, Robinson and Morris estates were confiscated and sold by the Commissioners of Forfeiture, and Mary Morris' furniture and silver were sold by auction in New York in 1783. The Phillipse estate alone was valued at £600,000. Mary Morris' estate eventually passed into the hands of the Astors.

In an old diary there's a story told that an acquaintance remarked to one of Mary's nephews, "It was such a pity that Mary Phillipse missed the chance to become first lady of the land." The young Robinson replied, "Ah, Sir, you don't know my Aunt Morris! She is a very fascinating person and a woman of great strength of character; had she married General Washington he never would have been a rebel."

Two of Susanna's sons went to New Brunswick with the Loyalists. John first settled at Douglas, building his "Pine Grove" home there. Then he went to Saint John, where later he was appointed Mayor of the city.

Beverly Robinson, Junior, who had married Nancy Barclay, daughter of another Rector of Trinity Church in New York, lived in Fredericton while building his home at Nashwaaksis. The doors and window frames for the new house had not arrived when the Fredericton house burned. With no other shelter to be had, the Robinsons moved into the unfinished house, and through that bitter cold winter, blankets were all they had for doors and windows.

Here, in those early days, massive mahogany tables sparkled with gleaming silver, and gracious ladies were escorted to dinner by stately men.

Many visitors enjoyed the Robinson's generous hospitality and the comfort of good featherbeds after a hard day's riding. There were no roads in New Brunswick then; but the loyal colonists got around on horseback, and they had boats — slow durham boats and rowboats.

Bishop Inglis, the first Bishop of North America, was used to having transportation difficulties in his efforts to reach all parts of his diocese which included Newfoundland, Bermuda, Nova Scotia (where he made his headquarters), Quebec and part of Ontario. But even in Saint John, when he had finished laying the cornerstone of Old Trinity Church there in 1788, he had to bargain with fishermen to take him to Fredericton. He hired "two men and a row boat at a dollar and a half a day" and stopped at Inns along the river. "Rogers", thirty-three miles from Saint John, was a good Inn. "Flaglor's" at Oak Point was another worthy of mention, but the good Bishop was not so complimentary about others with their soiled bed linens and poor meals.

Bishop Inglis was a guest at "Colonel Robinson's excellent farm" and Governor Thomas Carleton and his Lady often stopped over for tea, while planning the first official Ball ever held in Fredericton.

It was a gala affair. "The Governor was so animated and Mrs. Carleton so anxious to please that they showered every attention on their guests", is recorded in an old diary. Our great-great-grandmothers stepped the minuet in the low-timbered rooms of Government House to the music of flutes and violins. At supper they were served "rare and delicious foods," after which they "danced again until three o'clock in the morning." A scandalous hour for pioneer folk!

Of the beautiful gowns worn that night, Mrs. Carleton's was "of elegant tea-coloured satin, with a white satin petticoat embroidered in pastel shades. Her hair was dressed in light curls tied with a silk bandeau embroidered with "Vive le Roi", which had a pearl brooch on one side and ostrich and peacock feathers on the other. . . . [She] carried a large bouquet of Jasmine and Carnations."

Regimental drum, powder horn and cutlass of the 2nd Battalion New Jersey Volunteers. The three battalions of this regiment came to New Brunswick in 1783-84.   *Courtesy of The New Brunswick Museum*
Photo by William Hart

Another gown had "a train and body of cerise satin with vandyke points richly embroidered in silver, and an elegant gold muslin petticoat and sash of same, and a cape of white crepe with epaulettes of gold and silver bullion." For jewelry the lady wore "brilliant pendulum earrings", and over her light curls "a crepe bandeau trimmed with blonde lace and ornamented fancy plumes."

No mean display for Fredericton in 1795 with four hundred inhabitants in the town besides the officers of the garrison!

The house Beverly Robinson built at Nashwaaksis, a two-storey peaked-roof building, stands deserted now. Some of the willow trees he planted still cast cool shadows over the once-tilled fields of his "excellent farm." Of Beverly Robinson, Member of the Legislative Council, Trustee of the College of New Brunswick, and organizer of the King's New Brunswick Regiment, only memories remain. While his tall ghost walks the deserted gardens on windy moonlit nights, all across Canada there are Robinsons bearing the family names of Beverly, Morris, de Lancey, Cortlandt and Barclay, for Beverly and Susanna's descendants are legion.

The old Manor House on the Hudson where Susanna and Mary spent so many happy years has passed through the hands of many owners. Today the dignified old landmark, repaired and restored, is a cherished relic of Anglo-Saxon civilization in the New World.

A tablet in the hallway reads:

Phillipse Manor House, erected in 1682 by Frederick Phillipse, Esquire, Manor of Phillipsburg created in 1692. Confiscated by Act of the Legislature of New York in 1779. Sold by Commissioners of Forfeiture 1785. Occupied as a private residence until 1868. Purchased by the Village of Yonkers in that year. Became the City Hall of Yonkers in 1872.

There is glamour, romance and sacrifice in the life story of Susanna Phillipse who married Beverly Robinson and whose sons went to New Brunswick with the Loyalists. Strong, self-reliant, far-sighted men, they were proud of their loyalty with a quiet assured certainty that this new land would be a great nation in the days to come.

Susanna Phillipse Robinson died at Thornbury near Bath, in England, at the age of ninety-six. Today her descendants in New Brunswick cherish those heirlooms she brought from Beverly House on the Hudson so long ago. The massive silver tea urn, the first of its kind in America, still graces a mahogany sideboard. The little golden deer set with diamond, emerald, ruby and pearls that the Lords of Phillipse Manor wore on State occasions, still reposes in its velvet-lined casket. Over the fireplace in the living room of a lovely old New Brunswick homestead hang the miniatures of Colonel Beverly Robinson and his wife Susanna — and they're a very handsome couple.

BIBLIOGRAPHY

Incidents in Family History, Courtesy of Mr. John Morris Robinson, Rothesay, N.B.

Joseph Chew Letters, from 'Letters to Washington, 1758, 1770' by Stanislaw Murray Hamilton, Vol.3, Courtesy of the New York Historical Society, New York City.

Phillipse Manor Hall, by Edward Hagaman Hall, L.H.D., New York.

Yesterdays in Little Old New York, by James H. Callendar, Courtesy of the Museum of the City of New York.

Trips and Trails of Historic Interest, Courtesy of the Museum of the City of New York.

Dictionary of American Biography, Scribners New York.

Loyalists of The American Revolution, Sabine.

Historical Material — Early New Brunswick, Archives Department, New Brunswick Museum, Saint John, N.B.

Ann Mallard

Ann Mallard crept out of the rain-drenched tent in Parr Town one June morning to listen to the conversation between her husband and the tall stranger in the tattered uniform. This was the second time that William Ryan had come to offer his lot on King Street to Lieutenant Thomas Mallard.

Certainly her husband was not satisfied with the lot he had drawn in the city. Almost anything, Ann thought, would be better than that land so far away from the Landing Place. Perhaps Thomas could make a trade this time.

Life in the city had no attractions for William Ryan, formerly of the Royal Fencibles. King Street indeed! With its forty-foot lots; houses all crowded together, ships tied up at the foot of the street; everyone getting in everybody else's way. William longed for the wide open spaces. Already he had petitioned for part of an Island down Passamaquoddy way, where he could farm as he liked, and fish when he wanted to, not dependent on the others to supply him with food.

Lieutenant Thomas Mallard, late of the 37th Company of Militia, listened to Ryan's grumbling, then clambered over the rocks and stood beside Ann. A lot on King Street for nine guineas was what Ryan offered, he told Ann. She thought of their good home in New York City seized by the mob; their furniture smashed while she helplessly looked on. Nine guineas! What a price for a lot in this forsaken spot! Ann was all for bargaining.

But Ryan wanted to be off and Thomas Mallard was anxious to begin building before the summer was gone. The British Government had promised supplies, lumber and bricks and shingles. They must decide at once.

Nine guineas for a lot in the city, either that, or keep the place they'd drawn in the woods.

Rain came down in grey sheets as Ann and Thomas stood on the hillside. Ann thought of their children in the rain-soaked tent and made her decision quickly. So, "William Ryan, formerly of the Royal Fencibles and now of the City of Saint John, Cooper, sold to Thomas

Mallard, Lieutenant in the 37th Company of Militia, now of the said City of Saint John, Mariner, for the consideration of the sum of nine guineas that lot of land being 40 x 100 feet, Number 393 on King Street."

Then William Ryan went off to his Island, to gather the silver harvest from the sea, far from the tribulations of the market place, while Thomas and Ann Mallard talked things over in their tent.

Since the War was over and the regiments were disbanded Thomas would have to look elsewhere for a living, and besides his wife, he had Nancy and Margaret to provide for. Would he go back to sailing ships and leave his wife to bring up their children? Master mariners could always get a ship. He had sailed brigs and schooners and sloops in and out of New York on long and treacherous journeys. He knew fogs and storms. He had shared courage and fear along with maggoty biscuits and foul pork with his men.

And when the Revolution began he had joined the Militia, leaving his family, safe as he thought in New York, only to find, after years of struggle, another bitter journey with his Loyalist friends to their refuge in New Brunswick.

But Thomas was done with roving. All he wanted was a good roof over his head, where he could live unmolested with his family and earn enough to keep them from starvation.

Now the Mallards were essentially city dwellers. Ann liked having people around; Thomas was at his best in a crowd. And Thomas was a good trader; he'd handled his ship's cargoes at a good profit for their owners. Then again, Ann was a good cook. So they decided that the new city would need an Inn. Ships would come bringing travellers needing lodging, and everyone has to eat. Here was opportunity staring them in the face. So the Mallards built their Inn on the King Street lot.

It was a substantial building, this pioneer hotel. Two and a half stories with a huge kitchen and outbuildings connected with the main house by a covered passageway. And there were eight fireplaces. On the first floor was the tavern and dining room, and upstairs a large room was reserved for assemblies. In the bedrooms were huge canopied beds with straw mattresses and feather ticks.

Probably those beds were made by Thomas Nisbet, a cabinetmaker who, in 1785, advertised to "make beds and bed and window curtains" and advised "that a quantity of baked hair had arrived and he was prepared to supply sofas and mattresses of the best workmanship." He also "had considerable mahogany on hand and would be happy to execute orders for furniture."

So, with rooms furnished and the tavern and kitchen well-stocked, Ann and Thomas hung out a sign over the front door and

"Mallard's Inn" was open for business.

And business came. Passengers from the ships, with boxes and bundles and trunks smelling of tar and bilge water, climbed the narrow stairs to those bedrooms. Travellers on horseback rode to Mallard's door after covering miles over narrow paths through the forest that followed the old Indian trails; for there were no roads in New Brunswick at that time.

Ladies in rustling silk petticoats and ostrich feathers bobbing on their bonnets drifted through the hallways leaving a trail of perfume in their wake. And colorful young dandies in their velvet breeches, bright waistcoats and frilled shirts all stopped over at Mallard's Inn.

Owen's Gout Chair

Courtesy of The New Brunswick Museum
Photo by Gordon Anderson

Down in Ann's kitchen, long-handled skillets and spiders and huge copper pots, well-polished with sand and "elbow grease" shone in the firelight; for the flames in that huge fireplace seldom went out. There would be rich puddings bubbling in copper kettles that swung from a heavy iron crane over the open fire; and often a whole shoulder of beef would sizzle and sputter as it roasted on the spit.

Many pioneer homes used bake kettles in which pies were dropped and the bake kettles placed on the hearth, then covered with hot ashes. But Ann Mallard had a bake oven as big as a trunk built in the side of the fireplace, where pies and cakes and bread came out steaming with tantalizing odors.

Those were the days of hearty foods. There was no cold storage poultry, no radish roses or celery curls. Vitamins were unheard of. But Ann had some knowledge of food value — she knew that one pound of bread equalled two and a half pounds of potatoes, and rice was the most nutritious of all foods.

Ann's desserts were something to get one's teeth into. Besides boiled puddings she baked huge rice puddings with eggs and molasses. "Apple bread" with warm stewed apples added to bread dough and baked to a golden crust, she served with honey.

"Clapbread" was a favorite too, and so easy to make. Just oatmeal and salted water mixed to a thick dough, then rolled in thin cakes and spread on the hot hearth stones to bake. Kept in a covered crock they lasted for weeks. Many a traveller set out from Mallard House with a pocket full of Ann's "Clapbread" and a raw onion or two to sustain him on his journey. Yankee sea captains smacked their lips over the good "Kedgeree" Ann made, with fish boiled with rice and butter and mustard.

Pork was a staple food. "A pig should have its ears and tail covered with buttered paper." says the ancient cookbook used in Ann's day, and "a bit of butter tied up in a piece of linen to baste the back with; otherwise it will be apt to blister." Ann may have boxed the kitchen boy's ears if he loitered over the basting, but she saw to it the pig did not blister.

For Ann Mallard there was no eight-hour day. The energetic pioneers of our great country believed strongly in free enterprise and hard work. Ann never heard of the hillside being 'dew pearled' and 'morning's at seven'. Long before that hour found Ann down at the "Landing Place" where the fishermen and market folk brought their wares to the old brick building in Market Square.

Good bright silvery mackerel and gleaming pink salmon slithered into Ann's basket. And the servant carried home fresh vegetables and greens and herbs and faggots of shallots. And at Mallard House they would serve crimped salmon, collared salmon, curried, pickled or potted salmon for dinner. Another favorite dish was: "Fifteen sheep's tongues, simmered with strips of pork, bay leaves and thyme." Then Ann served it piping hot, with a "faggot of Shallots".

"Jugged Hare" was a 'piece de resistance' in those early days; for rabbit was plentiful and cheap. From yellowed pages the recipe is complete:

How to Jug an old Hare

Skin, paunch and wash a hare, Cut it in pieces and dredge with flour, fry in boiling butter. Have ready 1½ pints gravy of any sort, thicken with a little flour. Put this into a jar, add pieces of fried hare and an onion stuck with six cloves, a lemon peeled and cut in half, a good seasoning of pepper, cayenne and salt. Cover the jar down tightly, put it up to the neck in a stew pan of boiling water and let it stew until the hare is quite tender, taking care to keep the water boiling. When nearly done pour in a half pint of wine and add a few force meat balls or baked in the oven a few minutes before they are put to the gravy. When done serve with currant jelly.

Recommended as a breakfast or luncheon dish "Jugged Hare" required two and a half hours to stew. Small wonder that those early cooks were early risers!

That was Ann's kitchen. But that wasn't all there was to innkeeping. There was sweeping and dusting, huge featherbeds to be shaken up and turned every day, washstand pitchers to be filled with water, and fresh candles to be placed in the little brass candlestands.

Often when Ann Mallard supervised the bed-making, she would steal a glance across King Street. From the front windows she could see General Arnold's groom holding a frisky horse at the mounting block. Then Peggy Arnold, the General's wife, in her smart velvet riding habit would come down the steps, mount her horse and be off for a morning canter.

Shrill cries of street vendors penetrated Ann's bedrooms while market boys, their baskets slung on their backs, with carrots and beets draped over the edges like a vegetable waterfall, climbed the steep hill.

And if Ann pushed open the window on a hot morning she could smell something more than the clear sea air blowing up King Street. For early as it was, Mr. Evans, the hairdresser, would be bowing his patrons to their carriages, and the odor of Frangipani and Bergamot hair-powder wafted across the street.

Perhaps more than Mr. Evan's hair-powder assailed Ann's nostrils. For garbage and refuse lay for days in the streets and frequently a dead animal lay in the gutter far longer than decency permitted. Perhaps Ann had a fiendish desire to catch a city alderman and rub his nose in that garbage, but being a very tidy person she justly complained, like the rest of the citizens.

In winter from those same windows Ann watched travellers gathering at the corner across the street to go by "post sleigh" to Fredericton; for in 1787 John Droust, Courier, advertised in the *New Brunswick Advertiser*, "Saint John to Fredericton, mail sleigh. Leaves Saint John every Thursday at 10 A.M. Arrives in Fredericton the second day. Four dollars through passage. Way passengers three pence per mile. For seats apply Mr. John Masteng at Kent's Tavern, corner King and Germain Streets. Parcels entrusted to his care will be faithfully and punctually attended to."

A transportation centre in 1787, on this same location the Canadian Pacific Railway now carries on the old tradition. Here in the 1780's passengers for Fredericton, huddled in fur robes and with hot bricks at their feet, shivered along the adventurous eighty-mile journey. Today on this same spot, the travel-minded can arrange passage to far-off India, Australia, or any other place in the World and be transported swiftly, safely and comfortably in a well ordered luxury, never dreamed-of by pioneer travellers.

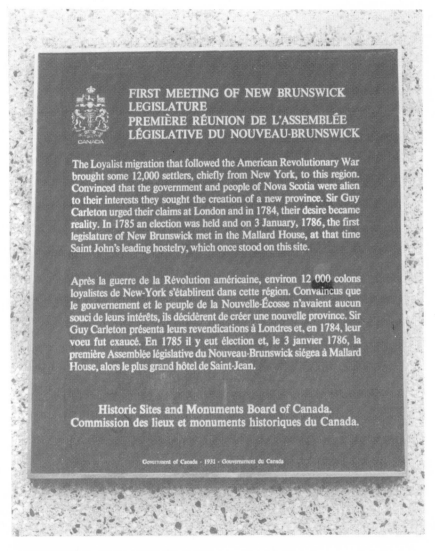

Plaque on the Brunswick Square Building on King Street, Saint John

Courtesy of The New Brunswick Museum
Photo by William Hart

93

When New Brunswick's first Governor, Thomas Carleton, arrived in Saint John, Mallard's Long Room housed the first General Assembly of Legislature. Gentlemen in velvet coats and wigs and swords waited at Mallard's door. It was cold that January 9th, 1786, but the gentlemen did not wear their three-cornered hats, for Mr. Carleton was King George the Third's representative and all heads remained uncovered in his presence. Shouting crowds lined the streets, hand bells rang, drums beat. There was a din of cannon from ships in the Harbour, and guns thundered salutes in reply from Fort Howe.

It was strictly a gentlemen's party. But while Thomas Mallard kept an eye on the door to prevent outsiders entering, Ann slipped upstairs to the Long Room, to give the spotless table a last-minute flick with the turkey-wing duster and see that the decanters and inkpots were filled and the sanding box for drying ink on the documents and sealing wax were at hand.

Then His Excellency sent a message to the House requesting their presence in the Council Chamber; accordingly Mr. Speaker with the House attended. Amos Botsford, Esquire, the representative from Westmorland County, was Speaker of the House and there were twenty-three members "in attendance".

Shortly afterwards, one night when all decent folk were asleep in their beds, a crowd of disorderly ruffians led by some Government opponents staged an election riot in front of Mallard's Inn. They stoned the windows and battered down the door with a heavy log and only the arrival of the Militia prevented further destruction.

For two years Mallard's Long Room was the Official Council Chamber, then the Legislature was moved to Fredericton because, as Governor Carleton explained, the City of Saint John was not a safe place; being a sea port it was more vulnerable in case of enemy attack.

Famous and interesting events took place in that Long Room. It was on May 28, 1789, that Saint John citizens attended the first play ever staged in New Brunswick — a performance of "The Busy Body" done by an entirely male cast. It was advertised in the newspaper: "Doors to be opened at half past five. To begin precisely at half past six o'clock. Tickets selling at three shillings each to be had at Mallard's. No money will be received at the door, nor any person admitted without ticket." Lady patrons were asked to come with their hair dressed as low as possible, for the low ceiling of Mallard's Long Room did not permit raised seats. And "no children on laps" were permitted to attend.

The Drama critic of the day reported that "'The Busy Body', by a company of gentlemen Saturday evening last, was presented before the most numerous and polite assembly which has appeared in this town. Mallard's Long Room on this occasion was converted into a very Pretty Theatre. The scene, decorations and dresses were in general well cast and the characters supported with great life and humor. Some of the Company displayed comic talents which would have done honor to a British Theatre, and it is in justice to say that all exceeded the expectation of the most favorable of their friends."

Jonathan Sewall, who was reading law with Ward Chipman and later became Chief Justice of Quebec, played his part "exceedingly well". But Jonathan had taken part in theatricals while attending school in Bristol, England, and his acting attracted the attention of the illustrious tragedienne, Mrs. Siddons, who wrote a note to Sewall beginning:

The World is dull and seldom gives us cause

For joy, surprise or well deserved applause.

And she went on to compliment Sewall on his clever performance. During the intermission of "The Busy Body" that May evening, gentlemen clattered down Mallard's narrow stairway to refresh themselves at the Tavern and stroll on King Street. Jewelled snuffboxes glittered in the setting sun and sleeve ruffles fluttered as they thumbed their snuff elegantly and exchanged opinions about the performance.

The Mallards were not without competition in their business; for there was Mr. McPherson's Coffee House at the foot of King Street, and just around the corner stood Thomas Mullin's "Bunch of Grapes", where, "he was known to keep a plentiful stock of the best liquers, and a hospitable table induces him to hope for a share of the public confidence." But Mr. Mullin had a sideline — evidently he was less of an innkeeper than a blacksmith, for on August 5, 1784, he advertised that he carried on "A Blacksmith Business in all its branches and has particularly laid himself out for heavy work, edge tools and ship work and will always be provided with a tolerable stock of hardware, etc. etc."

Ann Mallard had to contend with another "Lunch Room" just two doors below Mallard House, for in the *Royal Gazette and Nova Scotia Intelligencer* of (Christmas Day) December 25th, 1798, was advertised: "Mr. Marriott begs to inform the public that he sells Soups, Broths, Beef or Mutton Steaks at the lowest prices at a minute's warning, at the sign of the Red Cross in King Street, Nota Bene,-Also showing hairdressing, etcetera on the most reasonable terms." Another competitor with another sideline.

Ann Mallard had to cope with the servant problem too, but it is not recorded that she bought or sold slaves. That slaves were bought and sold in Saint John then, advertisements testify: "October 3, 1788, A stout, likely and very active young black woman, late the property of

John H. Carey, is not offered for any fault, but is singularly sober and diligent. James Hoyt, Auctioneer."

Again in the *Saint John Gazette* March 1, 1799: "For sale,- A Negro wench and child. The wench is about nineteen years old; has been brought up in the country; is well acquainted with a dairy and understands all kinds of housework. She is sold for no fault. Enquire at the Printer's Office." Servants in those days were not as reliable as we are led to believe. Light-fingered folk edged into even the best regulated households. One "Martha Maloney, by favor of a Magistrate, was helped to her new lodging in the Gaol on charge of making too free in several establishments with silver spoons and wearing apparel."

Money was a problem, as always, but in a different way. Those big silver Doubloons (worth $15.72 at that time) often had their edges shaved away until they were worth only half their value. And the Mallards had to make out accounts in Sterling and Dollars for both systems were in use then.

But Ann's business partnership didn't last long, for Thomas Mallard died in 1803. Now any other woman would have sold out and retired to live comfortably, free from business worries, but not Ann. She continued the business of innkeeping and made it profitable too. Her daughters, Nancy and Margaret, were now able to take over supervision of kitchen and upstairs, while Ann devoted her time to accounts and purchasing supplies.

And as it was a fashionable custom, Ann had her "day" when friends came to call and chat over the teacups. Ann didn't envy them as they told of voyages they'd made. She didn't have to go travelling, for as she sat at her desk inside the entryway the World came to her door. Blustery old sea captains, in their long tailed coats and brass buttons, swaggered in with wide strides bringing stories of far off lands. West Indian traders with colourful bandanas and gold rings in their ears came north to sell their rum, mahogany, sugar and spices. Travellers of all sorts, shades and sizes stopped at Mallard's Inn.

And Ann didn't miss much of local gossip either. She could watch big business being transacted over a glass of rum and she kept an ear to the ground as political intrigues were hatched across the Long Room table.

Then there were the dinner parties. Such dinners! Such parties! The Members of Saint John's Lodge met in Mallard's Long Room for years and invitations to their celebrations were published in the newspapers. "The Masters, Wardens and Brethren of St. John Lodge, Number 29, respectfully, acquaint their Brethren that they attend to celebrate the Festival of St. John the Evangelist on the 27th inst., at Mrs. Mallard's Tavern. All the Brethren, not belonging to the

Lodge who mean to favor them with their company, are requested to give their names at Mrs. Mallard's by the 24th inst. The Lodge meets at eleven o'clock at the Lodge Room: from thence they intend to go to church to hear prayers after which dinner will be provided."

After the procession and a three-hour church service the Brethren attacked the heaped dinner plates as if starvation were just around the corner. Then replete with roast beef, poultry, plum pudding, custards and wine, they sat in Ann's comfortable Georgian chairs, dozing before the open fire.

With so many patrons coming and going at Mallard's Inn many an eye turned to Ann's attractive daughters. But it was Captain Robert Farquar who captured Nancy's heart and in June 1805 Nancy and the young captain were married by the Rev. Dr. Mather Byles. There was a gay reception party; toasts were drunk to the popular young couple and the Long Room echoed with laughter and music. Then when Captain Robert sailed off on his voyages, Nancy remained at Mallard House, bustling about efficiently helping with the work.

And there in the Inn Thomas and Ann Mallard had built, and she had managed so well, Ann Mallard died at the age of forty-nine on March 17, 1807. But Mallard's Inn continued to serve the public; for Ann's daughters carried on the work for years. And on January 27, 1813, Margaret Blair Mallard married George Bonsall and together they took over the management of the old Inn.

In 1829 the Inn was partially destroyed by fire, but was rebuilt and altered both inside and out. In 1850 John D. Frost purchased the property from the Bonsall estate, removed the old buildings, including the house on the next lot. Here he erected a brick structure, using portions of the staunch old foundations of the original Mallard House. Eventually the building became the property of Thomas Reynolds and known as the "Royal Hotel."

And on the site Thomas Mallard purchased for nine guineas the old tradition of service established so long ago by Mallard House is still carried on. For "Royal Hotel" menu cards of festive days, glittering with tiny glass stars and Christmas scenes, tell of December celebrations.

The 1898 Christmas dinner card offered everything from oysters to coffee along with an assortment of ten different wines. The May 24th, 1900 "Queen's Birthday" menu offered: Soup, Fish, Boiled Meats, Roast Meats, Entrees, Cold Dishes, nine varieties of Vegetables, Relishes, Pastry, Desserts, and finally Buttermilk, Tea, Coffee, Port and Sherry.

The 1906 Christmas celebrations concluded with the singing of an old Anglo-Norman carol dating back to the 13th century: "Lordlings listen to our Lay", the first of all carols known to have been written in England and discovered on the front leaf of an ancient manuscript in the British Museum. Four verses of this carol, beautifully illustrated, were printed in the Christmas Menu booklet for the benefit of Royal Hotel guests, who wished to join in the good old custom of carolling at Christmas.

Today there is a small brass tablet on the wall of the Royal Hotel at the corner of King and Germain Streets in Saint John. It tells us that "Here stood the Mallard House where the first Legislature of the Province met in 1786."

Of course there is no mention of Ann; it was a man's world in those days! But Ann Mallard literally carved a career for herself back in those early days. And down through the years comes another chapter of pioneer history written in that early Loyalist kitchen of Mallard House. It tells a story of smoke-blackened fireplaces; hearths well swept with turkey wings and birch brooms; of cooking implements crude and cumbersome, and the hearty foods that were prepared there to gladden the hearts and satisfy the hunger of our ancestors.

And of Ann Mallard? We cannot afford to underestimate the example she set. For out of defeat came courage, and Ann Mallard, Pioneer Innkeeper, certainly had plenty of backbone.

BIBLIOGRAPHY

Story of Mallard House, Archives Department, New Brunswick Museum.

Advertisements, Saint John newspapers, New Brunswick Museum.

First General Assembly of New Brunswick, *History of the City and County of Saint John* by D.R. Jack. Provincial Legislative Library, Fredericton, N.B.

Recipes, from early Cook Book, courtesy Miss Estelle Vaughn, Saint John Public Library.

Menus, etc. — "Royal Hotel", courtesy Mr. T. Ernest English, Saint John, N.B.

Mehetible Caleff

The door closed quietly. With her mother's final warning ringing in her ears Mehetible Caleff, bonnet strings tied firmly under her chin, shoulder cape buttoned neatly, wide skirts flaring down to small slippers, paused for a moment at the broad white steps; then she went down the walk without looking back.

Along the streets of Ipswich, Mehetible scuffled through bright dry leaves that crackled and swished at every step. Demurely she walked past the gossips gathered at the street corners.

It was the year 1780. Even the Revolution with its noisy street mobs couldn't change the weather; and Mehetible rather enjoyed these frequent walks through the neat little town of white houses. Now and then she shifted the basket from one arm to the other. It was heavy; far too heavy for a little twelve-year-old, but Mehetible was going on an errand. And such an errand! She felt gay and excited and she had an answer ready for any inquisitive grown-up. Grown-ups might be stopped and questioned; they might even be pelted with stones. But nobody bothered a little girl carrying a basket; it was too common a sight on Ipswich streets, even in those hectic days. Her mother had been sure of that, or she wouldn't have trusted Mehetible on so dangerous an errand.

Along the streets and over the bridge, down beyond the last white house straggling at the edge of the town, she went, past the woods in their bright autumn colors. At a spot on the broad road she paused and waited. From the woods came a familiar whistle; suddenly the bushes on the roadside parted and Mehetible looked up at the smiling bronzed face of Captain David Mowat, Loyalist. Without a word he reached for the basket. Mehetible followed him through the woods until they came to the big tree, where they slid under the wide branches and sat down.

Then Captain David Mowat lifted the cover of the basket, took out half a chicken and ate ravenously. Two days in the woods without food was enough to give anyone an appetite and Captain David was healthy and young; and handsome, so Mehetible thought. She waited for him to finish his meal and make a parcel of the remaining food.

In a few days he would have to hide in the barn again. Soldiers were searching the woods he told her, and Mrs. Caleff must leave the doors unlocked. Mehetible promised to tell her Mother. Then Captain David settled down to tell stories of the wild Orkney Islands where Spaniards from the Armada had been wrecked on the rocky coasts. Mehetible was fascinated and all the way back home she thought of those wrecked sailors hiding in the caves and the cliffs with the wild winds howling above the noise of the sea.

It had been a disturbing day for Mrs. Caleff and Mehetible's message increased her fears; for she well knew that nothing would please the Revolutionists more than to capture Captain David and lodge him in one of their filthy jails. And her own family wouldn't be safe if the Captain was traced to their home.

Mrs. Caleff was alone in Ipswich with her children. Her husband, Dr. John Caleff, had left for England, sent as a representative by the Penobscot Loyalist Association to help settle the matter of the boundary line between the British and American territory. Before sailing for England, Dr. Caleff had undergone all sorts of indignities at the hands of the Revolutionists; for the Caleff family had always been staunchly British. The Doctor's grandfather, Robert Caleff, had enjoyed the doubtful distinction of having one of his books, "More Wonders of the Invisible World", burned on Harvard Campus in 1692. Dr. Caleff had been Ship's Surgeon on the ALBANY, which took part in the siege of Louisbourg. And he was present at the siege of Penobscot, afterwards writing the only published account of that action — the book may now be found in Harvard University Library.

And Dr. John Caleff was one of the famous "Seventeen Rescinders" who figured prominently in newspaper reports and cartoons. One such cartoon printed in 1768, captioned "A Warm Place Hell", depicts a group of Tories huddled on the flaming brink, while Satan with a pitchfork urges them forward saying, "Now I've got you, a fine haul, By Jove!" Dr. Caleff is protrayed with a calf's head, as his name was then pronounced "Calf". And the verse below began:

Oh brave rescinders! To yon yawning cell,
Seventeen such Miscreants sure will startle Hell!

So, Dr. John Caleff, being proclaimed a traitor and with a price on his head, sorrowfully departed for England. But before leaving he asked his life-long friend, Captain Henry Mowat, to keep an eye on his family. But, because Captain Henry had his hands full in those trying times, with sailors refusing to man his vessels and mobs storming the docks, he passed on the duty of "keeping an eye on the Caleffs" to his young cousin, Captain David Mowat.

When Captain David arrived in Ipswich he learned that some

100

enthusiastic rebels were on the lookout for him too, so he had to keep under cover. He dodged around from the Caleff cellar to the attic and barns; then he'd skip out to the woods where the Caleffs supplied him with food.

Dorothy Caleff felt anything but safe. Neighbours' homes were going up in flames; Loyalists were being dragged off to prison on any pretext. She was ever anxious for Captain David. Finally she could stand it no longer, so she hired a vessel, and secretly night after night stowed the family belongings on board. Grandmother Dummer's armchair and massive mahogany chests of drawers were trundled aboard; and along with them went the memories of the days spent in the big mansion in Rowley that Grandfather Dummer built in 1716.

Happy and carefree were the days of the Colonial era, when William Dummer, Governor of Massachusetts, entertained notables from home and abroad. The valuable silver tankard that had graced Grandfather's massive sideboard, silver candlesticks and platters with the Dummer coat of arms, Dorothy Caleff carefully wrapped in patchwork quilts and handwoven blankets. As she stowed away the cargo, Dorothy Caleff could see again every nook and corner of the old mansion. Its broad mahogany stairway, where William Dummer rode his horse upstairs to the second floor the night he brought Katherine Dudley home as his bride. All the treasures brought from the old home were stowed aboard — all except the portrait of Katherine, the Governor's lady, painted by a celebrated artist, which still hangs over the fireplace in the panelled drawing-room of the old mansion, now "Dummer Academy", founded by William Dummer and still in use today as a centre of learning.

With her children, Dorothy Caleff sailed off for Nova Scotia. She was sick and tired of the 'boundary question' too; but Captain David Mowat must wait in Ipswich to meet Dr. Caleff on his return and tell him of their new hardships and help him reach their new home.

Everything went well until Mrs. Caleff's vessel reached the Bay of Fundy, when a heavy storm blew up. The small craft was lost in the blinding snow and blown away out of its course. Then suddenly through the swirling eddies of snow they saw huge breakers alongside and the vessel pitched forward with a sickening shatter as it stranded on the shore.

Somehow Mrs. Caleff managed to bundle the children up in warm clothing. Somehow they managed to get ashore, and all through that cold winter day Dorothy Caleff and her children stumbled along twelve icy miles to the shelter of Parr Town, where kind friends gave food and warmth. But fortunately the vessel did not break up, and shortly afterwards Dorothy Caleff salvaged the precious cargo.

Meanwhile Dr. Caleff had been in England for two years. He

did not know of the hardships his family had undergone; letters were few and far between and his wife did not want to worry him. He had enough troubles of his own. He wasn't successful in his errand, although he had been hopeful at first, the boundary question was still unsettled.

One morning on entering the office of Lord North, the Premier of Great Britain who had done his utmost to support the Penobscot claims, Dr. Caleff was greeted by the Premier exclaiming, "Doctor, Doctor, we cannot secure the Boundary, the pressure is too strong." For the Americans had used all the influence at their disposal and overruled the Penobscot Society's claims.

But it was not until 1842 that the question was finally decided, for the King of the Netherlands, invited to settle the dispute, conceded the American claim, and the Saint Croix River was decided as the Boundary, giving the Americans several thousand additional miles of territory.

Heartbroken and discouraged, the good Doctor sailed for Ipswich not realizing conditions there had grown from bad to worse. But young Captain David was on the look-out for him. He chartered a ship, cruised around the coast, intercepted the vessel with Dr. Caleff on board, took him off and landed in a secluded spot on the coast of Maine.

Here they disguised themselves as Indians and began the long journey to the Saint John River. Living on fish and squirrels, through woods they trudged, circling away from the settlements. They swam rivers and endured unthinkable hardships. Then finally the two 'Indians' stumbled into Parr Town, more dead than alive, and found their way to Mrs. Caleff's door.

If Mehetible found the bronzed adventurer's tales more interesting than before, Captain David knew that this charming Loyalist maid "sealed his fate"; so, in 1786 Mehetible Caleff became the bride of David Mowat. She was just eighteen and he twenty years older.

Anne Hecht, Mehetible's best friend was the bridesmaid. And Anne, who was poetically inclined, composed a lengthy poem to her friend. In fine script on silky birch bark (later to be copied on parchment) Anne gives her friend excellent advice.
"Dear Heyy," it begins,
> Small is the province of a wife
> And narrow is her sphere of life.

The bride was expected to,
> Grace the home with prudent care
> and properly to spend and spare.

Anne concluded with a warning,
> Abroad for happiness ne'er roam

True happiness begins at home.

For several years the Caleffs lived in Saint John, where Dr. Caleff was attached to the Fort Howe Garrison as surgeon with the troops. In spite of his long absence from practice, he was quite prepared for his duties. For his wife had salvaged his medicine cabinet, surgical instruments and books, as well as the big mortar and pestle for preparing medicines. Even today that same mortar and pestle is used in the Mowat household, not for medicinal purposes, but for grinding breadcrumbs.

The Caleff house was at the lower end of Saint John and no roads had been built, but the valiant old Doctor (he was 62 years old then) never missed a day attending his patients at the Fort. Sometimes he would hire a row boat to take him up the Harbour. Often in winter he waded through snowdrifts to his armpits, but more frequently the Doctor in his blue military coat, with huge brass buttons marked with the initials G.H., could be seen clambering along the rocky shore, or striding along streets in the newly cleared sections of the city. And Mehetible, her seafaring husband away so frequently on long journeys, made her home with her parents.

When Dr. Caleff retired from military duties he moved to Saint Andrews, built a house and planted a row of fine elm trees that stood until recently, when they were cut down to make room for modern sidewalks.

Even with her four children, Mehetible found it lonely in Saint John, so she moved to Saint Andrews. Then Captain David sailed his vessels to the little wharf there, where the only harbour light was a candle in a small lantern hung on a post at the end of the wharf. And always there was a warm welcome for the handsome Captain, who brought gifts from faraway places. The beautifully lacquered snuffbox, embossed with the head of a King; an inlaid walnut writing desk; an Apostle pitcher, made long before Wedgwood was popular; and dozens of other souvenirs from abroad.

Kindly, neighbourly folk were the people of Saint Andrews; they still are. And next door to the Caleff house stood the big brick residence of Colonel Christopher Hatch. The Colonel had an old coloured slave, Violet, a wonderful cook, who served the most sumptuous dinners for her Master's guests. Voilet was so old she had forgotten her age, but she had a keen memory for stories of pre-Revolutionary days. Youngsters from all over the town came to sit on Christopher Hatch's doorstep and nibble Violet's crisp molasses cookies, while Violet told them hair-raising stories of plantation days, and frequently added a few ideas of her own about runaway slaves.

Gala gatherings provided entertainment for those Saint Andrews pioneers. Always on the fourth of June they celebrated with a grand ball in honor of George the Third's birthday.

Ladies in their short-waisted dresses and flowing skirts, their hair piled high and fastened with jewelled tortoise shell combs, gathered for the event. From Deer Island they came, those belles of years ago, to flirt and dance the Lancers and Polkas and Mazurkas with the velvet-coated beaux and officers of the garrison, so resplendent in gold-braided scarlet uniforms. Early garden flowers graced the banquet tables; and to prevent the lilacs from blooming too soon for the great event they tied paper bags on the white scented clusters.

In winter there were sleighing parties and dances with country fiddlers' music keeping the young folk out till the 'wee sma' hours. Even in those days young folks' frivolity was lamented; for an old letter predicts, "when good roads are built all the young people would want to drive in wheeled vehicles and forget the use of their legs."

Dr. Caleff's old friend, Captain Farrell, from Deer Island would come to Saint Andrews. These two old gentlemen were the last to wear three-cornered hats. Time and again when they met on the street they removed their hats, made a profound bow and one would say, "Be covered, Sir", while the other protested gallantly, "Not before you, Sir". And while this went on these two old gallants would bow themselves half way up Front Street.

The first "Quizz programme" originated in Saint Andrews; for every Saturday night the gentlemen of the town met and discussed topics of the day. The old minute book discloses that "spirits and water shall be the only form of refreshment allowed in time of meeting." Debates covered a variety of subjects including "In what manner female education may be made to contribute to rendering them [the ladies] better. Is knowledge of dead languages absolutely necessary in what are called the learned professions?" "How could Sampson catch three hundred foxes so soon when he sent them with firebrands to burn the corn of the Philistines?" and "Whether it is better to prune fruit trees in the Autumn or the Spring?" All these questions were debated and answered by these gentlemen.

But for Mehetible sad news had come; for Captain David Mowat died and was buried at sea. Sad too, the day when solemn seamen trundled their Captain's belongings to the big house; his trunks and books and the desk he had on the ship.

For a long time Mehetible sat with folded hands before the little desk with its fluted columns. Then gently she moved one of the columns and the secret drawers swung out — her letters; a lock of bright hair carefully wrapped in yellowed paper; other treasures. . . The room was too quiet in the chill November dusk and the loneliness in her heart was almost more than she could bear. Then slowly Mehetible put the secret drawers back again, fitted the fluted column in place and locked the desk. All this was over; now there were other things to be done.

All summer long Indians roamed the streets of Saint Andrews bringing their baskets and bead-trimmed moccasins for sale. Tagging along behind them, like the tail of a kite, came their solemn-faced, nearly naked children.

Long into the late frosty Autumn they called at the big white house at the head of the town. So it was no surprise to Mehetible when one cold evening she was summoned to the kitchen where an Indian waited to speak to "the lady". Motionless he squatted on the floor, huddled in his blanket. Knowing there was always a prelude of food to any transaction with the Indians, Mehetible put tea and biscuits on the table. Not a word was said until the last crumb had vanished — then he spoke: "White lady in woods near stream far down shore", he told Mehetible. "Many children, pick berries, get clams all summer. Now no berries, shore all ice, no eat. You ketchum lady before snow."

Questioning him, Mehetible pieced the story together and discovered where the "white lady's" shack stood. Early next morning Mehetible packed a hamper of food and saddled her horse. With the hamper strapped behind, off she road miles across the sands when the tide was low, to discover the Goldsmith family all huddled together in the shack trying to keep themselves warm.

As Mehetible unpacked the hamper those ravenous children almost gobbled the food; they hadn't tasted bread and butter, nor milk and eggs for months. Then she learned the story of how Mrs. Goldsmith and her family had managed to live all summer while her husband was away in England.

Henry Goldsmith was a nephew of the celebrated Oliver. Henry had inherited his uncle's talent in a small way, but as a business-man left much to be desired. He had big ideas of developing a lumber business and had gone off to England to organize a company to develop his dream. He had left his wife and six children in this shack in these desolate woods, and to make matters worse, there was no road. Only a few Indians ever passed by the place. Henry had left them some money, but it was useless under these conditions.

Thanks to clams and berries they had managed to exist; but with winter coming on, the children always hungry and cold, and no word from her husband, poor Mrs. Goldsmith was frantic. Mehetible promised to help and the next day sent men in a boat bringing the unfortunate family to share her home for the winter, or until Henry returned.

Six children, added to Mehetible's seven, fairly made the old house bulge. And even when Mehetible was an old, old lady, her memories were strewn with those crowded days. Children scrambling noisily over the place all day, and the long quiet winter nights when all were in bed and no sound, except the flames hissing in the fireplace and the frost cracking sharply cold outside.

The old King Street Burial Ground in Saint John

Courtesy of The New Brunswick Museum   *Photo by William Hart*

In October 1812 Dr. John Caleff died, leaving his possessions to "that mirror of love and patience, my daughter Mehetible". Sadly they laid him beside his beloved Dorothy. And the elm trees planted in her memory now reach high their branches over the moss grown stones in the old King Street Burial Ground.

When the War of 1812 was in full swing, Mehetible's grown-up sons decided that Saint Andrews, with its good Harbour, was far too vulnerable a spot; so they built a house farther out in the country on some land their father had owned. There Mehetible went to live with her eldest son, as the rest of the family were now married and in homes of their own.

One night when her son was in town on business suddenly there came a knocking at the door. Thinking it was some neighbour in trouble, Mehetible hurried to open the door. A bright shaft of light streamed wide into the dark, and there on the steps loomed five towering figures — American soldiers, armed to the teeth! Before she

106

could speak, rough voices were demanding food and shelter. For a moment Mehetible stood blocking the doorway. Then sharply she ordered them to the kitchen as she backed inside and bolted the door. Terrified, she hurried to the kitchen and began preparing a meal, while all the time she could hear them tramping about in the yard.

Mehetible heaped their plates and while they ate she slipped upstairs and returned with an armful of blankets. "You may sleep in the barn tonight", she said sharply, "but be gone early in the morning". They argued between themselves for a while, then picked up the blankets and went out.

Hurriedly she cleared the table, it would never do for her son to know she had fed the soldiers, nor find them for that matter; for she knew how hot-headed he was, and the Americans were well-armed. She could still hear their voices, but they quieted down before her son returned. It was several days before the blankets were found and Mehetible's secret was out. "Never again", thundered her son, warning her against such dangers. "Promise!" and promise Mehetible did, but with inward reservations.

Gravestones in King Street Burial Ground, Saint John

Courtesy of The New Brunswick Museum
Photo by William Hart

Seedtime and harvests came and passed. Wide acres grew from the wilderness under her son's sturdy plow. Mehetible busied herself spinning, weaving and knitting, and the years sped on etching fine lines of strength and patience and kindliness in her fine old face.

Then one winter day word came to Mehetible that her daughter was ill in Saint John. Nothing would do but she must go and care for the family. Reluctantly her son brought out the sleigh. It was too long a journey for an old lady; but he put hot bricks in the straw at her feet and covered her well with a buffalo robe, and with a grandson to drive for her, off they started.

The short winter afternoon faded, darkness came on and with night came the wolves. Mehetible could hear their cries as they raced along; but, her grandson, a husky lad of sixteen, stood up in the sleigh and whipped the old farm horse along at breakneck speed.

With woods on either side of the narrow road escape seemed impossible. One swerve of the sleigh and they would be out on the road at the mercy of the beasts. Mehetible prayed as she never prayed before. Then suddenly they saw lights flickering in the windows ahead of them. Lepreau! With a last frantic effort the old horse galloped into the village and the wolves, howling, disappeared into the forest.

That was Mehetible's last adventure. Home again, Mehetible would sit snugly by the fireside in Grandfather Dummer's armchair. The chair that had survived Revolution and shipwreck. She had the chair legs shortened so her feet could rest on a stool, for she was such a tiny little old lady, and she did love to be comfortable.

Across the hearth her son would sit mending harness, or oiling his guns on winter evenings, while the young folk sprawled on the floor reading by the firelight, all comfortable and sheltered. Mehetible's nimble fingers flew as knitting needles clicked and soon a sock would dangle from the busy needles. Faded old letters tell, "Grandma is starting the fall knitting." "Grandma has a troublesome cough, but does not complain." "Grandma is dozing by the fire."

But Grandma was not dozing — she was just remembering. Long, long thoughts of the streets of Ipswich and a small girl scuffling through the leaves underfoot. "Tory! Tory!" The sound of windows crashing rang in her ears. The Autumn woods — a handsome young Captain and his wonderful stories. Night in the Bay of Fundy — the wind and the cold. Run! Run! Fall and scramble up again — over rocks — through bushes. Stamp your feet, swing your arms to keep warm! All those twelve long miles to Parr Town.

Satin and flowers. Captain David standing beside her. Anne Hecht's poem, "Never roam . . . Happiness begins at home." Mehetible's head would nod, yes, yes. They thought she slept in the old armchair beside the fire; but no, she was off to the Goldsmiths, urging her horse across the red sands. A log would fall in the fireplace — was that a knock at the door? Quick, open it! Soldiers; noisy, threatening! How sharp her voice had been! And she was afraid — so very much afraid. Mehetible sat bolt upright in the old chair and peered across the room to the hallway. No, no soldiers at the door. Just this cosy room with the family gathered around.

Then one day Mehetible sat no more in Grandfather Dummer's armchair and the knitting needles were quiet. From "Beech Hill" they carried away the courageous little form on the last journey. Another stone was placed beside those of her parents inscribed, "In memory of Mehetible, Relict of David Mowat. Died December 1860 In the 93rd year of her age. Blessed are the dead who die in the Lord."

Just off the main highway near Saint Andrews is a quiet lane, where a stone wall, grey with moss and age is sheltered by tall fir trees. At the end of the lane stands lovely old-fashioned "Beech Hill".

In the drawing room Mehetible's armchair still stands by the fireplace and nearby is the little pedestal table she loved so well. There is the massive mahogany highboy, beautiful in proportion and workmanship with its carved brass fittings, gleaming bright. The inlaid desk, where Mehetible wrote her letters, looks as if she had just laid down her pen. Captain David's desk is there too, and the darkness of a secret drawer still shelters a lock of bright hair wrapped in yellowed paper. Near the fireplace hang coloured engravings and a miniature of Captain David Mowat in his blue uniform, with bright buttons of the Merchant Service; and silhouettes of Mehetible and her children. There is a the huge Family Bible brought from Ipswich with the names of generations inscribed on its pages. Legacies all, to Mehetible's descendants — those robust seafaring men, who brought their ships to safe anchorage — those tillers of the soil, whose strong hands guided the plow, and those kindly, courageous and thrifty women, who have carried on this goodly Canadian heritage.

BIBLIOGRAPHY

From letters, documents and diaries; courtesy Miss Grace Helen Mowat, Beech Hill, St. Andrews, New Brunswick.

Sara Frost

"May 25th, 1783, I left Lloyd's Neck with my family and went on board the 'Two Sisters' commanded by Captain Brown, for a voyage to Nova Scotia with the rest of the Loyalist Sufferers. This evening the Captain drank tea with us and appeared to be a very agreeable gentleman. He expects to sail as soon as wind shall favor. We have very fair accommodation in the Cabin, altho' it contains six families besides my own. There are 250 passengers on Board."

So wrote Sara Frost in her "Journal" that May day nearly two centuries ago.

Many who embarked that day wrote of their experiences; letters are still in the possession of their descendants and diaries were a favorite indoor sport in the eighteenth century. But Sara's Journal is a complete story of that voyage, intimate and unvarnished, perhaps never intended to be read outside the family circle. If authors are born, not made, then Sara was an author by accident, with her tale of her forced journey to the northern wilderness "with the rest of the Loyalist Sufferers."

William Frost, Sara's husband, was one of the earnest patriots who served with the Loyalist forces. Losing home and property, he fled with his family from Stamford, Connecticut, to the temporary safety of the British Garrison on Staten Island. William was thirty-four at the time and Sara twenty-nine; their children, Henry and Polly aged nine and seven, and Sara was again to become a mother.

The TWO SISTERS was one of thirteen ships, with two brigs as convoy, of the Second Fleet which left Sandy Hook June 16th, 1783. Several vessels of the First Fleet had returned to New York, as a newspaper of June 7th, 1783 records, "Yesterday arrived the Camel, Capt. Wm. Tinker, in eight days from the River St. John in the Bay of Fundy, who at the time of his departure left the new settlers there in good health and spirits."

And an address presented to Capt. Adnet of the Transport BRIDGEWATER, also recently returned, testified, "Your humanity and the kindness shown to render as happy as possible each individual on board your ship, during the passage and till their disembarkation, has filled our hearts with sentiments of the deepest gratitude."

The spring of 1783 had been wet and cold. To the unhappy people quartered in all sorts of temporary lodgings, the prospects were far from encouraging. It was with foreboding and bitterness the Loyalists prepared for their journey, for all through the winter they'd watched their cherished possessions sold for little or nothing to the patriots who knew no consideration and took advantage of their plight.

The newspapers were full of advertisements of Auction Sales. At 516 Hanover Square, Duncan, Barclay and Company announced the sale of "Mahogany Dining and Card Tables, Japanned Tea Tables, Elegant Silver Candlesticks of the newest style, Table and Tea Spoons, Silver handled Knives and Forks, Watches very neat, Elegant Silver, Mounted Small Swords and Hangers, Very Neat Tea Sets of China, Large Pier Glasses, Elegant Wilton Carpets, Girandoles, Small Looking Glasses and Pictures, Large Assortment of Decanters, Tumblers, Goblets and Wine Glasses. A variety of Copper Kettles and Pots, Sauce Pans, etc., a very large Kitchen Grate fit for a Tavern or Mess House."

Down in the field behind the Bull's Head Tavern in Bowery Lane, Barrack Hayes had for sale "Eleven Milch Cows, twenty-four ditto old and young, some fit for killing. Three very fine horses."

The Royal American Gazette, printed by Alexander Robertson at the printing office in Queen Street near the Coffee House Bridge, offered "Two elegant Tentenague Tea Urns also some Coffee and Chocolate Pots of the same ware with a variety of Japanned Copper and Tin Ware neatly finished."

By the following year the *Royal American Gazette* became the *New York Journal and State Gazette*, published by Elizabeth Holt, Printer to the State at her office No. 13 Queen Street, four doors from the south corner of the Fly Market where subscribers at Two dollars per annum, Essays and Articles of Intelligence were "gratefully received and every kind of Printing Work [was] performed with accuracy and dispatch."

Long lists of "Ships for Sale" filled entire pages of James Rivington's *Royal Gazette*. The Schooner EAGER; Brig REPRISAL of Richmond, Virginia; the Copper-bottomed TYGER; the Snow ANNA MARIA; Schooner DELANCY; Brig CHARMING POLLY and the sloops RANGER and BETSY. No longer would their proud owners watch them lift their sleek bows along the wharves of Whitehall, Beekman's and Peck's slips.

That year of 1783 was the busiest the port had ever known. While the auctioneers disposed of Loyalists' goods and chattels, Sir Guy Carleton, Commander of the British Forces, was arranging transport for the refugees. New York harbour was crowded with ships, gear clattering, chains rattling as goods were lowered into their holds. The Lloyds Neck refugees ferried out to the ships in small boats, clambered aboard with their few belongings.

On the deck of the TWO SISTERS stood Sara Frost in her neat linsey-woolsey gown, her hair snug under her bonnet. In one hand she carried a satchel, and to the other clung little Polly, the exact counterpart of her mother from bonnet to shoe buckles. Young Henry, feeling quite grown up, helped his father guard their luggage while he watched the crowds with wide-eyed wonder.

Then Sara Frost went down to their cabin, already crowded with other families, but she stowed away her family's best clothes in their corner, opened her satchel and took out her Journal, and ignoring the discomforts around her, began to write:

"Monday, May 26. Nothing happened today worth mentioning. We lay at anchor in Oyster Bay the whole day, having got all our passengers on board.

"Tuesday, May 27th. At 8 o'clock we weighed anchor at Oyster Bay with a fair wind for New York. Half after eleven we were brought to by the Guard Ship at City Island. Our Captain was very angry that they should bring him to, but they did not detain us long. We went on with a fair breeze through Hell Gate, but just as we got through, the wind and tide headed us out and we had like to have gone on shore. They tried twice to go on, but at length were obliged to anchor south of Harlem Creek where we lay that night.

"Wednesday, 28th. Weighed anchor at six o'clock, tide being low struck a rock but got off again. Ten o'clock anchored at lower end of New York City. Went ashore in Captain Judson's whale boat and went to Mrs. McKay's and from there to Mrs. Raymond's and Mrs. Partelow's, where we dined and spent the afternoon."

And although the passengers embarked on the 25th of May it was not until 22 days later, the 16th of June, that they finally set sail for Nova Scotia.

New York was not such a grown-up city when Sara Frost called on her friend, Mrs. Partelow. It didn't have six hundred miles of water front, nor fascinating, glamorous nightclubs and theatres. And it was many long years before the 'Elevated' roared its way along Third Avenue making a gloomy cavern of that narrow thoroughfare.

But New York was even then a fascinating city. The Bowery, a fashionable carriage drive for the rich merchants, extended to meet the Great Road to Boston. Near 42nd Street were free meadows used as a common pasture for the Knickerbocker cows. Along Wall Street's flagstoned sidewalks edged sedate red brick residences with their elegant colonial doorways and coloured glass fan-lights. Wall

Street follows the line of the old Stockade built in 1653 and then, as now, has a graveyard at one end and a river at the other.

Trinity Church, at the end of Wall Street, one of the largest and most splendid churches on the Continent, with its noble spire of 180 feet, had fallen a victim to the flames of the Great Fire of September 21, 1776. Its ruins, known as "Burnt Church" remained until 1788 when the second church was built.

The Parish of Trinity Church received its Royal Charter May 6, 1697, in the reign of William III, designating "a certain church and steeple that hath been lately built within our said city of New Yorke, together with a certain piece of parcell of ground thereunto adjoyning, scituate, lyeing and being in or neere to a streete without the north gate of our said city commonly called or known by the name of Broadway." To the ground "adjoyning", then known as the "King's Farm", Queen Anne added another section in 1705, which was known as the "Queen's Farm."

Past "Burnt Church" Sara went, with little Polly clutching her hand, along crowded Broadway to where St. Paul's chapel stood in Georgian splendor. Sara knew this Colonial British-built church with its British crest of Prince of Wales feathers over the pulpit and the Waterford cut glass chandeliers with their myriad candles. Prince William (afterwards William IV) had attended services here, as did Lord Howe with his British officers.

Further along on her way to Mrs. Partelow's they passed the great freshwater pond which stretched from Chatham to Great George Street, and where tea-water vendors were busy dipping up their morning's supply for thirsty citizens. By evening, gentlemen in three-cornered hats, velvet coats and snug breeches would take their ladies a-rowing for pleasure. But Sara hurried on, eager to reach Mrs. Partelow's. There was a good dinner awaiting them.

Returning to the TWO SISTERS that night, Sara writes: "In the evening we enjoyed a game of cards with Billy, my husband, in whom I take much delight." But the excursion to the city was too much for Sara, for next morning: "a headache obliged me to go to bed."

It was then William's turn to go ashore and he took Henry along. "I long to have them come on board again," writes Sara, "to hear what observations the child will make, for he has not been in town for some years now."

If they went to the Bowling Green, Henry may have seen the celebrated Wax Works, if his father could spare the shillings for that display of historical figures. But Henry did not gaze in amazement at the immense gilded statue of King George III in Bowling Green, for that famous image had been "levelled with ye dust by ye Freeborn Bands" some time previously. And George's head, which was mostly lead, had been carted away in a wheelbarrow to be melted down into bullets for the cause. But eight-year-old Henry found plenty of interest in the big city, for later Sara observes: "He has returned and pleases me very much with his disclosure about all he has seen."

The following day the Frosts dined at Mrs. Partelow's. It was a family dinner party. Mrs. Partelow was resplendent in black taffeta and jet brooch, while Sara wore brown cashmere, not quite so elegant, but more practical for travelling. There was good food on the candle-lit table and fine sherry in blue etched glasses. Then writes Sara, "Mrs. Schofield and Miss Lucretia came towards evening and gave me an account of my parents' welfare and my friends in the country. I am afraid I shall not hear from them again before I leave New York."

On Saturday, May 31st, Sara "got up early in the morning at Mrs. Partelow's, waited for some breakfast and then I went out amongst the shops to trade." The streets bustled with activity. Apprentices were taking down shutters from shop windows. Maids and serving men were scrubbing down stone steps and cobble sidewalks to be ready and clean for Sunday. Markets were crowded as well as shops. One could buy gloves and sailor jackets, nutmegs and taffeta, loaf sugar and copper kettles, rum, molasses and whale oil, all in the same shop, which proves that department stores are not such a modern idea.

When Sara returned to Mrs. Partelow's to pick up her husband and children she had a basket full of parcels as well as a "quantity of green peas" which she cooked for dinner that night on board the TWO SISTERS. With a steady diet of boiled beef and none-too-fresh biscuits, dried fish and tea, small wonder Sara writes, "Vegetables are so agreeable to the stomach."

Pandemonium reigned on the TWO SISTERS at meal time, with two hundred and fifty passengers all hungry at the same time, supplying much of their own food as well as doing the cooking on the little wood-burning galley stoves. It needed a steady hand and clever footwork to carry those soups and stews over heaving decks to the cabins below.

On the fourth of June Sara wakened to the firing of guns. It was "the King's birthday and such a time among the ships as to astound one." Flags went up on all the ships and the Loyalists celebrated lustily.

But the Captains had not received orders to sail and the second Fleet continued to lie at anchor off New York. There was a bad storm and the ship tossed very much. In the evening her father, Mr. Schofield, dined with them. "We have got green peas for dinner, but I could eat no dinner, tho' I have a great liking for green peas," Sara laments.

Then one day, tiring of ship's fare, William Frost with several other men went ashore for dinner at a nearby Tavern. William called for a glass of Punch, "and the landlord forgot to put any sugar or rum into it; it was comical Punch I can assure you," Sara writes with amusement.

Could it have been Fraunces' Tavern which still stands at the corner of Broad and Pearl (then Great Dock) Streets? It's very probable, for the landing place, Whitehall Slip, was almost at its door.

The original mansion of yellow Dutch brick from Amsterdam, built by Etienne deLancey in 1719 was one of the finest in New York City. Here, we are told, no hostess was more hospitable, gracious or popular than Mrs. deLancey. Here Susannah deLancey's wedding to Sir Peter Warren, Vice Admiral of the Fleet, was the social event of the season. And later when deLancey built a new home on Broadway the old residence was taken over by Henry Holt, a dancing-master who held public balls in the deLancey drawing rooms and advertised "Pantomimes and Plays", with tickets selling for "five shillings each".

Then Col. Joseph Robinson, merchant and warden of Trinity Church, occupied the house and later used it as a warehouse for goods from Europe and East India brought by the ships of deLancey, Robinson and Company, until Samuel Fraunces paid his two thousand pounds and opened his "Queen's Head Tavern" in 1762.

Soldiers of both armies patronized "that Tavern near the Ferry at which for seven years the officers of the British Army, including poor John André, had gloried and drunk deep." Here General Washington bade farewell to his officers in the Long Room that memorable December day in 1783.

This storied old hostelry called "Fraunces Tavern" since 1783, when landlord Samuel Fraunces with an eye to future business, tossed into a nearby alley the old wooden sign bearing the portrait of Queen Charlotte, has continuously dispensed food and drink (with plenty of rum and sugar) since April 1763.

But in spite of Sara Frost's visits ashore the waiting on board ship was exhausting. "We are so thronged that I cannot set myself about any work. It is not comfortable for anybody. Our people are cross and quarrelsome, but I will not differ with them if I can help it," Sara resolves. And often long after night fell Sara kept a vigil "at the entry way of the cabin as it storms and I cannot sit on deck. My husband and children are sleeping and I am here sitting quite alone."

Then the ship sailed as far as Staten Island and anchored and Sara "went ashore and got some gooseberries." Later she went ashore with Mrs. Mary Jones, who shared their cabin. Mary carried a bucket and Sara a large bundle. In a secluded spot on the shore they did the family washing, hanging it on the bushes to dry.

It was 5:30 on the morning of June 16th when the guns signalled the ships to get in line.

The Captain stamped along the deck, coat-tails flying, bawling orders to the sailors. Could this be the agreeable gentleman who drank tea with them? Sara scarcely believed her eyes — and ears!

But Captain Brown got his ship in line and past Sandy Hook went the leading Frigate with the two Brigs and thirteen ships streaking out behind like the tail of a comet. On every ship, passengers crowded the rails to watch the green meadows until the last blue line of headland faded from view.

The Atlantic was none too kindly on that voyage; for the next day the sky suddenly darkened and a squall hit the TWO SISTERS almost heeling her over. As the ship staggered and plunged, passengers and baggage rolled about below decks, while pots and pans clattered about in the galley. Rain came down in sheets, the wind grew fiercely cold, and hailstones "as big as ounce balls" fell. At sunset there came another squall and it hailed faster and heavier than before.

When pallid faces appeared above deck again and Sara saw the hailstones lying thick on the deck, she had an idea — for the drinking water was not all one could hope for. So, "Billy went out and gathered a mug full of hailstones and made a bowl of punch. And the ice was in it till we had drunk the whole of it. Such an instance I have never seen before in midsummer."

Amid storms and hail and seasickness the TWO SISTERS sailed on. In three days the unhappy voyagers were 150 miles from their former homes.

Then to add to their miseries measles broke out amongst the children. "We bear it pretty well", writes Sara, her nerves near the breaking point, "but at night one child cries in one place and one in another until I think sometimes I will go crazy."

All through that dreary voyage the women patiently tended the sick children while the men, their faces stern, played cards and fought old battles over again. Courageously they planned what they would do in the new land, while their hearts were secretly linked with the old.

Then one day excitement ran high as a rebel Brig was sighted. "She crowded sail and put off from us, but our Frigate knew how to speak to her, for she gave the stranger a shot across the bow, which caused her to shorten sail and lie to." And that evening in celebration of the event, "Mr. Enslie, the mate, drank tea with us," writes Sara. Afterwards "Mr. Whitney and his wife Betsy, and Bill and I have been diverting ourselves with a few games of cribbage."

Sylvanus Whitney and his wife Betsy were also from Stamford, Connecticut, and Mr. Whitney had been arraigned before the committee of that town charged with the offense of buying and selling tea.

Soldiers searched Mr. Whitney's warehouse and a quantity of the forbidden leaf was found. Sylvanus was forced to make a "confession" and his stock of tea was confiscated. Not content with that, the patriot committee made quite a ceremony of its destruction.

An effigy was made, large bags filled with tea to represent a body and a gallows was constructed in the market place.

Through the dusty streets of Stamford the soldiers paraded Mr. Whitney, unarmed and under heavy guard.

Two captains led the van with the unfortunate "tea" hung across a pole. Then followed the council of observation to see that full justice was done. Drums beat and pipes played doleful airs as the procession marched along. Supplemented by curious townsfolk, the rabble and dozens of small boys, the parade grew until a large crowd assembled at the market place. Around the gallows they crowded, shouting and jeering while the town hangman performed his duty.

But it was not wise to leave such quantities of Hyson, Oolong and Souchong dangling there for fear the people might be tempted to replenish their depleted supplies. So, a huge bonfire was built, and though secretly many a mouth watered for a steaming cup they stoically watched "Traitor Tea" go up in smoke.

Mr. Whitney, forced to witness this "act of justice, behaved himself as well as could be expected". And small wonder, for had he made a move to recover his property the soldiers would have knocked him on the head with their rifle butts. After much cheering the people returned to their homes, "without any bad consequences whatsoever."

Sylvanus Whitney was then permitted to go home, where for very good reasons he packed his silver, mahogany, and expensively tailored clothes and with his wife Betsy made his way to New York to join the refugees.

There were days and nights of fog, dense, gray and cold, when the TWO SISTERS drifted in the dark Atlantic. Bells were rung constantly and guns fired to keep the ships in line, but they lost touch with each other and for "three days heard no sound from any ship".

Then came sudden sunshine, and when the Frigate rounded up the straying vessels they found they were near Cape Sable, but the Captain assured them they would be in the Bay of Fundy before morning. With 240 miles to go, the wind turned against them and they made only some ten miles a day. "How I long to see that place, even tho' it is a strange land", Sara confides to her Journal. "I am so tired of being on board ship, tho' we have as clever a Captain as ever need live."

On Saturday the 28th of June, Sara "got up in the morning with renewed hopes to find land on both sides." Soon after ten o'clock "a pilot came aboard and our ship is anchored off Fort Howe in the Saint John River."

With a rousing salute from the guns of the Fort, the exiles crowded on deck. Some women wept with sheer relief that the journey had ended. Men with stern faces gazed morose and silent at the small clearings in the rocky hillsides, the tents and the wilderness beyond. Was this their reward for all those years of battle and privation?

"People went ashore", writes Sara, "and brought on board some pea vines with blossoms on them, also some gooseberries, spruce and grass, all of which grow wild. They say this is to be our city. Our land is to be five and twenty miles up the River. We have only a building place forty feet wide and one hundred feet back. Billy has gone on shore in his whaleboat to see how it looks. He returns soon bringing a fine salmon."

The last night on shipboard few slept. There was no card-playing, and when the men spoke it was in quick gruff tones. Women hushed the children's excited questioning and held their babies closer, while they tried to hum little lullabies, lullabies that had comforted in the old homes they would never see again, but the song died in their throats.

Sara and William Frost left the stuffy cabin and stood together on deck leaning against the rail. All around them ship's lanterns bobbed and twinkled across the harbour waters and the dark hills loomed beyond.

William's toil-hardened hands gripped Sara's and held them close. He spoke quietly, but with conviction. For himself he cared not; but life would not be easy beyond those hills. They would have to make do; a tent in the woods until he could build a house; his Sara, who had been used to so comfortable a way of life! After what they had been through it was a lot to ask of any woman; but they would, at least, be on British soil. Sara looked up at her husband with tears in her eyes, but there was no wavering in her voice as she answered as Ruth had done, "Whither thou goest I will go," as William's strong arms encircled her.

"Sunday, June 29th. This morning is very pleasant. I am just going ashore with my children to see how I like it."

Later, "It is afternoon now and I have been on shore. It is I think the roughest land I have ever seen; it beats 'Short Rocks'. I think that is nothing to this. But it is to be the city they say. We are to have our land up the River. We are all ordered to land tomorrow and not a shelter to go under."

Then Sara closed her Journal, put it in the satchel and followed her husband ashore.

On July 30th, 1783, in a tent on the rocks, Sara's daughter, Hannah was born. The second female child to be born in Parr Town after the coming of the Loyalists.

Then across the hills Sara went with her husband and children and household goods and her diary in the satchel. Gagetown knew Sara and William Frost, and St. Stephen and Deer Island. Then they went to Kingston on the Kennebecasis River where they stayed.

The rest is a story of heartbreak and courage, when swords were exchanged for ploughshares and women, reared in luxury, toiled at unaccumstomed tasks.

Kingston Church with graveyard where Sara Frost is buried

Courtesy of The New Brunswick Museum
Photo by Gordon Anderson

But from lonely wilderness clearings, farm lands spread across the countryside — neat frame houses replaced the log huts chinked with moss and clay that sheltered the refugees that terrible first winter.

Often at the end of the day when Sara sat before the fire with her open diary the words would blur as she read some well-remembered episode to her grandchildren.

Back in New York a new 'Trinity' raises its lofty spire over the ruins of Burnt Church, and streets that had known Sara's footsteps echo with the babble of Europe, Asia and Africa.

Today in Fraunces' Tavern a doorman in revolutionary costume conducts patrons up the lovely old colonial stairway which Susannah deLancey descended as the bride of Sir Peter Warren. Perhaps at night when a cool breeze blows across the river, ghosts of red-coated soldiers steal into the taproom and loyally raise their glasses in a silent toast to the King who had forgotten them in their hour of need.

And down in Macdougal Street near where Sir Peter Warren's mansion stood and Susannah strolled in her English gardens, a magnificent old elm tree tosses its green mantle over the hurrying throng of Greenwich Village.

The old tree still waters its thirsty roots in Minetta Brook (now running underground as a nearby hotel can prove.) This brook fed the "Fresh Water" pond Sara Frost passed on her way to dine with Mrs. Partelow. And the elm tree was full grown when Captain Brown sailed the TWO SISTERS out of New York harbour in 1783.

Sara Frost's diary is dog-eared and torn and some of its pages are missing. But it tells of a voyage to a wilderness that challenged courage and resolution of both men and women.

Under the shade of the trees in Kingston's beautiful pioneer churchyard, a tall grey stone marks the resting place of "Sara Frost, wife of William Frost in her 64th year".

A peaceful, well-tended spot, the white church surrounded by hills and the river gleaming bright below, harmonizes well with Houseman's verse:

> How green the earth, how blue the sky
> How pleasant are the days that pass
> Here where the British settlers lie
> Beneath their cloaks of grass.

BIBLIOGRAPHY

The Diary of Sara Frost, Archives Dept., The New Brunswick Museum.
"Revolutionary Times in New York"; The Royal American Gazette, Jan. 13, 1780; The Royal American Gazette, Aug. 8, 1780 and July 21, 1781.
The Royal Gazette, November 19, 1783.
The New York Gazette and Universal Advertiser, Nov. 29, 1783.
The *New York Journal and State Gazette*, Mar. 25, 1784.
All from "Collections of American History"; Courtesy of New York Historical Society, New York City.
Early days in New York; Shipping; Trinity Church; and St. Paul's Chapel; "Trips and Trails of Historic Interest". Courtesy of the Museum of the City of New York.
Fraunces' Tavern, by Henry Russell Drowne.

Elizabeth Russel

When Elizabeth Russel sailed away from the green fields of Ireland that autumn morning in 1819, it was not just another day in her life; it was the beginning of a great adventure. A pioneering adventure in New Brunswick, where terror lurked in the deep forests and loneliness shrouded the isolated homes, but adventure beckoned stout hearts.

The quay was alive with people. Tall masts of ships lined Belfast Lough. The little sailing vessel bound for the Miramichi lay in midstream; its canvas flapping in the wind. Decks were piled with boxes and bundles, and crowded along the rail, passengers stood anxious-eyed and tearful as they waved farewell to their friends on the shore.

Then the wind filled the sails and the vessel moved past the steep crags of Antrim on its way to the sea. Ancient Carrickfergus and its hoary Castle rose above the blue waters of the Lough. Elizabeth and John Russel stood watching the green fields and headlands disappear in the haze. She shivered in the cold wind, and loneliness surged over her like a dark cloud, as she looked at those green fields she would see no more.

Sadly she went below deck to find bunks and store their luggage; for this was no comfortable passenger vessel, but a small timber carrier, its hold lined with rough board bunks, where adventurous woodsmen, farmers and cattlemen with their families now huddled together for the six-week-long journey to the new land.

And rolling along the bleak Atlantic, with seas pounding and waves pouring into the hold soaking the unfortunate voyagers, Elizabeth had plenty of time to think about that land of promise and pray fervently they would reach it safely.

But those staunch little vessels had been sailing across the ocean to Newcastle on the Miramichi for almost fifty years before Elizabeth's time. It was in the 1770's that William Davidson and John Cort of Scotland had begun their timber operations. And from Davidson's Grant on the shores of the Miramichi mighty trees were marked with the King's broad arrow to be felled for masts for the British Navy. Newcastle was the thriving little village where the carriers loaded masts and spars and squared timber for Davidson's trade.

When William Davidson died in 1790 the business was carried on by James Fraser and James Thom, and after them came Alexander and James Fraser, who brought settlers from the old country to carry on the timber operations, and John Russel was one of these.

For Elizabeth Russel one long dreary day followed another. Nothing but the boisterous Atlantic as far as the eye could see as the vessel plunged through the waves. Then one evening, when the sun blazed a crimson path across the waters, the banks of Newfoundland rose ahead. Land at last! Past the headlands of Cape Breton the little craft sailed and fishing boats were heading homeward with their catch. And at long last the Miramichi Bay with isolated homes strung along the shores. A strange land and dark, with the deep forests edging the shores all the way up the River to Newcastle.

But here were little white houses and stores and a Military Barracks with a slim church spire towering over all. The wharves were stacked with timber and ships lay alongside. Traders and woodsmen in deerskin jackets, women and children crowded on the shore to greet the newcomers. Copper faces, framed in dark hair, stared at Elizabeth as she followed her husband across the gangplank into the crowd. Loneliness and fear surged over Elizabeth as she waited for her husband to finish his business with Fraser's agent. There were no familiar faces anywhere.

Soon they left the little town with its white houses. Down a dark forest trail they went to a small log cabin in a clearing. Tears blurred Elizabeth's eyes as she looked at their home. So bare, so isolated, not a neighbour for miles. She scarcely heard her husband telling her of the trees to be felled — the barn they would build. If she ever longed for the green hills of Antrim she longed for them now. But as the days sped by, somehow she was ashamed of her tears. Other women had managed to live in this wilderness, and so would she; for here was her home, here was her husband and here she would stay.

Day after day Elizabeth was alone in the cabin, for John Russel worked in the woods. Acres of timber had to be cut in that two thousand square miles of forest.

Wild animals scurried down the trail to the river at dark. Indians came silently from the forest and suddenly appeared at the cabin door. There they'd squat pointing at the shining copper pots that hung over the fireplace, their beady black eyes following Elizabeth's every movement. Elizabeth hated their brown nakedness, their smells, their necklaces of shells and bear's teeth. She was scared to death, but didn't dare show it. At times she would give them food, or a bit of ribbon to get rid of them; but it was her copper pots they wanted and they'd go off reluctantly.

In that little cabin, with the snow drifted to the roof, one

February day her son was born. A neighbour woman from across the river stayed with her for a few days, then went off to tend her own little family.

John Russel would come home from the woods and eat enough for two men. "Potatoes and fish is an Irishman's dish!" he'd say, passing his plate back for the salmon heaped with snowy potatoes. Then he'd toss his son to his shoulder. "The strong legs of him," he'd say. "Hey laddie wait till ye grow a bit and I'll be makin' ye a woodsman yet!" And at night when they sat before the fire and talked of the future, Elizabeth was content.

Summer passed and their meagre harvest was safely stored in the new barn. John Russel was making good his promises — there would be plenty for those willing to work, and John went off to the woods again.

One night, when Elizabeth had barred the door and lay in her bed cradling her son in her arms, there came a scratching at the door. What would anyone be doing out at this time, Elizabeth wondered. Perhaps some one was lost on the trail; or a neighbour in trouble.

"Who's there?", she called. But there was no answer. The scratching came again. Elizabeth repeated the question. Again no reply, but the scratching. She sprang out of bed, bare feet on the cold floor, and shivered as she lit the candle. Better find out what it was than worry all night. But her fingers shook as she unbolted the door and cautiously peered into the darkness.

There on the doorstep stood a huge black dog wagging his tail. The night was cold so Elizabeth let him in and bolted the door again. Round and round the cabin the big black dog went investigating every corner. Then apparently satisfied he curled up on the floor beside her bed and lay quiet. Where did he come from, this dog, at this time of night? It was a long time before Elizabeth dozed off to sleep. Then suddenly she was aroused again. Footsteps making the rounds of the cabin. Someone trying the latch of the door. Terrified, Elizabeth prayed as she never prayed before — then a hand appeared at the window trying to force it open. Suddenly the big dog was alert. Barking furiously he jumped at the window, snarling at the form outside. Then, thankfully, Elizabeth heard the footsteps crackle in the brush and die away. But there was no more sleep for her that night, and all the next day she kept the door bolted and the big dog with her in the cabin.

"There's something queer about the whole thing," John admitted as he sat by the fire with Elizabeth a few nights later; the dog curled up comfortably at their feet. "Sure an' there's no dog like him for miles around an' I know them all clear to Newcastle." John's strong hands fondled the big black ears. "I'd better be stayin' here awhile."

But nothing happened. After a few days John announced, "It's goin' back to work I am." And when Elizabeth protested "Wisht woman!" he replied, "Would ye be havin' me like a pig's tail goin' round all day and nothing done at night?"

The dog stayed on, evidently quite at home. Then one day he disappeared and was never seen again. And no one ever knew who owned the big black dog that came from the forest that night to protect Elizabeth and her baby.

All through those dense Miramichi woods settlers' cabins were scattered, and often, when John was away Elizabeth would go off to visit a neighbour. She'd pack a lunch and with her son start off bright and early. All along the trail the little lad would run ahead and play hide and seek between the trees. But one day he ran further than usual and when Elizabeth came to the bend in the trail he was nowhere to be seen. Perhaps he was hiding under the bushes. Elizabeth called to him, but there was no answer; no movement in the brush, nothing but the wind swishing high in the trees, and the distant call of the birds. Along the trail Elizabeth ran calling frequently and frantically. Then, leaving the trail, she scrambled under brush where timber cruisers had blazed a narrow path. Suddenly she came to a well-worn track, the road to the Indian camp. The track widened and she saw ahead wigwams scattered over the hard baked ground.

Cautiously she went towards a group of squaws. "Have you seen a small white boy?" she asked. They looked up blankly and went on scraping their deerskins pretending not to understand. But they understood very well, Elizabeth knew, for she recognized a fat squaw who had come begging to her cabin. "Where is the white child?" she asked sharply.

Soon she was aware that the whole tribe was watching her, and Indians appeared to come from nowhere and stood around motionless. Suspicious now, she ran to the nearest wigwam calling for her son. He was not there. Terrified she dashed around the campsite, searching under the bushes while the Indians and squaws watched her without moving.

Doubt surged in her mind. Had he really come this way? Had he been carried off by a bear? Perhaps the Indians had not seen him after all. Then she heard voices in the distance, children's voices. She went towards the sounds and suddenly there was a child's voice, crying, piteous, terror-stricken. She ran down a path and there in a clearing under the trees a small white figure twisted and strained against a tree trunk, while a group of little Indian boys stood at the edge of the woods getting bows and arrows ready to use on the small white captive for their target.

Elizabeth screamed as she rushed across to the tree. Fiercely she tore at the thongs binding the little white body. Gathering her naked little son in her arms she ran from the place as if Satan himself were after her; across the camping ground, between the groups of squaws and braves and down the hard packed road. She was over a mile away before she dared stop and look behind. And there was no visiting that day.

In pioneer days on the Miramichi, the churches were social as well as spiritual centres; and in spite of the long prayers and longer sermons church-going was lots of fun. It brought the people together, for whole families from grandfathers to babies would come by canoe from along the Miramichi and go u p to Newcastle. They'd take picnic baskets full of good things to eat and a jug or two or rum, for they never could be sure they'd find a well handy.

Canoes would be hauled up on the beach and they would gather in the graveyard with its little white fence. A safe playground for the children while the older folk sat around resting their backs against the headstones; a real holiday for one and all, but quite dignified, of course.

Now, the church stood in a clearing and not far down the road was the minister's house. Most of the people could tell time quite accurately by the sun, and watches were still a scarce commodity — only the rich could afford them. Naturally, the church sexton didn't own one. So, when it was time to ring the bell for service the minister's wife would hang a pair of her husband's trousers out of the window as a signal. The old sexton would watch the window closely until the trousers appeared and then he'd swing the bell rope vigorously; and the congregation would file in and sit solemnly on the benches for the two-hour sermon.

Afterwards there was an intermission for the noonday meal. Picnic baskets and rum jugs were dragged up from the canoes and everyone ate heartily. Then at the bell's signal they'd file into church again, well-fortified for another two hours' discourse, while the children squabbled and played around the graveyard.

That sturdy old pioneer, Samuel Peabody, always brought his snuffbox along to church; a huge tortoise shell and silver affair — for he was an inveterate snuffer.

He'd come stamping up the aisle with his heavy gold-topped cane; the corner of a bright red handkerchief peeping from his coat-tail pocket. If it happened that the preacher expressed views that did not agree with Mr. Peabody's, click! would go the snuffbox like a report of a bullet, and the long sermon would be punctuated with hearty ka-choos and a waving of the bright red handkerchief.

Schooling for the settlers' children was a problem to both parents and teachers. Often the teacher went from house to house along the river to stay for a week, or a month, if the family was large. Fees were seldom paid in cash and the instructor would take whatever the family could offer. If they could spare neither grain, nor firewood, he had to be content with board and lodging, scant as it was.

Books were as scarce as fees, but in one school at Newcastle an ingenious teacher printed the alphabet and shorter catechism on strips of paper and then pasted them on a shingle thus preventing the precious paper from wearing out with constant handling, for these 'shingle books' were passed on from one scholar to another for years.

Slates and pencils were unknown and quill pens a luxury. Birch bark copy books were quite popular in those days, and some schools had a large wooden box, the bottom covered lightly with earth, and by using sharpened sticks they would write in the earth, and that way many future leaders of the Miramichi district learned to write and "cypher".

Every year the fields grew wider along the riverbank. Ships from Greenock, Liverpool and Belfast tied up at Newcastle wharves to load masts and spars from the green gold of Miramichi forests for the staunch ships of Britain.

Fishermen were kept busy at the weirs, and hundreds of tierces of salmon were exported as Davidson had done years before, when he exported 3,800 tierces of salmon in one year.

And in the cabin by the river Elizabeth Russel rocked her second baby, Nancy, in the little cradle that John had built. It was the year 1825. The summer had been very hot; wells had dried up and the parched ground grew gray and dusty. Even the mighty Miramichi had receded, leaving long stretches of pebbly beaches along its shores. It was a dangerous time of year; for, when trees were cut in the forests, the woodsmen lopped off the branches and there they'd lie, getting dryer and crisper in the hot sun until the whole forest was like a tinder box. But the settlers' barns were full with crops harvested and everyone was getting settled for the winter.

October the seventh dawned hot and still. Elizabeth Russel had been in Newcastle that morning, while a neighbour's daughter stayed with the children. Tired from her long walk home in the heat, Elizabeth took off her shoes, but found little relief, for even the floors of the cabin were too warm for comfort.

The air was stifling and the sky a pale orange hue. The woods seemed empty with a silence so uncanny she could almost feel it. But Elizabeth went about her work as usual and all the time she was wishing that John would come home, for she began to feel afraid.

Only that morning James Wright had walked the streets of Newcastle beating his drum and calling to the people, warning them of an approaching fire. Erect and sprightly, in spite of his seventy years, he stepped out briskly, well remembering the days he had drummed for the Volunteers long ago.

Clerks in the shipping office paused their quill pens and wandered to the doorway to see what it was all about. They laughed when the old drummer told them the Indians had fled the forest and were gathering on the river banks and advised them to do the same.

"Old scaremonger!" they said, as James beat his drum along the crooked old streets with the town's children trailing along behind him kicking up little spirals of dust with their heels. "What if the summer had been dry?" They had had dry years before, they argued. "What if the sky was black and the air stifling?" It was only the forerunner of a thunderstorm and, God knows, rain was needed. "James and his Indians!" "Always fishing and hunting when he should have been attending to his work!"

"Who did he think he was? An old spae-wife with a teacup foretelling things to come?"

And back to their ledgers and their shops went the townsfolk. A ship was loaded ready to sail, and neither Peabody, nor the Frasers, would put up with delays, so the pens scraped down the long sheets of manifest.

Back in the cabin it was getting darker and a gentle wind began to blow; but instead of bringing relief, it brought only scorching heat, as if a huge furnace door had suddenly been opened. The sky was dark now with great rushing black clouds. Suddenly a terrific gust of wind blew through the open door carrying twigs and leaves into the cabin, and leaving a strange smell of warm balsam in its wake. Anxiously, Elizabeth stood in the doorway, almost hoping to see John coming up the path. She watched the swaying trees. This was no thunderstorm! If only John were here! Then the wind came again, acrid and pungent now, with the smell of wood smoke. Terrified, Elizabeth rushed to the cradle and snatched up her baby and a blanket, shouting to the girl to bring William.

Down the trail they raced. Sticks and stones cut Elizabeth's feet, for she had not taken time to put on her shoes. Frantic animals crashed out of the forest and ran along beside them and overhead the wind roared like thunder. Branches and blazing twigs swirled through the air setting small fires in the dry leaves, while behind them was a lurid glare as the wall of flame roared on.

Elizabeth tripped and fell and scrambled up again a dozen times before they reached the outskirts of Newcastle. The choking haze took her breath away, for her the smoke was so dense she couldn't see a dozen feet ahead; the fences were her only guide and even some of them were on fire.

All Newcastle was in an uproar. Half-dressed men, women and

children ran screaming along the streets. Terror-stricken, Elizabeth joined the crowds in their mad race to the marshes above the town.

The river was lashed to fury by the gale, and those who had tried, too late, to get away in canoes were tossed about like chips in a millrace, while many were drowned.

In the marshes crowds scrambled upon logs or anything they could get hold of. Hastily constructed rafts were swarmed to sinking with terrified humanity. Children whimpered piteously and Elizabeth clung to her little ones, praying for her husband's safety. People with blackened faces and staring eyes crowded the rafts, only to slip off into the water. Then dimly through the roaring wind that almost drowned the shouts of the refugees, Elizabeth heard her husband calling. He staggered waist-deep through the reeds and the water and reached out strong arms to hold his son. Horror-stricken, the little family clung together all that wild night. The wind hurled burning faggots that fell hissing into the marsh. Young people stood neck-deep in the water holding up the feeble and sick, while cattle and wild animals struggled beside them trying to keep their heads above water.

All night long the flames swept on. Forests, farms and houses disappeared as if they had been melted.

Smoke and embers from that holocaust were carried by the wind to Newfoundland. Warm cinders fell in the streets of Halifax, and in the morning everything for miles and miles in that green and pleasant land was black desolation.

For days hollow-eyed men and women wandered around homeless, or searched for their scattered families. Nothing was left of the town of Newcastle but gaunt, ruined chimneys and heaps of still-smouldering ashes. No food, no clothing, except what they stood in, the sufferers wandered aimlessly around until help from outside came to ease their distress.

But Elizabeth Russel remembered the field of potatoes that had not been harvested. Back along the blackened trail the little family went as soon as the ground was cool enough for travelling, and there, sure enough, they found the potatoes all roasted in the ground.

But their home! Their farm! The smoke-blackened man put his arms around Elizabeth as she sobbed on his shoulder. Nothing left but timbers and the chimney standing tall over the ashes like a grim monument.

That day John Russel found a canoe floating inshore on the Miramichi. He paddled across to Beaubear's Island, where a few dilapidated shacks stood, remnants of Davidson's once-prosperous lumbering settlement, but long since deserted.

He brought Elizabeth and the children to a cabin with crazily sagging walls. With axe and poles he repaired the roof and filled the chinks in the walls with sod. He brought potatoes from their field and there was fish in the river. Elizabeth salted and dried the salmon and somehow she hung on through that terrible desolate winter; for John was away again, deeper in the woods now, cutting timber and hauling it by slow oxen to the landing place. When he did come home he was busy with his axe, making tables and benches and beds for their new home, and leaving a huge pile of firewood just outside their door.

Back in the town of Newcastle other sufferers covered the cellars of their burned homes with logs and crowded into them for shelter. Few came to Beaubear's Island. Perhaps they were afraid, for there were weird tales of the place.

For Beaubear's Island had sheltered many since the days of Charles des Champs de Boishebert, the Quebec-born aristocrat and his band of adventurers. Even his battery, with its good French cannon at the east end of the Island, had been no match for wily Indians on the warpath. They swooped down on the refugee Acadians Boishebert had brought in 1755, and all who could scattered and fled from the settlement.

The Scots, who came with William Davidson in 1764 for fur trading and fishing, built the first vessels on the Miramichi, but they too abandoned the Island after frequent raids by American privateers during the Revolutionary War.

On long winter nights, when the snow piled eaves-high and the frost cracked like cannon and the wind wailed like a tribe of banshees, Elizabeth would lie trembling in her bed. Often she thought she could hear voices drifting on the wind. Voices of Boishebert's men, and wild cries of savages as their hatchets struck down the helpless Acadians.

But when the sun came stealing out of the east, making the frost-covered trees a very fairyland, Elizabeth would say to her four-year-old William, "Look, yon's a castle, and there is a ship," and she'd croon haunting little Irish folk songs to Nancy while William played on the floor making houses with little sticks.

And when March gales cracked the ice and spring spread its healing green blanket over the scorched land, John Russel built another cabin around the old chimney and they began homesteading all over again.

Swift years sped on behind Elizabeth Russel. Children and grandchildren heard her tales of the Great Fire and that heart-breaking winter on Beaubear's Island. But when she spoke of the green fields of Antrim her voice would drift off to a whisper. "Och, ochone! The green of it! And the fairy glens with the early morning mist on the hills." Elizabeth's eyes would grow moist as she told of the land she would never see again; for Elizabeth Russel lies sleeping in a little churchyard on the King's Highway in Newcastle.

Nearby her resting place rises the tall white spire of Saint James Church, where she worshipped, a successor to the church destroyed in the Great Fire. The same church where, for many years, the Reverend William Aitken ministered to the staunch Presbyterians of the Miramichi. And the whole town of Newcastle speaks with friendly familiarity of the son of Reverend William, that seven-year-old newsboy of days gone by, Lord Beaverbrook now.

But it's a far cry from the pioneer log cabins on the Miramichi to the summer camps of today. Mansions they are, of almost unbelievable luxury. No fishing nets are allowed above the tide line as they were in Davidson's time; but anglers may hook salmon, grilse or sea trout from the still teeming Miramichi. All for a price of course, varying from the "rough it" camp in the woods or modest cabin and one-man-guide at moderate cost, to the sumptuous "de luxe" establishments, which charge from seventy-five to one hundred dollars a day. Millionaires often bring their secretaries to keep them in touch with the world, while they play a mighty fighting salmon in the streams, or travel the forest lands in search of game.

On cool spring evenings the frogs chant their chorus, and sunset spreads a rose-coloured scarf over the river as it shimmers between its green banks, just as it did in the days when Davidson carried on his "masting industry". The Miramichi is still a great timber centre, with three large mills, though not so much long timber as pulp. There are still fortunes to be had in pulpwood and a large pulpmill is under construction.

And roaming about the elm-shaded crooked streets of Newcastle, with their basket and splint chairs for sale, are the descendants of the same Micmacs, who kidnapped Elizabeth Russel's son. Quiet and inoffensive now, the Indians of the Miramichi have marched with time a long, long way from the days when their enemies named the district "Maissimeu assi", meaning "country of the bad people" and Champlain spelled it "missamichi;" the only Indian place name in all Canada to continue in permanent use. And on the riverbank today, overlooking Beaubear's Island, a monument recalls the tale of that brave soldier Boishebert and the refugee Acadians who sheltered there.

The perilous days are gone. But our great country was not built by gold lace and swords and fine words. It was built by brave men and self-reliant women, whose calloused hands guided and cared for their sons and daughters. Women, like Elizabeth Russel with her homespun gown and homesick heart, who tackled her job and made good.

BIBLIOGRAPHY

From the "Historical account of the Russel Family, William Russel, narrator, Born Feb. 3, 1822, Newcastle. Moved to British Columbia 1891. Died at Victoria, B.C. 1906."

From "Historical-Geographical Documents, Foundation of modern settlement of Miramichi" Edited by Wm. F. Ganong, Ph.D.

Elizabeth McColl

It was in St. Stephen, a little settlement on the St. Croix River in New Brunswick, that Elizabeth McColl began her career as a minister's wife.

The first church service in that community was held in the McColl cabin and for over one hundred and eighty years there has never been a break in those services that Elizabeth's husband, Duncan McColl inaugurated that November Sunday in 1785.

Elizabeth McColl's life was not drab or dull just because she was a minister's wife, for she lived in a world of drums and soldiers and ships and guns.

St. Stephen, when the McColls arrived, was a hive of industry. Soldiers of the 74th Argyle Regiment had settled in and around St. Stephen and patched and faded uniforms were seen everywhere. From the spruce clad hillsides came the sound of axes and saws as men, working from dawn till dark, cleared their land and built cabins, and the skirl of the pipes echoed in the streets when the remnant of that proud battalion gathered to celebrate.

From the ships at anchor in the St. Croix River — that boundary line between Canada and the United States — came the satisfying rattle of hoisting gear, while cartmen and sailors with tarry pigtails jostled and shouted as they wheeled barrows of food and tools and clothing along the streets.

To Elizabeth McColl the scene brought back memories of Philadelphia where she had spent seventeen years. The narrow streets with their bustle of trade and gloomy little two-storied houses with shuttered windows. The wharves along the Delaware with schooners' masts towering above the storehouses; sailors and tar, and smell of bilge, carts rolling along Front Street; and that August day in 1774 when she stood beside her father on Chestnut Street watching the Sons of Liberty march along with their banners protesting against the British.

Afterwards, Elizabeth's father, John Channel, told of meetings in dark shuttered rooms, guns hidden down wells, and rebels planning a blockade against Britain which closed every port and ruined British merchants with interests in the colonies.

When the streets of Philadelphia were no longer safe for loyal supporters of the King, Mr. Channel quietly moved away. He wasn't going to wait for the shooting to begin. It would be impossible to get transportation then and he had no stomach for soldiering. Then he stowed his family and his belongings on board a ship and sailed for Bermuda. As a result John Channel lost a fortune in the Revolution and Elizabeth forfeited all the property left to her by her grandmother.

After the drabness of Philadelphia Elizabeth found Bermuda an exciting spot. The brilliant birds, gorgeous flowers and soft warm air were a pleasant contrast to the cold northern climate. Strange fruits from tropical gardens and delicious fish from the bright blue sea challenged Elizabeth's skill in cooking. She was very happing keeping house for her father and brother, who was a doctor and had soon established a good practice.

Here in Bermuda were traders and merchants and a solid British Fort garrisoned by British soldiers who protected them from buccaneers who sailed the seas. Coal-black negroes unloaded the ships that sailed into the harbor and red-coated soldiers marched out to the tune of fife and drum along the dusty white road.

Even the strong British Garrison, however, with their muskets and bayonets could not protect Bermuda from the fierce tropical storms that roared across the Island and washed battered ships and wreckage in their wake. One of these Atlantic hurricanes washed a ship ashore that changed the whole pattern of Elizabeth's life.

On this ship was young Duncan McColl, a British soldier who had fought with the 74th Argyle Regiment at the siege of Castine, Maine, during the Revolutionary War; and Duncan McColl had had a narrow escape in that engagement. He was carrying dispatches that day. Bullets fell all around him as he crossed a field, but Duncan McColl went on, dodging around bushes, dropping behind boulders. The American soldiers were good marksmen too, but they couldn't hit him. Suddenly there came a shout, "Cease Fire!" The officer who gave the order remarked to the men nearby, "God must have some work for that man to do." McColl crossed the field unharmed as the Americans watched. It was a miracle.

Thus Duncan survived that siege of Castine and lived to reach New York with the retreating British troops. Then, his services as paymaster in the Regiment no long needed, he sailed from New York November 14, 1783, for England as he did not intend to take a grant of land in Nova Scotia with others of his regiment.

The ship had reached Seal Island at the mouth of the Bay of Fundy when a raging hurricane swept the decks and carried the ship southwards. For twenty-seven days they were at the mercy of the winds. Short of water and provisions (they were down to one biscuit and half a pint of water per man a day), they were finally swept to Bermuda. It took all winter to repair that ship, and as Duncan had been in business before he'd been a soldier, he stayed on in Bermuda to keep accounts for the ship's owners.

After he had put away his ledgers for the day, Duncan would have supper with some of the merchants of the Colony. Very likely he found it a pleasant change from the ship's fare of biscuit and dried beef. It was then he met the Channel family. Perhaps Elizabeth's cooking lured him to the Channel home so often. Perhaps her father's learned discourse on experimental religion and the principles of Methodism was interesting. For although the Channels came from Philadelphia, they were Methodists, not Quakers. After three months in Bermuda, Elizabeth and Duncan were married in spite of the opposition of both Elizabeth's father and brother who believed that Duncan's prospects were not encouraging.

In the spring the ship was ready to sail north again. It took Elizabeth and Duncan up to Halifax, and Duncan decided he wanted to be a minister of the gospel. Nevertheless, Duncan McColl unpacked goods, wrote invoices — in fact, did any sort of work to provide a living. Then they decided to go to Saint Andrews where many of Duncan's comrades of the 74th Argyle Regiment were already taking up land.

To Elizabeth, Passamaquoddy Bay looked even less promising than Halifax. Thick dark forests rising above the shore, no wharves; no husky black boys to unload cargo and sing their plaintive songs. No neat white houses as in Bermuda, only a row of queer-looking cabins stretched along the shore. These were the birch bark houses built by the Government for the new settlers.

These flimsy cabins cost ten pounds each and often when a settler had paid for his home he had no money left. Land was being allotted to the settlers on condition they build homes, but supplies for building had not arrived. From a "License of Occupation Register of Ungranted Town Lots in Saint Andrews", under the date August 28, 1784, "permission is given Duncan McColl to occupy Lot No. 6 upon express condition that he erect a house there, equal to at least sixteen feet square and exactly six feet from the street, before the first day of October next, in which case he will be recommended for a grant of the place." That would give Duncan only one month to build, so one of the birch bark cabins costing ten pounds became Elizabeth's new home. All that long, cold winter those settlers had to heat up birch logs and put them in their beds to keep from freezing. They didn't have enough blankets, and often snow was six feet deep.

How those pioneer mothers ever sang lullabys to their babies through that awful winter we'll never know; but Elizabeth McColl's courage never failed her as she went from cabin to cabin trying to help the sick, often with a jug of soup, or some cornmeal mush for the children.

Still Duncan wanted to be a minister. These men and women who had sacrificed so much must have a church. He had no money, however, and after that first terrible winter the McColls moved to St. Stephen further up the St. Croix River, about twenty miles from Saint Andrews.

Duncan had learned that one of his officers from his old regiment had a store in St. Stephen and needed a man to look after his business while he returned to Scotland, so Duncan McColl became a businessman again.

The McColls drew a town lot when land was being divided in St. Stephen, and the whole neighbourhood turned out to build them a cabin. With Duncan working at the store and a sound roof over their heads, Elizabeth counted herself lucky. For some reason, however, Duncan couldn't collect his pay for managing the store, so it was then that he took up the ministry in real earnest.

On the last Sunday in November, 1785, Duncan McColl held a meeting in his cabin. Six people came that day, and from that Sunday on there has never been a break in the weekly church services of that congregation.

That was the beginning of the Kirk-McColl United Church, and the present edifice built on land given by the McColls stands today as a monument to the faith and courage of those early settlers. Back in 1785 sixty people came to McColl's cabin for the second church service the following Sunday and Elizabeth had to hustle around to borrow benches, for that one little room was packed.

His mission now begun, Duncan travelled throughout sparsely settled Charlotte County, carrying his Bible in a saddlebag. He walked, for he couldn't afford a horse, and for the first few years Duncan McColl had no salary whatever, for his congregation was as poor as himself.

One year, Duncan McColl received three dollars and fifty cents as a salary, and the women sent Elizabeth two cheeses as a gift. These Duncan carried home on his back. Elizabeth could buy moose meat in season at a penny a pound, if she had the penny, and there was always fish for the catching in the river. Then every settler grew a few potatoes among the burnt stumps around the cabin, and in summer they could dig for clams — for in those sandbars that connect the little islands and all along the shores of Passamaquoddy Bay the wet red sands are full of clams.

Long before the white settlers came, the Passamaquoddy Indians used to roam the shores all summer, fishing and digging clams. They had a primitive form of dehydration for storing clams for winter use. The squaws would string them on long grasses, dry them in the sun and tie them in bunches. Even today those temporary camping grounds of the Passamaquoddy Indians can be traced by the great heaps of clam shells they left behind them. They're worn down level with the shore by the waves, but they show up in grey-white spots on the red sands.

One time a grateful congregation gave Duncan McColl a suit of good broadcloth. He wore it only on special occasions and it lasted a lifetime. The rest of the time he dressed in homespun and leather breeches — they survived the tramps through the woods better than cloth ones — and Elizabeth patched and mended and patched again.

Year after year Duncan tramped the forest trails preaching to the settlers. Often he had to cross deep creeks in water up to his waist. Once, in a winter, he went through the soft ice, but scrambled out, made sure his precious Bible was safe, then with his clothing frozen stiff, he ran as fast as he could to the Meetinghouse where he lit a fire and dried out his clothing before the congregation arrived.

Another time he spent two days and three nights in an open boat on a trip from St. Stephen to Saint John; and often when there was only one room in the cabin where he stopped overnight, he would sleep on the floor near the fireplace with his saddlebag for a pillow.

Many a bright Sunday morning as the tide was coming in, the candidates for baptism would kneel on the shore before the open-air service began while Duncan McColl performed the ceremony.

Elizabeth McColl had a busy life in her career of helping her husband. Sometimes at night there would be a knock on their cabin door; a lantern would flash in the dark; then a voice would explain that someone was in trouble. Duncan and Elizabeth were needed, and dawn would find them walking home together along some lonely road.

At first Duncan travelled alone, but later Elizabeth accompanied him on preaching tours. He didn't stop on the Canadian side of the Saint Croix River; he went across to the American side and preached in the towns and villages there. On Sundays people came from miles around to join the services in the McColl cabin. What a strange sight it was: those British soldiers and rebel Americans all gathered to worship together!

Elizabeth was proud of her husband as he preached the gospel of brotherly love. He told them that they must work together and build a church, for the cabin was too small for his congregation by this time. Elizabeth had a vision of a strong tower above the clustered rooftops of a town, for she knew there would be broad fields and villages and towns where now the great forest stood.

The McColls got their church. That was a day to remember. The congregation overflowed the church and spilled right through the door to the roadway. Elizabeth was there that day in her plain dark gown and scoop bonnet, for Methodist women in the early days wore a special garb; a cape or cloak of drab or dark gray and a scoop bonnet with no bright colors or ornament of any kind. This costume was indeed sober and dignified.

Now that they had their church, Elizabeth wanted her husband to be an ordained minister, and Duncan had to go to New London, Connecticut, to attend the Methodist Conference. It began July 15, 1795 and lasted for three days.

Travelling in those days was both hazardous and expensive. The fare from St. Stephen to New London was two pounds eight shillings. You paid your money and took your chances, for often a ship would lie over for days waiting for a fair wind. Sometimes a storm blew them miles off their course, and there were always privateers lurking around ready to pick up a good ship and its cargo. The fare was for transportation only and each passenger provided his own food for the journey.

Nevertheless, Duncan McColl went to New London to be ordained. Elizabeth mended his old suit for travelling and the black broadcloth was safely stowed in the saddlebag, for she wanted her husband to look his best when he met the gentlemen from Connecticut.

The ceremony over, Duncan headed for home, and as he didn't have enough money to pay his fare back by ship he started to walk. Through the woods of Massachusetts, across the hills of New Hampshire and along the coast of Maine he trudged. It's five hundred and twenty miles from New London to St. Stephen by today's road map, but Duncan added many more as he stumbled through forests and detoured around bogs.

Day after day Elizabeth went down to the shore to watch for his ship. Days lengthened into weeks. Still no word came, Elizabeth was in despair for she had not even heard if Duncan had reached New London. Letters took so long in those days.

Then one day a tattered old man with birch bark tied over his shoes to replace the worn-off soles, and a ragged old saddlebag slung on his back, stumbled along the road in Maine and finally reached Calais. Someone rowed him across the river. Duncan McColl was home again! His clothes were in ribbons and he was so bruised and weary that Elizabeth just put her arms around him and wept. Years afterwards in his memoirs Duncan McColl wrote, "I had had many days of fatigue, but never harder than what I encountered on this journey."

In time the little settlements of St. Stephen and Calais on the St. Croix River grew up, and friendship grew between the Canadians and Americans. Young folk met and married. It didn't make any difference to Cupid which side of the river they lived on.

Then came the War of 1812. History books tell us all about Brock and Tecumseh and of Laura Secord's trek through the woods with her milk pail. They even tell about the march of the 104th New Brunswick Regiment that marched on snowshoes all the way from Fredericton to Quebec, 435 miles, in the dead of winter without losing one man. One of the greatest marches in history, it proves the vigor of those hardy pioneers. But the story of the truce between Canadians and Americans along the St. Croix River receives little or no publicity. But it is a fact.

Martello Tower in Saint John West, built for the defense of British North America in the War of 1812

Photo by William Hart

Back in 1812 the people of the border towns went about with serious faces. Women gathered in little groups. They had watched their men march away to War before.

The Administration of New Brunswick issued a Proclamation forbidding anyone to molest United States citizens living on the borders of the Province. A public fast was proclaimed, but while they fasted some were already cleaning their muskets and sharpening their swords. This war was very unpopular with the New Englanders too, for when the Declaration reached Boston all ships in port there hoisted their flags at half-mast. It meant the end of trade with Canada.

In her home Elizabeth McColl talked it over with a group of friends. She knew that the people in Calais and St. Stephen were friends, even relatives. So why should James take a shot at his uncle Henry just because England and the United States had declared war?

Elizabeth and Duncan sat up talking long into the night. Duncan knew all about war. Perhaps he prayed as he paced the floor that night. Maybe it would work. Perhaps it wouldn't, but they'd try. Elizabeth got out the quill pen and put the inkpot and paper on the table. Duncan sat down and wrote two notices. He tacked one up on their church door in St. Stephen; then he rowed across the River to Calais and tacked the other on the door of the Town Hall. He had invited everyone to meet at the church.

Then he went back to his church and waited. They came, from Calais and Scotch Ridge and St. Stephen and all around — men and women. The little church wouldn't hold them all and the old gallery in that Meetinghouse sagged a few inches with the crowd, but no one except Duncan saw it.

Elizabeth sat in the front pew, cold fingers clenched together. Her heart beat wildly as she watched Duncan standing straight and tall in the pulpit. How pale he was! The crowded church buzzed with voices. But when Duncan raised his hand the noise died into a stillness so intense one could hear a pin drop.

When Duncan McColl began to speak his voice came clearly, earnestly across the Meetinghouse. He told those people how he had christened many of them, and buried their parents, and married some of them, and he asked them to stick together. Why should they take up arms against their best friends? From the back of the crowd someone shouted, "To hell with war!" Perhaps Duncan thought the same.

Then and there the people of Calais and St. Stephen made a truce of their own. They would have no war! Elizabeth listened as if in a trance. She never before was so proud of her husband. Someone then touched her lightly on the shoulder, and her eyes were misty as she made her way through the crowd and out into the sunlight again. On their knees, in that little cottage that night Elizabeth and Duncan gave thanks from the bottom of their hearts.

Although there was no fighting, there was the Blockade. British frigates cruised along the coast of New Brunswick, for Halifax was the base of the North Atlantic Squadron in 1812. Trade suffered; no cargoes could be sent to the United States; no fish could be sold. Lumber piled up on the wharves, and the cold grip of poverty closed in on the St. Croix settlement.

There was no tea, no sugar. Molasses cost one dollar a gallon and flour sold at twenty dollars a barrel, so bread became a luxury.

One winter night the McColls sat down to supper with their last loaf of bread on the table. There was nothing else except the bitter brew of dried wild berries that served for coffee. After grace was said Elizabeth and Duncan sat quietly looking at each other. Neither dared to break the loaf.

Now that they shared hunger they remembered that pledge made in sunny Bermuda so long ago, "for richer, for poorer". Yet in their little cabin that cold winter night for Elizabeth and Duncan there was no self-pity, no bitterness; only understanding and faith. No words were needed as they began their meal.

Suddenly the quiet was shattered by a fierce knocking at the door. Before Duncan could move, the door swung open and a strange man, stamping the snow from his boots, stepped into the room.

Huge and burly, he paused for a moment while Duncan rose and stood beside him.

"McColl," he said abruptly, "how are you off for beef and bread?" Duncan cleared his throat and began to speak while the man stared at the sparsely-set table.

"Good God," the stranger interrupted, "is that all you've got?" He turned and bowed to Elizabeth, "Beg pardon, ma'am." Then to Duncan he said, "I'll be back!"

The door slammed and he was gone. Duncan and Elizabeth stared at each other. Who was he? Where did he come from? Did it really happen? They thought perhaps their imaginations were becoming too vivid, yet there on the floor was the snow melting in puddles. Elizabeth fetched a mop and cleaned it up. Then they sat down to their supper again.

In no time their visitor returned dragging two sacks.

"A tierce of good flour and another of beef," he announced as he dumped the sacks on the table. Duncan began to thank him but the stranger said gruffly, "No, after what you've done for us here! Anyway, if I don't give it to you those damned drunken sailors will find it and steal it!" And he was off again as suddenly as he had come.

Duncan and Elizabeth never discovered where the food came from though they believed it was contraband. The next day Elizabeth McColl went visiting and there was beef and bread in the basket she carried under her grey cloak.

Although during the War of 1812 both nations had troops stationed in those border towns, not a single shot was fired across the

St. Croix River.

Through the war years people were hungry, but they never despaired. All that time Duncan McColl held services in Canada and the United States, just as he had always done. For forty-five years he carried on the work of the Church. For his strenuous labors in a circuit, which comprised a large part of western Charlotte County and the adjoining settlements in Maine, his salary only averaged one hundred and fifty-seven dollars a year. In a letter written near the close of his life in 1830 he says, "I received no earthly support but the contributions of my hearers together with my own property, which was under the management of Mrs. McColl; but that supplied my wants."

When peace came the border towns were prosperous again. For thirty-five years Elizabeth McColl continued her career as a minister's wife. She died on March 23rd, 1819.

Today from an old square tower a bell rings across the roof tops of St. Stephen on the banks of the St. Croix River. Its deep tone calls to worship the descendants of those pioneers who built this country and made it great.

And on the spot where Elizabeth McColl's cabin stood is a solidly built church called the KIRK-McCOLL UNITED CHURCH.

BIBLIOGRAPHY

From collections of notes by Mrs. A.E. Vesey, St. Stephen, New Brunswick.
Newspaper articles by Ian Sclanders, Archives Dept., New Brunswick Museum.
Court Records of Charlotte County, New Brunswick.
Moreau de St. Mary's "American Journey" 1793-1798 (Philadelphia).

Charlotte Haines

There is a dainty beige kid slipper with a silk bow on the toe and a quaint little portrait painted on glass in the New Brunswick Museum. Once they belonged to Charlotte Haines. The slipper she wore when she was ten years old; the portrait was done when she was an old, old lady, but from the years between comes a tale as romantic as anything in fiction.

Charlotte Haines was born in New York City in 1773. Her grandfather was an Amsterdam merchant, who had set up in business in the new Colony of New York and Charlotte's father, John Haines, inherited the substantial brick house and warehouse established by his father. Charlotte would have spent the rest of her life in New York, if she had not gone to visit her cousins one day. John Haines was a rebel who supported Congress and the Union, while her uncle was loyal to old King George. So the Haines brothers were not on speaking terms and Charlotte had been forbidden to have anything to do with her Loyalist cousins.

But Charlotte knew what was going on in the country, even if she was only ten years old. She watched soldiers marching through the streets and heard the roar of British cannon from Battery Point. And she saw the British refugees, who had been chased from their homes, come crowding into the city for protection, for New York was headquarters for the British army then.

Many a time Charlotte listened to her father growl about "Royal Governors" and "Lobster backs" and mutter things about tar and feathers, while her mother went about tight-lipped and silent, her eyes strange and pitiful.

And while John Haines railed against the Loyalists he took revenge in overcharging Loyalist customers, now that the guns were silenced. For on that grey November day of Friday 25th, 1782, General Washington and his American soldiers marched into New York and took over the city; and John Haines in his Sunday best, with a Union cockade of black and white ribbons on his hat, pushed through the crowds on Broadway and Wall streets down to the "Blue Bull

143

Tavern" to watch the sights.

That night while Charlotte and her mother sat in the parlor working embroidery, John Haines stood before the blazing fireplace warming his coat-tails. With a grim smile he told about ships being readied to deport the Loyalists; there was nothing else to do with so strong-minded a lot — and good enough for them. Charlotte shuddered as she thought of her cousins going off to a strange country; forests and wilderness, so they said, no cities, no houses; they'd be scalped by Indians or murdered in their beds. Charlotte's eyes blurred with tears, she couldn't see the pattern on her sampler, so she put it in her workbasket and sat quietly with folded hands listening to her father.

All that winter Charlotte heard stories about the Loyalists. The girls at school whispered about them too, when they weren't too busy chattering about beaux and small scandals. For Charlotte Haines, along with daughters of other wealthy merchants and shipowners, attended a fashionable school for young ladies.

Every morning Charlotte went vamping over the cobblestoned streets, stiff-starched petticoats around her ankles as she stepped primly along as a young lady of quality should. Her slave, straight and handsome in bright colored turban and kerchief folded over her dark woolen gown, followed just a step or two behind "missy", carrying books and lunch.

Though the Revolution separated families and friends forever, school went on just the same; but one by one the Loyalists' daughters disappeared from the classroom. Charlotte missed her lively cousins, classes were dull without them, and she made up her mind to visit them, even though her father had forbidden it.

Church services went on too, and Charlotte's father was strict about religious formalities. Every Sunday Charlotte and her brothers, David and John, dutifully walked to church with their parents and listened to sermons as high and dry as the three-decker pulpit. John Haines permitted no work to be done on Sundays. No horses of his in their shining harness and netting pranced along the streets. Other coaches might pull up before the church with Sunday-dressed occupants, but John Haines followed the fourth commandment to the letter. And every Saturday the servants scrubbed down the wide front steps so they would be fresh and clean when the Haines family stepped out next morning.

Winter passed. A bright March sun brought new life to naked branches of shrubs and trees, and slender green sprouts pushed their way through the brown earth in John Haines' garden. Charlotte wore her new slippers and the new red pelisse with its little shoulder capes to school. Spring was here.

But to the hundreds of unhappy Loyalists huddled in Howe's camp on Staten Island, Spring meant only one thing, exile. New York Harbour already was crowded with transports and men-of-war; and Charlotte watched the white sails with a sinking heart, for she had not seen her cousins all winter, and soon they would be going away forever.

Even on her way to school Charlottte saw furniture piled on the sidewalks in front of some staid brick house. Often there would be stacks of books and pictures and clothing; and all day long men pushed handcarts piled with goods, as if it were one vast moving day. The Loyalists were preparing to leave the city. She must see her cousins before they went away! She must!

So off she went one morning as usual, pausing dutifully at the gate to wave to her mother at the window; then down the street with her black girl behind her. At the school door she paused, watching her servant loiter along on the way home. Then she too went down the street.

Past block after block of tall houses, their pansy-edged lawns green in the bright sun, their lilacs nodding over iron railings. Up the stone steps of a shuttered house on tiptoe, Charlotte sounded the heavy knocker. Then books, lunch and all, she was in her aunt's arms, and down the stairs with a flurry of petticoats rushed her cousins to greet her.

Curled up on the wide canopied bed, the girls chattered excitedly. So much to talk about and the time so short. Servants clattered in and out banging drawers open and shut while her aunt tied up dresses in bundles.

From the hall below came snatches of conversation and Charlotte heard her uncle's voice sharp and angry. It was bargain day for the rebels, but for the Loyalists there was no mercy. Mahogany, silver and paintings changed owners for a mere pittance, but David Haines was determined to get all he could before Union committees moved in to confiscate the house.

Dinner was meager. When they had finished her uncle took a newspaper from his coat-tail pocket, spread it on the table and spoke sharply, "Listen to this." It was as if a town crier had shouted "Hear ye! Hear ye!" "Relating to embarkation," he read, "Notice to Refugees. The following Transports . . . [then came a list of ships' names that Charlotte scarcely heard] will certainly fall down on Monday morning. It will be absolutely necessary for the people who are appointed to go in these companies to be all aboard to-morrow evening." The silence that followed was like the hush of doom. Tears rolled down her aunt's cheeks as she rose quickly and left the room, the girls tiptoeing out behind her.

It was late afternoon before Charlotte started homewards; the girls wept and clung together as they said good-bye. And long after Charlotte disappeared around the street corner her cousins stood on the steps waving moist handkerchiefs.

The fine spring day was clouded now and a chill wind swept down spattering great coins of rain on the cobbles as Charlotte hurried along. Suddenly she was afraid. What would her father say when he learned of her visit? She dared not lie. She picked her way around puddles in the street wishing she had worn her pattens. How vexed her mother would be if her slippers were ruined; already her new red pelisse was quite damp. Perhaps she could slip down to the kitchen where black Phoebe would rub her feet with a comforting warm towel and fetch her dry clothes. The good warm kitchen with its savory smells! Baked meats and hot gingerbread! It made Charlotte hungry even to think of it.

The wind almost blew her up the path when she opened the gate. Then her heart stopped, for there stood her father in the doorway.

"Where have you been all day?" he demanded angrily. And Charlotte gasping for breath answered she had visited her cousins. Terrified, she stood in the rain while her father shouted and threatened. Never before had she seen him in such a rage. Never before had he used such words to her. There he stood, blocking the doorway and Charlotte wanting desperately to get in. But John Haines would not forgive his little daughter for her visit to a Loyalist home — he would not allow her in the house.

Charlotte stood speechless gazing at her father, while hot tears streamed down her face. Suddenly she picked up her petticoats, ran down the wide front steps and along the street with her father's words ringing in her ears. Back to her uncle's home for shelter raced the terror-stricken little ten-year-old that wild windy night. Charlotte's aunt and uncle looked very grave as she sobbed out her story and later that night the Haines brothers had another argument; but John Haines would not be reconciled.

Next day, even on tiptoe, Charlotte could scarcely see the Harbour, so thick were the ships. Trumpets sounded as soldiers who had fought for King George, marched down to the wharves. Drays and wheelbarrows loaded with goods were all mixed up with men and women carrying bundles, and babies cried while their mothers sobbed good-byes. Charlotte, clinging to her cousins, searched in vain for a glimpse of her mother in that sea of faces, then she was hustled on board.

That night, crowded in a bunk on a rough mattress she shared with two cousins, Charlotte wept bitter tears into the bundle that served as her pillow. Oh! For her own cosy room at home; the friendly firelight and her mother's soft voice as she tucked her in bed! The sampler with its flowers and birds would never be finished now. She would never hear the friendly chatter of the girls at school again, now she was sailing away on this smelly old ship. Such a nasty crowded cabin with boxes and bundles stacked all around and old black Susan moaning on the floor, for the Haines negroes would not stay behind. It was a confused, unhappy journey for Charlotte Haines.

But the confusion on shipboard was nothing compared to the day the Loyalists arrived in Saint John Harbour. Twenty ships at anchor with over three thousand people and not a roof to cover their heads. Saint John was only a fort and a forest then, with a small clearing where New England settlers had established a Trading Post. That day in May 1783 was never to be forgotten.

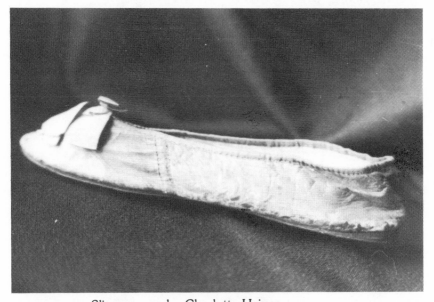

Slipper worn by Charlotte Haines

Courtesy of The New Brunswick Museum
Photo by Gordon Anderson

Charlotte stood on deck with her cousins and watched the soldiers line up when tattered little drummer boys beat a tattoo. Puffs of smoke floated from the guns of the Fort and the noise was deafening. Everyone rushed about collecting children and bundles in that mad scramble off the ships; for the Captains were in a hurry to be off to New York again.

Charlotte tried to hold up her petticoats and carry the bundle as she followed her aunt along the shore. It was rocky and wet and slippery. Mud was everywhere and Charlotte wore no pattens. As she slithered along in her little kid slippers, down went one foot in the mud and when she pulled it out again her slipper was gone. No time to hunt for it either, for tents were going up all over the hillside and everyone was hurrying to find shelter for the night.

That first night ashore, Charlotte's aunt rummaged in the bundles for shoes she could wear until the cobbler could make new ones. So Charlotte packed her one little slipper away, fine slippers were of no use in this country of rocks and trees. For soon Charlotte was one of the little procession led by her uncle over the old Indian trail to where boats waited to carry them on the river of the Loyalists to the river settlements.

Amos Botsford, an agent for Loyalist settlement, wrote in 1782, "They cut down the trees, burn the tops, put in a crop of wheat or Indian corn, which yields a plentiful increase. These intervales would make the finest meadows. The uplands produce wheat, both of summer and winter kinds, as well as Indian corn."

Tree by tree, stump by stump, those fertile uplands were cleared to wide fields, black men and their masters working together. And Charlotte Haines grew up with the country.

Then on the first day of June 1791, when she was seventeen, Charlotte became the bride of William Peters, just one year her senior. William had come with his Loyalist father James Peters from Hampstead, Long Island; another family whose allegiance was divided.

The Peters home at Hampstead, Long Island, built by Dr. Charles Peters in 1720, was Sir Guy Carleton's headquarters during the Revolution. Still a landmark today, visitors speak in hushed tones as they tiptoe across the parlor floor, where gay dancers stepped the minuet and Carleton's officers trod those same wide floor boards. Soldiers of revolutionary days tore up gravestones in the Peters family burial ground to make hearths for their fires, but the garden has a grape vine as old as the house.

Back in their Long Island home the Peters boys attended Seabury School, where masters "proposed to entertain and instruct young gentlemen in a genteel manner" for some "thirty pounds sterling per year."

William Peters began his education at Seabury, wearing knee breeches, silk stockings and a coat with wide buttoned cuffs, but not his own hair. For, like their elders, boys' heads were shaved and wigs neatly fitted by the barber. And when one little gentleman slugged it out with another little gentleman on a point of honour, a third little gentleman stood a few paces away holding coats, hats and wigs.

Topboots replaced the silk stockings and buckled shoes of

James Peters' sons, when they lived in the old house on Grimross Neck near Gagetown. It is a huge place built of fieldstone with two and a half foot thick walls, three stories high and a massive chimney containing three fireplaces, one above the other. It was built by Pierre de Joibert, Sieur de Soulanges et Marson, to whom Count Frontenac granted seigniories on the Saint John River in 1672. Madame de Joibert was a daughter of Chartier de Lotbiniere, Attorney General of Quebec, and her daughter, Louise Elizabeth, was born at Grimross Neck in 1763.

Another citizen first saw the light of day in that old stone house and James Peters took his quill pen and inscribed with flourishing capitals in the Family Bible, "Harry Peters, born Fryday 11th November 1785, half past ten o'clock at night at Gemross, St. John's River."

It was of "Squire Peters", as James was known, that Patrick Campbell in his *Travels in North America 1791-1792* writes, "Squire Peters has an extensive plantation on the same side of the river [Gagetown]. I asked several questions of this gentleman about farming, which he answered in a very satisfactory manner; among the rest, that they might cut two crops of hay in a season on the same spot, but as one cutting afforded them plenty for their own use, it was not worth any man's while to be at the trouble or expense of making hay for sale . . . A ton feeds a cow for the season."

James Peters built the huge barn which stands today, firmly held against the wind, weather and years by its wooden dowel-pins, where from a ramp leading to the top level Squire Peters' men forked loads of hay into the mows some thirty feet below to feed their "cows for a season."

Charlotte and William did not settle at Gagetown, but went farther down the river to where it widens to a magnificent view on the sloping hillsides of Hampstead, and here they built their home.

There was not ten miles of roadway in the Province then. A visitor described the country as "Heaven for women, a correction for men and Hell for horses." Travellers rode horseback through wilderness trails and there was great excitement in pioneer homes when a trumpet sounded and flying hoofs brought a courier with the mail. Not until 1809, when troops, "furnished with tools" and paid "six pence a day and found", began building the road between Fredericton and Saint John.

But the river was always a highway. Durham boats were succeeded by a regular "Scow-boat service". The FOUR SISTERS advertised "to sail from Saint John every Thursday, wind and weather permitting." The boat reached Fredericton in three days, while its some twenty passengers slept at night on deck wrapped in great coats or blankets. When bad weather prevailed, men, women, and children occupied a common cabin, the tired ones trying to sleep while more energetic fellow passengers enjoyed card games all night.

Farmers along the river did not rely on passenger sloops to take their produce to market. They had "market boats" of their own, like an over-sized rowboat rigged with a sail and a covered section up forward where a couple could shelter from the weather. All summer long Charlotte could watch these little boats as they passed Hampstead, heading downstream where they tied up at Market Slip. The city depended on this food supply.

Then steamboats came. THE GENERAL SMYTHE first chugged up the river in 1816, taking fifteen hours to reach Fredericton at "Four Dollars per person per trip." And William Peters decided time for competition had come.

Then, down on the riverbank at Hampstead, caulkers' mallets rang, and soon William Peters' one-hundred-foot-long side-wheeler slid into the blue waters. No sails, no engines, but definitely horsepower. Twelve horsepower to be exact, for the side-wheels of this craft were driven by a large capstan from which twelve bars projected, and to each a horse was attached. What a tramping and grinding those old dobbins made as they walked the deck up and down the river! What happened to the horses is not recorded, but the boat finally was taken off the river route and ended its days as a hotel for lumbermen in the Grand Lake area.

When William Peters, with his flair for politics, was elected as first representative of Queens County in the New Brunswick Legislature, he spent much time in Fredericton attending the sessions of Parliament; so Charlotte had the entire management of the whole household, and when winter shut down on the fields, food was plentifully stored and the spinning wheels began to hum.

When journeyman cobblers came they stayed for weeks, piecing together scraps of leather making dozens of pairs of shoes; for Charlotte had fifteen children — five sons and ten daughters. She not only clothed, fed and cared for them, but provided much of their early education as well. And she looked after the slaves, for often they were sick, as the cold climate did not agree with them.

There were no luxuries in the early days, no hot water from shining taps, no telephones or electric power. But people were happy. Saturday night wasn't the loneliest night in the week; it was then the fiddles struck up rollicking times and on those long summer evenings there was tapping of dancing feet in big houses and cabins alike.

Long after the slaves were given their freedom they stayed on working for the families who brought them to the new country. Often they took the names of their masters and today there is a settlement called Elm Hill, near Hampstead, where their descendants all have farms of their own. One of these, James Haines, a son of Harry Haines, who came with Charlotte's uncle, lived to be one hundred and four years old. And what stories that old man could tell!

On fine summer days Elm Hill seems like a bit of the sunny South. The hunting and fishing are good, and they have plenty of time there for "pleasurin'." If you visit Elm Hill to see one of the older inhabitants perhaps you'll be told "Grandfather isn't around." "Could it be rheumatism that keeps Grandfather indoors?" "No Sir! Grandfather has no rheumatism, but he isn't around either. Grandfather is out pleasurin', huntin' birds in the woods and he won't be home till after dark." And Grandfather is probably well over ninety.

But the happy life at Hampstead was shattered by tragedy. Charlotte's son, John Haines Peters, was drowned while trying to rescue a negro lad from the river. And when her beloved William died in 1836 leaving his will that said, "my worldly estate I give and bequeath to my wife Charlotte and all my personal and real estate for her use and benefit during her life," Charlotte went to live with one of her daughters. For her children were married and in homes of their own scattered along the Saint John River valley. And the little girl who lost her slipper in the mud of Saint John Harbour lived to see one hundred and eleven grandchildren grow up.

One of Charlotte's grandchildren was a founder of this great Dominion of Canada, Samuel Leonard Tilley, later Sir Leonard. (His mother was Susan Ann Peters.) He was born at Gagetown, a beautiful village where fine old elm trees line the streets. The original Tilley homestead, continuously occupied for over one hundred years, is still to be seen. Its vine-clad porches and shuttered windows have an old colonial flavor and beside the fine old doorway a bronze tablet was placed on the Diamond Jubilee of Confederation.

Charlotte's grandchildren were always delighted to visit her. Then she would sit in her neat black dress and fine white cap with crisp starched bows tied under her chin. But she was never idle. Her graceful hands would be busy winding yarn or knitting a sock, and she was never too busy to answer a small boy's question.

Leonard Tilley often visited his grandmother and heard her tales of early days; how, when roads were only forest trails, she rode horseback when she went visiting, perched on a pillion behind her husband as they galloped along; and now she could look from the window while she talked, and there was the great road from Saint John to Fredericton right at their door.

Young Tilley learned that "the fear of God is the beginning of wisdom," for Charlotte knew all the Bible stories by heart. She had a very real and intelligent influence over all her family, for she believed that their heritage carried great responsibility to others. And Charlotte may have had a great deal to do with the naming of our country; for, later, Sir Leonard Tilley was in London with the other Fathers of Confederation at a Conference where it was planned to unite the Canadian Provinces.

Perhaps it was the memories of those early days that led him to open his Bible at the 72nd Psalm and read: "He shall have dominion also from sea to sea and from the river unto the ends of the earth." For it was Charlotte's grandson, Samuel Leonard Tilley, who suggested the name "Dominion" for our vast country, back in 1867, and also the motto on our Canadian Coat of Arms "A mari usque ad mare."

But Charlotte did not see Confederation; her interesting and useful career ended in her 78th year, February 5th, 1851.

Today in the quiet loneliness of the Loyalist Cemetery at Gagetown, a tall grey stone marks her resting place and fragrant wild lily of the valley mingles with the grass over the graves of pioneers.

The old Peters homestead still stands on the slopes of Upper Hampstead. Apple orchards bask in the sun, cattle graze in the emerald green intervales — those lands laid out by early Government surveyors — and the Saint John River flows past the fertile fields and valleys that Charlotte Haines Peters knew so well. And the little girl who lost her slipper in the mud of Saint John Harbour left hundreds of descendants, who are scattered all across our great Dominion of Canada from Halifax to Vancouver.

BIBLIOGRAPHY

Material from "A Peters' Lineage, Dr. Charles Peters of Hampstead, Long Island". by Martha B. Flint.

Documents from Archives Department, New Brunswick Museum, Saint John, N.B.

Family History, courtesy Mrs. Wade H. MacBride, Saint John, N.B., present owner of Charlotte's slipper, which is now on loan to the New Brunswick Museum.

Martha Owen

In the age-yellowed records of the Province of Nova Scotia, a Minute of Council dated, 13th March 1767, states, "Read the memorial of Captain William Owen and others for 4,000 acres of Land at Passamaquoddy. Granted." But it was not until September 30, 1767, that Sir William Campbell issued the Grant to "William Owen, Arthur Davis Owen, David Owen, and William Owen, junior, their heirs and assigns, a tract of land situate, lying and being an Island at Passamaquoddy". And here began the story of Campobello Island down in the Bay of Fundy, off the coast of New Brunswick; the Island that holds more of historic interest than any other New Brunswick island.

September 30th, 1767 was a memorable date for Captain William Owen of the Royal Navy. He had been exploring streams and lakes in Nova Scotia with his friend, Sir Thomas Rich, and returning to Halifax they dined with Sir William Campbell, the Governor of Nova Scotia.

Captain Owen liked what he had seen of the new country and he had petitioned the Admiralty for a grant of land in recognition of his services in the Navy, claiming his health had been broken due to service in the East India Campaign. And that night, while candles flickered in huge silver candelabra and the Governor's servants moved quietly about the panelled room, there was good food, good talk and good wines, and the Grant signed, sealed and delivered, was safe in his capacious pocket. Captain William Owen was well satisfied.

Sir William looked across the table at his guest; a picturesque figure he was too, with his empty right sleeve tucked into a pocket and a black silk patch where an eye should have been. And Sir William remembered that the arm had been sacrificed at the battle of Pondicherry on the Madras Coast in a naval encounter — the eye had gone for political convictions in an election brawl. He certainly was not handsome, this stocky, retired Captain, thought Sir William, but his one eye had a piercing glint and his jaw was stubborn.

Glasses were filled again and tobacco smoke fogged the room with blue haze. Sir William spoke of the Grant. "Very good Island," he said. "Very good indeed." "It was a very good arm", replied Captain Owen, looking at his empty sleeve, and "fair exchange is no robbery."

Sir William enquired about colonization.

"We'll form a Company," the Captain replied. "Mostly Liverpool merchants, shrewd men, but ready with their silver where there's profit to be found — and my nephews, good fellows, these Owens from Glausevern, Montgomeryshire."

Captain William Owen

Courtesy of The New Brunswick Museum   Photo by Gordon Anderson

So Campobello, or Passamaquoddy Outer Island, as it was then called, became the first British Feudal Tenure in all America.

It's a romantic spot, with its high cliffs and gleaming beaches swept by the great tides of Fundy. Evergreens and silvery birch edge its large freshwater lake; there are sparkling streams and winding roads with a story at every turn. From the time when "Lief the Lucky" with his Norsemen explored America, until today, legends of buried treasure, stranded ships and ghostly visitors are all interwoven with historical fact in a vivid and picturesque tale.

Not much is known of the Indian period on the Island, which the Passamaquoddies called "A-bah-guict." But in Champlain's map of 1612 it is clearly outlined and the harbour "Port Aux Cocquelles" (Harbor of Shells) was part of De Razilly's grant of Sainte Croix in 1632.

Between 1680 and 1700 there was a French settlement near Harbor de Lute, and on a map of 1733 houses were marked: "French Inhabitants." Here, later old cellars were found which may be the remains of the Seignory of Jean Ferreau, Sieur de St. Aubin who was the most influential man of that time.

In 1704 English cannon boomed across the waters, when Colonel Church from Massachusetts engaged the settlement in reprisal for terrible French and Indian massacres in New England.

The Island saw the first English settlers in 1776, when Robert Wilson came from Massachusetts and named that section Wilson's Beach, and his descendants are there to this day. Wilson, Hibbard Hunt and William Clark lived on the Island, fishing and farming in their thrifty New England way, until Captain William Owen arrived in 1770 bringing his vigorous English colonists to the first British feudal tenure in America. Afterwards Martha Owen inherited the quaint little Kingdom of Owen, and to this day only a few lots are freehold there; most of the residents pay ground rent to the owners.

Captain Owen did not set out immediately for his Island the night after the dinner party. Instead he sailed with Sir William Campbell in the ship GLASGOW for a tour of New York, Newport and Boston.

Of Boston he writes, "The country round about is exceedingly delightful and from Beacon Hill, which stands close to the back of the town within the Peninsula, there is one of the most beautifully variegated and richly grouped prospect it is possible for the human mind to conceive of. Arts and sciences seem to have made greater progress here than in any other part of America. Harvard College has been founded about one hundred years and altho' it is not upon a perfect plan, yet, it produced a very good effect. The Arts are undoubtedly much forwarder in Massachusetts Bay, than in Pennsylvania or New York. The Publick Buildings are more elegant and there is a more general turn for music and 'belles lettres'."

Then back to England sailed Captain Owen to recruit "settlers of all trades and callings" in Liverpool and Warrington for his Island. He bought a ship; named it the SNOW OWEN, and loaded with supplies, farm implements, building material and settlers, sailed for Passamaquoddy. When he first set eye on his Island June 4th, 1770, he was so impressed with its beauty he named it "Campobello" in honour of Sir William Campbell.

His first object was to build a temporary shed to shelter his people, to fell and burn wood and clear the ground for planting and sowing potatoes, turnips and all sorts of grain and garden seeds which had been amply provided in England. He named the village New Warrington, and established a brickyard, tannery, sawmill and gristmill; in fact everything for a self-supporting colony in that Kingdom of Owen.

Home of Captain William Owen
Courtesy of The New Brunswick Museum
Photo by Gordon Anderson

Comfortable houses were built for his 38 indentured servants, farmers, fishermen, tradesmen, cooks and housemaids. He even had a brewer to make his beer. Farmers were paid seven shillings a week; carpenters and boat-builders eight shillings; cooks and housemaids two shillings, and his tailor received six shillings.

Captain Owen's own mansion, "Man-of-War House", was like an English country home surrounded by orchards and gardens and deer parks, all fenced in by snake fences of logs.

On Sunday July 8th, he "performed Divine Service and in the evening read a sermon to a numerous audience in the newly built store." He solemnized marriages too. On March 30th, 1771, Mary Lawless, one of the cooks, was married to Andrew Lloyd. Their daughter Fanny, married Abijah Garrison of Maugerville, and their son was William Lloyd Garrison of New York, the great abolitionist.

Captain Owen kept strict discipline on the Island, just as he had done on board ship. Woe betide anyone caught poaching in the Park, or fishing in the big freshwater lake, for down in the village of New Warrington there were whipping posts and three pair of stocks where offenders sat with their feet locked in for punishment; and the Captain didn't hesitate to use them. October 16th, he writes, "Evan Williams stole rum out of the store, which he for some time obstinately denied, altho' he was exceedingly drunk and proof positive of his guilt. I ordered him to be put in the stocks for the space of one hour, with a label pinned on his back 'A thief, a liar and a drunkard'."

If Captain Owen was strict, he was also just. He had bought "a barrel of flour, some rum and onions" from a Virginia sloop out of Halifax, but he writes on Oct. 22: "On taking a survey of the quantity of spirits, provisions and warm clothing remaining in the store, I found I was not sufficiently provided for a long, tedious and perhaps severe winter; not even for the necessary supply of my own numerous family to say nothing of the impoverished Indians, many of whom I was certain if not occasionally relieved by me must be inevitably starved." So he sent the SNOW OWEN back to England for supplies, and in his small vessel, THE CAMPOBELLO PACKET, which "Sir Thomas Rich was so obliging as to sell to me" . . . (for 52 guineas) Captain Owen sailed for Casco Bay for stores and provisions, which were "nearly as cheap as I could buy them in Boston."

He ordered "the foremost fireplace to be taken down to make more room for stowage," and "took on board as much rum, molasses, flour and Indian corn as we could possibly stow in the hold and battened down the hatches; stowed in my cabin and lockers a quantity of fearnaught, milled caps, mitts, hose and blanketing; and on the deck I took carcasses of beef and lashed some casks of cyder and other articles." So the colony was prepared for the winter.

This strange pioneer lived in semi-royal splendor, ruling his Island; entertaining lavishly when ships anchored off Campobello bringing traders, visitors or friends.

Then, on that cold night of February 19th, 1771, (10 below zero by Owen's weather chart) while winds howled across Campobello and snow drifted high, Captain Owen's son was born. Who was the baby's mother? It's an historical mystery, for tho' the Captain kept a journal, the pages covering that month of February are missing. Who was this woman who left England for the love of a one-eyed, one-armed, retired Navy captain? Like other pioneer women, she would have no doctor, nor nurse. She would have no companions, for the other women were cooks and housemaids. The only clue rests in the list of servants where Sara Haslam is named as Housekeeper, but no salary is recorded. Why was Captain Owen so reluctant to mention his son's mother? It adds a note of mystery. (And the second son of the same mother, born at Manchester, England in 1774, writing 71 years later, is equally reticent.)

The baby was named Edward William Campbell Rich Owen in honour of the Captain's friends. And after the christening ceremony all work was stopped and a great celebration held with gifts doled out to settlers.

Throughout the winter the settlers had been busy cutting masts for the British Navy, but April 23, 1771 the Captain writes: "Began gardening, the frost being pretty well out of ground. Mounted the co-horns and swivels on Flagstaff mount and scaled them." On the 24th he "launched a fine large Gondola built by my people." On the 29th they "began to set potatoes."

May 20th Captain Owen learned that "the Snow Owen from England was working up back of the Island. She saluted with ten guns and I ordered an equal number returned from Flagstaff mount."

Bad news was brought by the SNOW OWEN: "For a certainty the probability of a rupture with France and Spain." And Captain Owen, knowing that the Indians favored the French, determined therefore to return to England. On Sunday, 9th of July, "I performed Divine Service both morning and evening and preached my farewell sermon to the people." Following which he "embarked on the Snow Owen with family, servants and baggage, leaving Captain Plato Denny to direct, conduct and superintend the affairs of the Island, I took command of the Snow Owen in his room."

Even in England he planned for his Island. In 1772 he advertised in a Liverpool newspaper offering settlers "a 99-year lease at four to seven shillings an acre for farm lots; twenty shillings for house lots and five pounds for water lots at Welchpool."

The Captain's second son, William Fitz-William, was born Sept. 17, 1774 at Manchester, England. But it is of his eldest he writes from Shrewsbury to Sir Thomas Rich. "The hereditary Prince of Campobello had not forgotten his God-papa. I assure you he often speaks of you and desires his duty to you. He is universally caressed by all degrees of people in this proud town and they all pronounce him to be the finest boy ever beheld, but what is infinitely more estimable to me, he is really a very good boy and makes rapid progress already at school."

Captain Owen was destined never again to see his beloved Island, for, on returning to India he was killed at Madras in 1778. His nephew, David Owen, a graduate of Cambridge University and co-grantee, took over the Island and ruled there in patriarchal fashion for forty years with his horses and hounds, tenants and livestock. The original Owen mansion, Man-of-War House, did not satisfy him, so he built Tyn-y-Coed (house of the woods) on a larger scale. In 1796 he was elected to the House of Assembly of New Brunswick and died in 1827.

Back in England William Fitz-William, the Captain's second son was attending school. A pathetic figure, this stocky little William, wearing a cocked hat and a suit of scarlet made from an old coat of his Father's. When asked his name by a visitor one day he replied "I don't know, but Mother can tell you." Friends cared for the lonely little lad, who made remarkable progress in his studies and whiled away the tiresome hours at Chapel by talking on his fingers with the girls from another school who sat in the adjoining pew.

Like his father and brother, William Fitz-William joined the Navy and made a name for himself. He was a Captain when he married Martha Evans in 1818. The hereditary Prince of Campobello, "Edward Campbell Rich Owen", having no family and no desire to colonize, gave up his Island rights to his brother.

So to Campobello came William Fitz-William and Martha and their two daughters, Portia and Cornelia. Back to Man-of-War House with its panelled rooms and huge fireplaces, its gardens and orchards and deer parks, back to the village his father had built with its whipping posts and stocks and quaint, snug little cottages. Then he too built a new house near the brow of a cliff, overlooking the sandy beach at Welchpool. He had a platform built like a quarter deck on the edge of the cliff, and often he paced that quarter deck between the two old brass cannon whose muzzles pointed out across the blue waters of Fundy, spending hours searching the sea with his telescope.

He was an admiral now, but he still followed the urge to make surveys and chart coastlines. He had charted the west and east coasts of Africa, Mauritius and Asia, and he now made a detailed survey of the Saint John River. His unpublished charts and plans of the river, so beautifully drawn, are now in the Crown Lands Office in Fredericton. Even the Admiralty Charts of Passamaquoddy region now in use are based on Sir William Fitz-William Owen's surveys.

When he wasn't on a surveying jaunt, Admiral Fitz-William improved the Island's roads and repaired the cottages. He sent homage gifts to England, masts for their Navy, timber for their ships. He established a Bank and for currency, bank notes engraved with the Owen Coat of Arms marked "payment at Welchpool" were legal tender in the Owen domain.

Social life in southern New Brunswick was never so gay as when Martha Owen was Chatelaine of Campobello. In the family carriage drawn by spirited horses, Martha and her daughters, Portia and Cornelia, went driving every fine afternoon. They carried little parasols to protect their complexions, for they were beautiful women, and all along the way cottagers doffed their hats and women paused to curtsey as the carriage passed by.

The Admiral's old friends steered their ships for Campobello, for they knew a warm welcome waited them and at the Mansion there were always house guests. When someone asked Martha why she didn't build a larger house, she replied, "I prefer to spend the money on hospitality." And spend it she did.

There was a great ball each year for the servants and their friends, when all the rooms were beautifully decorated with flowers from their garden. Martha Owen and her daughters provided music for the dancing, which lasted all night long. And the Admiral was an excellent violinist. Often he'd slip out for an evening and play for the village dances, which he enjoyed as much as the villagers. He often composed songs, and always encouraged theatricals — there was no lack of entertainment on the Island.

Twice a year there was a great housecleaning at the Mansion, and afterwards Martha presented each servant with a new dress for their extra work. And there was great excitement when boxes arrived from England with bolts of new material and fabulous dresses all ready-made. Martha was an excellent seamstress too, and her sewing classes for the servants and villagers were well attended.

Martha Owen ruled the kitchen and parlor alike. She was an excellent cook and often remarked that the first way to train a servant was to know how the work should be done. Morning after morning found her in the kitchen making a special sauce for some dish, sampling the spiced ham to see if the flavor was just right, or trying out some new recipe. Often the villagers would kill a goose in winter, pack it down in the snow and send it early in the spring to the Admiral's table.

Dinner every afternoon at four o'clock was an event. In the panelled dining room, the carpet, a gift from the King of Prussia, was a masterpiece of art. Heavy damask curtain draped the small paned windows. Beautiful rosewood and mahogany furniture glistened in the firelight as great logs burned on the tall andirons in the fireplace.

Martha, in a formal gown with her favorite black and gold scarf across her shoulders, would stand before the huge fireplace with the Admiral welcoming their guests. Candles in immense silver candelabra lighted the table with its fine linens and massive crystal goblets. The sideboard glittered with tall decanters filled with sparkling wines from the cellars and four or five courses were served on silver and gold-lined dishes at the meal.

The Admiral's friends were immersed in discussions of Navy affairs and surveys of the Saint John River and Passamaquoddy Bay; for the International Boundary question sizzled along with the roast at every dinner.

160

But boundary questions were far from the mind of Clement Henery, the handsome young wine merchant from Jersey. Clement could be quite eloquent about wines and the special flavors obtained from grapes grown on high slopes; but he was more interested in Portia's ruby lips than the color and bouquet of the wines on her father's table. And he was the first to catch Martha Owen's signal of dismissal at the end of the meal, for that meant a stroll in the gardens with Portia.

Afterwards there would be tea and a rubber of Whist in the drawing room, and music with Martha Owen at the piano accompanying Clement's passionate tenor in "Woulds't thou know my Celia's charms?"

So Clement Henery came hopefully to the Admiral one day and asked for Portia's hand in marriage, and he was so direct and business-like that the Admiral temporarily forgot Clement was "in trade." The wedding took place on September 7th, 1836 in the little church on the hill overlooking Welchpool, and after the ceremony Portia and Clement sailed away to Jersey.

It's a lovely little church, St. Ann's on the Hill, built and furnished by the Owens. The chancel carpet is of needlepoint worked by Martha and her daughters. There used to be brass sockets in the book-rests for candles — the church is lighted by chandeliers now — and when all the men were away at sea an old lady would come and ring the bell for weekly services.

The Admiral married the boys and girls in that church, for he was Chief Magistrate of the Island. (And Magistrates performed marriages in the presence of witnesses in the early days.) And he often demanded the first kiss after the ceremony too.

On Sundays he preached sermons and read prayers and frequently omitted the parts he happened to dislike; for he was keenly interested in theological questions and had vigorous opinions of his own. He even wrote a book "The Quoddy Hermit or Conversations on Religion and Superstitions", published in 1842, but the family were so displeased about it that it was recalled and destroyed, except for a few copies.

Martha Owen taught a class in the Sunday School at St. Ann's and distributed prizes to the scholars at the Christmas Festival, for she was kindly and generous and admired by all.

One day a friend of the Admiral's steered his ship to Campobello and going ashore he took along a bright, young lieutenant. As they dined sumptuously at the Admiral's table, Lieutenant John James Robinson fell in love with Cornelia and on July 9th, 1838, there was another wedding at St. Ann's. Young Robinson took the name of Owen, so he could carry on the tenure of the Island. In the Owen

Family Bible, is a pencilled note marked:
> Written 1860.
> Mrs. Robinson had four children:—
> Owen Campobello, born Campobello, 1840
> Portia Owen, Campobello, 1842
> John Herbert, Portsmouth, 1845
> Cornelia Ramsay, Campobello, 1847[or 9]

Owen Robinson died at an early age. Portia entered an Episcopal Sisterhood in New York. A tablet erected in St. Ann's Church reads: "In memory of Sister Portia, Community of St. John the Baptist A.D. 1889." John Herbert died at sea, while a Lieutenant on H.M.S. Endymion, Apr. 3rd, 1870. Cornelia married Admiral Cochrane, went to live in England and became the mother of another Admiral.

There are strange tales of buried treasure, mystery ships and ghostly visitors at Campobello.

One day, while Admiral Owen rode across the Island, he followed a path that straggled down to the beach and suddenly came across a group of men digging in the sand. When he told them they were trespassing, they claimed to be descendants of buccaneers and had a map describing the location of treasure buried over a century ago. The Admiral laughed at such folly and allowed them to continue digging. About a month later he went around again just to see how they were getting on. Imagine his surprise when all he found was a very deep hole in the sand, and on the bottom plain to be seen was the outline of a huge chest clearly marked by streaks of rust. The men were gone and if they found their treasure they'd taken it with them.

And there is the phantom who visits the Island at regular intervals, always at high tide on a night when the fog rolls up like grey velvet. One may stand on the shore and hear far off in the dark the rhythmic sound of oars. The sea heaves gently, there is no wind, and all is quiet, except the stroking oars which come nearer and nearer. Then on the beach is the eerie scraping of a keel on the sands, but never a boat can be seen. Only the fog swirls closer and there's a smell of seaweed in the damp air. But in the morning, if you take the trouble to look, there is always the mark of a prow in the sands, clear and deep as though some heavily laden craft had come ashore.

And once there was a strange old wreck lying far up in a cove high and dry where no ship could be stranded now. It was a huge craft of some thirty or forty tons, overgrown with weeds and bushes, but there was no trace of iron in all its fastenings; it was held together with wooden pegs. Where had it come from? Could it be a Norse ship? Those adventurous explorers were known to have landed on the shores of New England, and the Sagas of Eric the Red lead us to believe that the first child of the white race born in America was

Snorri, the daughter of Thorvald Erickson. Was this craft once manned by Lief the Lucky's men? No one knows. But the bleached bones of this strange old wreck lay undisturbed for years and years until it was finally cut up bit by bit and whittled into "charms" and "love tokens" by the Owens' settlers.

Picture of the Mallard House
Courtesy of The New Brunswick Museum
Photo by Gordon Anderson

The sea-going Owens ruled Campobello for more than a century. Then in 1881 the Island was sold to an American Syndicate and Martha's home is now the headquarters for the Campobello Yacht Club of which the late President Roosevelt was a member.

In 1890 Martha Owen's great-grandson, Archibald Cochrane, then a midshipman carrying on the family traditions of the sea, visited Campobello. All Welchpool was decked with flags and a salute was fired in his honour from the old brass cannon, with steamer whistles answering every cannon roar. Young Cochrane examined the sun dial on the old quarter deck, clicked the famous pistols and tried on his great-grandfather's ancient three-cornered hat.

There was a baseball game in his honour and a service in St. Ann's Church on the Hill, where he sat in the family pew while the bishop reminded one and all of Martha Owen's deeds of kindness.

Campobello today is an ideal summer resort, and fishermen, farmers and tradesmen live there all the year round. Robert Wilson's descendants may still be found near the beach that bears his name, but there are no Owens on the Island.

The old brass cannon (once stolen by privateers, but returned to the crusty old admiral) still stands in the village store. In the Library at Welchpool there is a portrait of the first Owen, Captain William; and Admiral William Fitz-William's pistols and cocked hat.

Sofas and chairs of rosewood and mahogany that once graced the Owen Mansion and a huge armchair with sockets in the arms for candles are now owned by the villagers.

Across the blue waters of Fundy, prim New England church steeples edge down to the wharves of busy Eastport in Maine, and as long as the sound of the sea remains, the saga of that ancient Feudal Island will never be forgotten, for the Owens left their storied footprints in the sands of Campobello Island.

BIBLIOGRAPHY

From "The Journal of Captain William Owen, R.N., during his residence on Campobello in 1770-71. Together with other documents and notes upon the history of the Island." Edited by W.F. Ganong. (Published by New Brunswick Historical Society.)

Glimpses of the Past. St. Croix Courier Series, by James Vroom.

"Campobello" An Historical Sketch, and "The Brass Cannon of Campobello", published in the New England Magazine by Mrs. Kate Gannet Wells.

All material from Archives Department, New Brunswick Museum.

Old prints — Owen House - Portrait Captain William Owen, Ganong collection, New Brunswick Museum.

Harriet Hunt

All across Canada every September, school bells ring calling the boys and girls back from their summer vacations — back to the modern classrooms in busy cities; back to the new brick school in tree-shaded towns and back to the little 'red school-house' on some quiet country hillside.

There will be gay gymnasiums and music classes, vocational departments and Latin and Greek, as well as those old standbys, reading, writing and arithmetic. And there will be plenty of 'pep' in the 'teen-agers' when they get together on Saturday nights.

But classes won't begin at six o'clock in the morning, as they did when Harriet Gale Hunt went to school; and small girls won't wear a stiff collar with prickly spiked edges to make them hold their heads up straight as Harriet did. Neither will they wear tightly laced stays and pantelettes and wide skirts with yards of ruffles as Harriet did, for Harriet began attending school in 1815, and when she finished was presented with a diploma that was more like a paper lace valentine than a document of learning; but Harriet managed to absorb an education and make good use of it.

Harriet was born in Gloucester, England, January 2nd, 1809, and when she was only two years old came to New Brunswick with the rest of the family.

Her father, Benjamin Gale, was the architect who designed and built many of Saint John's largest buildings in those early days, and at that time the architect's work was not finished when he drew the plans; back then the architect was also the contractor. He saw that the stone was cut according to specifications and ordered the lumber, glass, plaster and hardware. He even planned the interior decoration, for no room was complete without a concave moulding around the ceiling, decorated with plaster medallions of cupids and flowers. Walls were painted with scenes of forests and birds and flowers, or stately old castles with knights in armour in the foreground.

The more elegant residences of Saint John's wealthy ship owners frequently had the walls decorated in artistic designs with real gold leaf. And Benjamin Gale supervised the work down to the last bud and flower.

Benjamin Gale built the Officers Barracks at Military Headquarters in Saint John, which is still in use; and the old College Building at the University of New Brunswick in Fredericton is a monument to Benjamin's careful planning.

When Harriet came to Saint John it was a rapidly growing city. The people were proud of their ships and new buildings, and they laid plans for better educational facilities for the new generation. For, even in the city, schools were run on rather a hit-and-miss method. In the country districts the system was even worse, for only the English language, writing and 'cyphering' were taught. Often the schoolmaster was a retired soldier, who was more proficient in enforcing discipline than teaching the three R's.

The teachers in rural schools were supposed to receive four shillings a month for each pupil, but often had to take their pay in grain or muskrat skins, or be satisfied if the fees were paid in work done on their farms. And many a farmer paid his children's school fees with a barrel of vegetables, or a keg of salt pork. There were precious few Latin or Geography lessons and practically no History was taught; but the scholars did learn to read and write.

One little log school house near Penobsquis was so far back in the woods that it had to be moved by ox team a couple of miles nearer the main road, so the children wouldn't have to go through the woods.

There were no schoolroom clocks in those days, even the teacher didn't own a watch, so those resourceful pioneers cut notches in the window sills. When the sun's shadow reached one notch it was dinner time, another notch meant it was time to go home. What they did on stormy days, unfortunately, is not recorded. Today that pioneer schoolhouse is used as a pig pen, notched window sills and all; and generations of pigs, probably anticipating meal time, have watched for the shadows on that window sill with greedy little eyes.

In Saint John the City Fathers had provided schools for boys, but no prizes or certificates were given unless they could recite the Lord's Prayer and the Ten Commandments, as well as make a pass mark on their examination papers. But there was no provision made for little girls, except at small private schools, until 1820.

The first National School in New Brunswick was opened at Saint John on July 13th, 1818, in the old Drury Lane Theatre at York Point. Mr. West from Halifax was the first teacher. Evidently this system was popular for on the 24th of December 1819, the school was moved to larger quarters in a brick building on King Square and Mr.

George Bragg took charge. Shortly afterwards a school for girls was opened with Mrs. Bragg as teacher, and at the Christmas examination of 1820 medals were presented to honor students by Lieut. Governor, Major General Smyth. Harriet Gale won one of those medals, for already at the age of eleven she showed exceptional ability.

But Benjamin Gale was not satisfied with educational facilities in Saint John, so he packed up and with his family returned to England where the children could enjoy the advantages of a good education.

Harriet and her sisters attended a school in London. It was one of those schools in a dreary old house with a walled garden where pupils "took the air" as they walked sedately along flower-bordered paths. Here they were safe from any male distraction. Everything was very proper. Even on the way to Chapel each morning a stern-faced teacher shepherded her charges carefully along in solemn procession. Woe betide the rash young lady who dared lift her eyes to acknowledge the amorous glances of the bright young dandies who happened to stroll by. Bread and water would be her diet for a day or two as punishment.

And these respectable and well-trained young ladies never acknowledged a greeting from the other side of the street, if any acquaintance had the temerity to risk such a thing. There was no "Hi there!" or "Hello" exchanged in those decorous days, for deportment was a major subject strictly observed when Harriet attended school. And to teach them to walk gracefully with 'chins up', every young lady wore for an hour each day, a stiffly starched collar with sharp little whalebone spikes along the edge, quite uncomfortable enough to encourage them to hold their heads well up. The most strenuous of physical exercise was their daily walk along the paths in the walled garden of the school.

What those young ladies lacked in exercise and entertainment, they made up for in studies. The classics, mathematics, music and history was administered in maximum doses, and after that came painting and languages.

Harriet, who had unusual personality and skill became a 'pupil teacher' in that London school. With her long skirts sweeping the floor and a little black apron tied around her slim waist she went from one desk to another supervising the lessons and pointing out mistakes to the younger pupils; and Harriet herself had just passed her twelfth birthday.

Closing day at the London school was the event of the year. The young ladies in their best 'party' dresses and best party manners played little twiddly piano solos and recited long romantic poems for the audience of fond parents and friends, who applauded decorously at such display of accomplishment.

Afterwards they danced sedate quadrilles, and all the time the watchful headmistress and her staff kept an eagle eye on the entire assembly; for girls were so giddy, they might dance with too much vivacity, or even dare to stroll in the garden with a partner of the opposite sex. Closing day refreshments was an event of wild dissipation with lemonade and cake and even syllabub, made with wine and cream and beaten until foamy. After one or two servings of syllabub, one never knew what wild chances some daring young lady might take. Closing day indeed had its anxious moments for pupils and teachers alike.

After graduation and two years of teaching in private school in the great city of London, Harriet came back to Saint John. The whole family brought back extensive wardrobes, wonderful dresses of silk and satin in the latest London style, for when Mrs. Gale went shopping she always bought the best materials saying "they were cheapest for they lasted longer."

Harriet and her sisters were the envy of Saint John's young ladies, who wore cotton gowns, except on very special occasions. Even the Sheriff's wife went to church wearing a cotton gown. Over the tea cups Harriet's silk dresses were often the subject for gossip.

"London swells!" remarked the young ladies with a sniff and a toss of their curls as they nibbled daintily and sipped their tea, all behind Harriet's back of course. Punctiliously polite they were when they met Harriet out walking.

Suddenly romance stepped into Harriet's life and after a brief, exciting courtship, she married a charming musician and went to Boston. Here Harriet discovered that altho' her husband was a genius, he was also erratic and thriftless, so Harriet returned to teaching. Two children, in as many years, complicated matters and the Hunts returned to Saint John.

Even then fortune did not smile; for, when Harriet's husband set up a piano factory with shareholders' funds, the building and contents were destroyed by fire. This was the last straw for temperamental Mr. Hunt, who departed for the United States leaving Harriet to face the shareholders. Harriet accomplished the impossible. She opened a "School for Young Ladies" and met every claim with her own earnings.

Harriet Hunt's School had accommodation for sixty pupils, and a waiting list a yard long. The daughters of Saint John's elite did not have to go off to Boston, or New York, or London to finishing school now. Harriet's School provided the necessary education and requirements for fashionable finish as well. Pupils came from all over the Maritimes and Quebec, even from the United States and England. Harriet's fame as a teacher had spread far and wide.

With three 'age groups' in Harriet's School, English, History, and Geography from "Peter Parley's Geography Book" were essential studies. A little taste of Arithmetic was wedged in too, and those pupils who reached the mystery of Decimals were considered mathematical marvels.

But Harriet Hunt did not stop at the essentials of education, she introduced subjects never before taught at a school for Young Ladies. Fond mothers were astounded at her teaching of Physiology, considered quite improper in those days, for in polite society one never mentioned the processes of life, be it animal or mineral.

And when a machine to illustrate lectures on Natural Philosophy was required, and no funds were available, energetic Harriet organized a School Bazaar, where beaded pincushions, embroidery and hand-painted bookmarks brought in quite a tidy sum. But one year with increased expenses for books and appliances, Harriet balanced her accounts and found she had a net profit of exactly *three* dollars!

Schoolteachers today organizing and demanding higher salaries, would scoff at Harriet Hunt's determination to carry on under such difficulties. But this pioneer educator solved one of the problems by rising at six in the morning to give music lessons, and thus save the expense of another teacher.

French and Italian were taught also, but "Fasquelles French Grammar" contained no English translation, so Harriet read the Classics in French to her pupils. Perhaps the more romantic ones wept a little over the plight of ancient heroines, but Harriet dit not encourage 'vapors' or 'swooning' at the very thought of anything disagreeable. And although it was fashionable for 'young ladies' to be pale and fragile creatures, Harriet encouraged them to be active and energetic.

"What gives your pupils such wonderful complexions?" enquired a visitor one day. And Harriet Hunt, recalling her own school days (when they ate daintily for fear of being unladylike; those awful spiked collars, and the morbid forced strolling in the walled garden under the eagle-eyed duennas), replied, "I send them out walking and give them plenty of good wholesome food."

Music classes were conducted by the best teachers. Under the tuition of Professors Card and Rowe and strict old Count Wolawoski, scales and arpeggios echoed daily from nimble fingers on the grand piano in the parlor. There were painting classes and deportment classes where pupils learned the 'correct' method of entering or leaving a room and the proper position of placing the feet. Pupils walked about the room each day in a ten minute "grand march" to music with books on their heads to encourage correct posture.

And last but not least Harriet taught Astronomy — then considered far beyond the grasp of female intellect.

With large maps of the solar system studied at school, on fine starlit nights she assembled the entire class in the King Square right in the centre of the city. If the pupils needed to refresh their memories there was much running back and forth to the school which was four blocks away.

And if, as it frequently happened, the housekeeper was indisposed, Harriet was up at six o'clock in the morning and off with a large basket to the City Market. From stall to stall she went selecting the food for the day; for nearly half of the pupils were boarders and providing thirty dinners a day was no small undertaking.

Harriet's "Training School Journal" was a handwritten two-page school newspaper. The issue of June 15, 1866 reads: "The T.S. Journal is published on alternate Fridays. It contains a record of the condition and progress of the school, Useful Hints and Suggestions to the Students, Correspondence, Miscellaneous matter; the news of the day and original articles on various subjects allied to education."

And it warns, "Anonymous letters will not be inserted unless the author be known to our educational or reporting staff. And rejected MSS. can be had on application at our office. We do not pretend to return them unless called for."

Under the heading of Physiology we read: "On Wednesday of last week Miss Sara Brown delivered a truly admirable lecture on Respiration, which want of space prevents us from noticing more fully."

"On Wednesday last Mr. Jones gave his views on the Heart in clear and perspicuous language, altho' his pronunciation was not of the highest order."

"Miscellany" includes this note: "The Ladies attending the Training School wish to express their thanks to Mr. John Miller for the pleasure they enjoyed in listening to his interesting recitation of Tennyson's poem, Enoch Arden."

The "Local and Personal" column reports: "On Tuesday last Miss Smith wrote under the head of a criticism, one of the best essays on Education, which we have ever met with in so small a compass. This lady's success as a teacher is, we think, certain."

The next item reads: "We hope that none of our readers will allow themselves to be gulled by what is euphoniously styled the 'Babbitonian system of Penmanship.' The so-called system is, we have no hesitation in saying, a contemptible imposition and an open insult to common sense." And directly below this warning, "Mr. Josiah Murphy and staff recently made a complete survey of the triangular field near the Training School."

Under the head of "New Advertisements" is the notice "The Examination of Candidates for Licences for the Summer Term will commence on Tuesday 26th inst. at 9 A.M. The Regular Quarterly Convention of Teachers will be held on Saturday 30th. All the students will be expected to be present."

Closing day at Harriet's school brought visitors, and sixty young ladies in their wide frilly gowns, into the drawing rooms where tableaux, songs, piano solos and recitations proved the success of the pupils. Afterwards tea and sandwiches were served by the pupil-hostesses. Every graduate of Harriet Hunt's "Training School for Young Ladies" received a certificate. Beautifully printed in flowing script, lace edged, and embossed with flowers and birds, it looked more like a lace valentine than a testimony of educational ability.

And long after graduation Harriet Hunt kept in touch with her pupils, even urging them to continue further studies, for she was a great believer in higher education for women. But Universities were closed to women then. Even the Normal School wouldn't admit women students.

It was Martha Hamm Lewis who changed that regulation. She persisted in demanding entrance; finally an order-in-council was passed by the Lieutenant Governor of New Brunswick before she could attend the school.

The headmaster, Mr. Duval, simply walked the floor at night worrying about this new regulation. What was the World coming to! Women insisting on becoming licensed teachers when they should stay at home and learn to cook! The headmaster was sorely tempted to refuse admittance to this forward young woman. The Lieutenant Governor must be out of his mind passing such an order-in-council.

But even headmasters have to eat; and orders-in-council signed by the Lieutenant Governor were orders indeed. So Mr. Duval devised rules, strict rules at that.

This young woman would enter the classroom ten minutes before the men students and sit at the back of the room. She must wear a veil to hide her charms; she must make her curtsey to the teacher and leave the room five minutes before the lecture ended, and she must leave the grounds without speaking to any young man.

Promptly at ten minutes before the hour Martha arrived. Her skirts trailing, her books grasped in lace-mittened fingers, and how her bright eyes twinkled behind that black veil! Sedately she took her seat in the back row and gazed impishly at the display of masculine shoulders. There was at least some satisfaction in realizing how dangerous her presence was in that classroom.

Mr. Duval fervently hoped that Martha would grow tired of the lectures, the restrictions, anything, so he would have an excuse to expel this forward young woman from the school. He watched Martha like a hawk for any infraction of regulations. But in spite of his hopes, Martha proved a good student, for she completed the course and received her diploma, the first woman to graduate from the New Brunswick Normal School.

That was in 1849, and although no romance was tolerated in the classroom or on the grounds, somehow Cupid got around, for Martha married, and today her descendants value very highly that first diploma granted to a woman.

Back in Saint John, Harriet Hunt's Training School for Young Ladies was attracting more than ordinary attention. For Harriet's career as a teacher was an extraordinary example of individual initiative. Her keen mind not only conquered every obstacle, but her every effort was crowned with success.

But all through Harriet's domestic life there ran disappointment and heartbreak. She never heard again from her husband who had left her with two young children to care for. And during the terrible earthquake of 1868 in South America her son was drowned.

Harriet's daughter remained a loyal helper. She, too, taught at her mother's school. For thirty-three years the Training School flourished and Harriet's progressive, courageous influence reached far into the future.

Then one September day in 1890, Harriet Hunt closed her books, never to open them again. And her epitaph reads "Blessed are the dead that they may rest from their labours; and their works do follow them."

All across Canada every September school bells will ring again. Regional high schools in rural areas replace the little log shacks where the pioneer teacher was paid in muskrat skins, wood or vegetables. Fine school buildings in cities and towns prove that people are willing to provide better facilities for the education of their children.

And education for women has travelled a long way down the years from the days when Harriet Hunt pioneered in teaching. For like Harriet, women with vision and energy have helped develop our great treasury of knowledge.

BIBLIOGRAPHY

"The Training School Journal" by Harriet Hunt.
"National Schools" and others, Archives Department, New Brunswick Museum.

Margaret Jordan

Between timber-crested hills, a short distance from Saint John, lies a ten-mile chain of lakes, their blue waters dappled by cloud shadows and rippled by stray breezes; their cool depths an angler's paradise. Around the shores cluster trim summer cottages flanked by sturdy farmhouses set in fields divided by century-old cedar snake fences. This is Loch Lomond, one of the early settlements in New Brunswick, where, for thirty-four years lived Margaret and John Jordan with their five sons and six daughters. Today descendants of these pioneers still occupy the staunch old farmhouse built by John Jordan in 1818.

It was Lauchlan Donaldson, an adventure-loving Scot who, while trekking through the forest one day in 1810, first saw those spruce-clad mist-wreathed hills reflected in the broad blue water. It reminded him of the Highlands of Scotland and the lake where he too, had wandered by "yon bonnie banks and by yon bonnie braes". With sentimental nostalgia Donaldson promptly named the spot "Loch Lomond". He camped on the shores while he explored the surrounding country and then returned to Saint John to organize a settlement.

William Marks, of Cumberland, England, was the first settler. That was in 1813. Then came the Jordans and William George Cody, formerly proprietor of Saint John's Exchange Coffee House. John Jordan built his farm home while Cody established his inn, "Ben Lomond House", on the adjoining property at the foot of the lake.

John Munro and Ephriam Sentell soon arrived, so by 1819 the settlement of Loch Lomond was well started.

John Jordan was an up-and-coming young man, a tanner by trade. He also had a great flair for politics and was representative for Saint John City and County in the Provincial Legislature for twenty-seven years. When he met Margaret Melick it was love at first sight, and in spite of wars and rumors of conflict between the United States and Canada, they were married in Saint John in 1812.

Margaret's father, Captain William Melick, had served with the British forces during the Revolution. Of Dutch origin, the Melicks had emigrated to England and married into the famous Churchill family. As an exiled Loyalist, Captain Melick's contribution to the new home in Saint John included some furniture, an old Dutch stove, and his beautiful daughters.

John Jordan's father, Jean Jourdain, was a courier with the British forces and he too left New York with the first fleet destined for the Saint John River, bringing his family, his pewter dishes, books and mahogany furniture. John had been brought up with family military traditions ringing in his ears. Often he heard the tales of his Crusader ancestors, the Jourdains, Counts of Toulouse. His Huguenot great-grandfather, Ozce, fled from his comfortable *maison* at La Rochelle some time after the Edict of Nantes and came by way of Glasgow to Westchester, New York. This distinguished old gentleman, translating very literally the motto of the family crest, "Percussus Resurgo" "Fallen, I rise again", firmly established his family again in the New World.

Time and again John listened to the story of the American soldiers who searched the house in New York for his father Jean Jourdain, the courier. When Washington's minions could not find him, they decided he was sewed up in a featherbed. To make certain they cut it to pieces with their swords while his mother stood by protesting at such wanton destruction, knowing full well that her husband and his messages were safely hidden elsewhere.

From across the Atlantic had come the exploits of another member of the family. Brave and brilliant Jean Baptiste Jourdain, carrying family tradition to the heights, became General of the Sambre et Meuse division in the French Army. This right-hand man of Napoleon became a Marshall of France, a Governor of Grenoble and acting Governor of *Les Invalides*. His portrait in his uniform with gold epaulettes, high collar and snowy stock, now hangs in the Louvre in Paris.

Back in Saint John in 1812 John and Margaret Jordan set up housekeeping in a comfortable home on Union Street. The city was growing up then. From the two hundred and twenty-six houses erected in its first year it had expanded far beyond its planned street lines. By 1812 new homes crowded the hill beyond Union Street, which stretched across the city to the north, dipping its muddy length in Saint John Harbour at one end and Courtney Bay at the other.

Union Street was a fashionable neighbourhood even though it accommodated several livery stables, a brewery and a brickyard. Michael Weaver, owner of the brickyard, advertising in *The Royal Gazette and New Brunswick Advertiser*, "Informs his friends and the Publick that he continues the brick making business at his yard near Mr. McKay and Co's Brewery in this city and expects to have a kiln ready for sale on the most reasonable terms some time the ensuing week. He thanks all those who have heretofore favored him with their custom and begs a continuance of it".

But Union Street started off handsomely at the west end with the Honourable George Leonard's residence set in terraced gardens. Here, Thomas Carelton, first Governor of the newly formed Province of New Brunswick, was royally entertained in 1784. Later, when news of Nelson's victory at Trafalgar reached the city, Mr. Leonard's spacious dwelling glittered from cellar to ridgepole with "illuminations" which could be seen for miles. When Margaret Jordan lived on Union Street, the second governor of the Province, General Smyth, occupied the Leonard residence.

Just a stone's throw up the street, Captain George Colville had built the first framed house in the city with hickory brought all the way from Carolina. "A house of wealth and luxury, often the haven for distinguished visitors", it was purchased shortly afterwards by Mr. Cruikshank. Across the street stood James Fairchild's home with its wide windows and scenic interior decorations. On the hill beyond, now known as Chipman Place, Ward Chipman's mansion crowned the summit.

Another prosperous citizen, David Merrit, had timber specially selected, cut and rafted down the Saint John River for his well-proportioned residence with its four great chimneys at the corner of Union and Germain streets. Mr. Merrit's house with its fine curved stairway, beautifully carved cornices and mahogany panelling stands a silent tribute to the builders "who wrought with greatest care", and today the huge brass knocker announces the arrival of visitors to David Merrit's descendants.

Not to be outdone, Joseph Nutting, collector of customs for the city, erected the second brick house built in Saint John, where, in a city of two-storey wooden houses, it added dignity and elegance to the already fashionable Union Street.

Margaret Jordan's home was comfortable and spacious, but not as luxurious as the fine stone mansion of her neighbour, the Honourable Charles Peters. Built of stone brought from England, it raised its massive dignity in a setting of lawns and walled gardens.

While Margaret Jordan's family increased from year to year, her children never lacked playmates, for the Honourable Charles had married twice and there were twenty children in the Peter's family right next door!

So, in the early eighteen hundreds, Saint John presented a queer combination of dignity, disorder and dirt. Every back yard boasted an outhouse from where slops seeped into the streets; and garbage, not required to fatten the family pig, lay in heaps until the stench became so unbearable it was carted away by the "night brigade".

When Margaret Jordan, hatted and gloved and veiled and wearing her best taffeta, drove out to visit her friends in their neat parlours and chat over fine teacups, pigs, horses, goats and cows often disputed the right-of-way in the muddy streets.

Even the stout, wealthy Mr. Cruikshank, bouncing about on the red leather cushions inside his fine closed coach (the first in the city), on his way to some important function, had to put up with delays while his coachman, perched high on the box outside, spared neither whip nor curses on the straying animals impeding his progress.

Long and loudly did the citizens complain. Finally the city fathers passed a law ordering "that no Stallion or horse known by the description of Ridgeling shall be suffered to run at large under penalty of five pounds for each and every Stallion or Ridgeling that shall be found." Citizens gladly brought the strays to the Public Pound where "Twenty shillings for expenses of taking up the same", were collected by the finder. That took care of the horses.

It was not until 1822, however, that the mayor and alderman got around to the stray pigs. Then they decreed, "That no hog or swine of any description unless rung and yoked and no boar whether rung or yoked or not, shall be allowed to run at large in any of the streets, squares, lanes, alleys or unenclosed ground within the Said City, with a fine of fifteen shillings for each offence." The law was explicit. Porkers were kept at home more or less, but as late as 1840 "One horse, two cows, seven goats and one pig" were caught gamboling in King Square!

It was clean-up time with a vengeance in Saint John! But the waterfront gangs survived. Though advertisements for their capture offered up to sixty dollars a head as reward, the city still swarmed with deserters from the army and the ships. These drunken, rowdy transients roamed the streets at night, breaking into houses and shops, aided no doubt by the cheap and copious supply of liquor. Duty on rum was six pence per gallon, a tidy sum not to be winked at by customs collectors considering the amount consumed.

"Fine flavored Gin", advertised the Carleton Distilleries "could be had by retail at the rate of five shillings four pence per gallon at the south side of the Market Wharf at the Sign of the Butt, in any quantity from a pint to five gallons."

Just across the Market Slip, Henry Blakslee catered to citizens of more temperate tastes. "Water!" he advertised, "Those who wish water by the cask can be supplied by applying to store of Henry Blakslee, North Market Wharf". Saint John did not have a central water supply until 1837, and then, piped in from Lily Lake, it was available for only two hours each morning. Small wonder that the thirsty lined up two deep at the "Sign of the Butt"! Small wonder also, that respectable citizens locked their doors and barred their windows at sundown.

One night when John Jordan was in Fredericton attending Legislature, and everyone in the Union Street house was in bed, Margaret heard gruff voices and scuffling in the street in front of the house. For minutes that seemed ages she lay numb with fear. Then she slipped out of bed, threw a shawl over her shoulders, picked up her night light and crept along the hall to the stairs. There was no time to rouse the servants. In any case, they would be too terrified to be any help. If she could only get downstairs, she thought, before the rowdies broke in. All her good silver and pewter was in the sideboard within easy reach of thieves. She was almost angry with John for leaving her unprotected.

Halfway down the stairs, there was a crack of breaking locks. The front door opened slowly, and in the half-dark bulky figures stumbled across the threshold.

Desperately she shouted, "If you dare to come in here, I'll call all the men down from upstairs!"

Perhaps she looked like a ghost standing there in her light bed gown, the flickering candle in her hand. But her threat was real enough. The looters didn't wait for the "men from upstairs". They tumbled headlong into the street in their scramble to get away.

In her husband's absence, Margaret had the full responsibility of the household. Added to that the tannery foreman would come to talk of hides, machinery and workmen. There were supplies to be arranged for the farm too, for in 1818 John Jordan, persuaded by the amiable Lauchlan Donaldson, took up land at Loch Lomond, built his farmhouse and kept his men busy clearing land and planting crops.

Margaret's days were full, but she was never too busy to enjoy the ever-changing kaleidoscope of Union Street. From her windows she could watch Mr. Whitney's "Pleasure Coach" depart each morning from the "Sign of the Golden Ball", the Inn and Livery Stable at the corner. This "Elegant Coach with its span of horses devoted to Parties of Pleasure" attracted be-ruffled young ladies and their gentlemen in top hats carrying picnic baskets at the unearthly hour of seven in the morning. Mild expeditions according to today's standards. Mr. Whitney "paid strict attention to the comfort and conveniences of his patrons", and the jaunt into the country was very elegant and exciting.

Market carts too, jogged along the street with their crates of squawking hens, squealing pigs and fresh vegetables. Gentlemen galloped their horses between the wood vendors who pushed their two-wheeled carts and called their wares, for wood was the city's chief fuel then. More than once, pickets from the old fence around the Loyalist Burying Ground were lifted for kindling wood by some improvident citizens.

Then there were the quaint oxcarts of the freed slaves with their loads of birch brooms. From one stable to another and to the coach houses of the well-to-do, these exiles would jog behind their diminutive oxen on their spring journey. Their winter's output of brooms, birch twigs strongly laced together on a broom-stick, were clumsy things, but useful stable equipment. Margaret was to see more of these slaves when she moved to Loch Lomond.

Now Saint John was accustomed to negroes for many Loyalists had brought their slaves along when they settled in New Brunswick. More often than not they gave them their freedom, for life on the old plantation scale was impractical in their new homes. Many worked for their masters as long as they lived, but others ran away. "Nine guineas reward", heads an old advertisement, "Run away on the night of the 26th inst. three negro men, one by the name of Joseph."

The Royal Gazette and New Brunswick Advertiser of September 6, 1791, ran an advertisement for "Poll, Four dollars reward! Ran away from the subscriber on Friday the 26th inst., a negro wench named Poll about seventeen years of age very much pitted with the small pox. Whoever takes up the said wench and delivers her to the Subscriber will receive the above reward, signed, Alexander Morton. N.B. masters of vessels are forbid taking the said wench and all persons forbid harboring her as they may depend upon being prosecuted with the utmost rigor of the law".

The Postcript to the *Royal Gazette* of July 1791 listed entire pages of runaways from the south, believed to have escaped to northern ports. Amongst others, "Dolly, Neptune, Pompey, Scrub, Bungay, Coffey and Cato, all marked with their owner's initials on their shoulders," were sought.

There is no record of slave auctions in Saint John, but when Abraham de Peyster required extra help he purchased two slaves quite legally from Munson Jarvis, as recorded by a long and tedious document of sale, "signed, sealed and delivered on the fifteenth day of July, 1797". The trade in "Black Ivory" diminished to a vanishing point in New Brunswick after 1800, however, when slavery was made illegal, although as late as 1816 an advertisement appeared for a "runaway black boy."

In 1815, however, the city fathers had a problem to face, for when the British forces had chased President Madison from Washington and burned the Capitol in 1814, swarms of negro refugees from the Southern States descended on the ships lying at anchor in Chesapeake Bay, and begged to be taken away from slavery. When they arrived in Halifax, the Governor of Nova Scotia, already beset by many problems of such runaways, asked the Governor of New Brunswick to provide for some of these Chesapeake negroes who sought refuge in Canada.

On May 16, 1815 the *H.M.S. Regent* arrived in Saint John with over three hundred homeless negroes. With no preparation made for them they drifted around from one ramshackle shelter to another, dependent on individual charity for food and clothing. When the bitter cold of the northern winter added to their suffering, the almshouse commissioners supplied food for a while. Settling these unfortunates provided a two-year headache for the government which at length was only partially relieved.

In the *Journal of Assembly* February 14, 1817, is the "Petition of William Flood on behalf of himself and forty other black people brought to this province by order of His Majesty's Government in the year 1815, praying aid and assistance to form a settlement at Loch Lomond". Thus, a few miles east of the Lake in a spot known as Willow Grove, they were granted farm lots of fifty acres each. This was the only slave settlement established in New Brunswick.

But those unhappy fugitives were totally unfitted for life in a northern climate and their plight brought sympathy from Saint John's citizens. Time and again Robert Ray, a prominent sail-maker in Saint John, organized relief expeditions. Even through the storms of winter he sent sled-loads of flour, cornmeal, molasses, pork and salt fish for their assistance.

Since the welfare of their neighbours was of great concern to them, the Jordans of Loch Lomond sent from their own storehouse barrels of rice, molasses and flour to the needy blacks and whites alike.

Scratching away on their little farms in a wilderness of blueberry bogs and tamaracks, the refugees wandered like a lost tribe from cabin to cabin trying to recapture warmth and sociability. African melodies brought with the slave-ships, folk songs and haunting spirituals echoed across the lonely hillsides.

Sometimes they became obstreperous and raised a riot among themselves. One August day in 1818 no less than twenty-four coloured persons of the settlement were tried "for rioting and assault, pulling down a house, setting fire to a mattress and pelting the inmates Plato Loupee and his family from the settlement." Plato had been accused of some misdemeanor and, according to the gossip, his neighbours were determined to lynch him. Much contradictory evidence occupied the court's entire day, but the verdict was "acquitted".

It was not until 1868 when the Reverend Edmund Duval worked to improve their condition and the Society of Friends contributed funds, so a Baptist church was built for the negroes. There was always a large congregation, and though they had no organ, they sang Bible narratives set to well-known tunes along with their favorite hymns. Mr. Duval's sister taught the Sabbath School, trained the children's voices and organized concerts around the countryside to augment funds for their church.

Their hardscrabble farms could not support entire families, so many were employed as servants, sawyers, cabmen, stable boys and farmhands by the white settlers of Loch Lomond.

One old negro, going for the cows, had to cross a wide brook. Visiting city children tagged along with him, but he was careful for their safety.

"Now doan' yo cross dis brook," he warned as he began stepping from stone to stone.

Disappointed, the children paused a moment on the bank, then began the perilous crossing. The old man turned quickly, "Ah kin see yo' 'cause I'se got eyes in de back ob ma head." His skinny black fingers pushed up little circles in his wooly white thatch. "Jes yo' set. Ma back eyes are workin' on yo'!"

Back at the cabin "Ol M'am", a stiffly starched apron billowing over her homespun dress, would set out hot gingerbread and mugs of milk, while the children sat on the cool stone doorstep wondering about the old man with "eyes in de back ob ma head".

Hard times at the end of the Napoleonic wars brought throngs of settlers from across the Atlantic. Free land was the lodestone, drawing famine-stricken Irish, dispirited English and hopeful Scots. In January 1821, "Cheap passage from Ireland" was advertised by A. and S. McDonald in Saint John newspapers. "Persons desirous of getting out their friends from Ireland in the spring are requested to make early application at the store of the subscribers where a list for names is at present lying." The McDonalds were snowed under with replies.

The six-week wild Atlantic journey over, Irish immigrants stretched their cramped bodies and swarmed off the ships at Saint John with their little brass-bound cowhide trunks, their cook pots and bedding, and scarcely a penny in their pockets. Aided by friends, scores set out for Loch Lomond. With incurable Irish optimism they cut, hauled and sawed logs for their house. Soon fields of grain and pastures with a cow or two replaced the wilderness, for these intrepid colonists were real settlers.

The European depression stretched its tenuous fingers across the Atlantic and 1825 was a bad year, particularly for Saint John. Lumber, the backbone of New Brunswick's trade, sold for less than the cost of transportation, and other trades suffered in proportion.

180

It was then that John and Margaret Jordan moved to Loch Lomond. For weeks Margaret bustled around supervising the packing. One fine June morning when the old Dutch stove, mahogany furniture and the last trunk had gone, the Jordan carriage set out from the city. The girls wore miniature pelisses primly buttoned, and wide straw hats with huge ribbon bows. The boys were in their best Sunday clothes and beaver hats.

They set up the tannery beside the lake and loads of hemlock bark from the surrounding district came jolting by oxcart over forest trails. The old millstones groaned from morning till night, grinding the bark for the vats. With leather in great demand, processed hides from the Jordan tannery found a ready market in Saint John.

Not all the leather went to market, however, for many settlers at Loch Lomond followed a trade as well as a plow. Ephriam Sentell, once a shoemaker in Saint John, continued the same trade for the settlers at Loch Lomond. Thus, Margaret's children were assured of always being well-shod with stout cowhide boots.

John Jordan was the "Squire" now and, added to his other duties, he was one of the three magistrates appointed in New Brunswick to perform marriages. Clergymen were few and far between in those days and only the ministers of the Church of England and Scotland along with Roman Catholic priests were authorized to perform marriages in New Brunswick.

Time and again Squire Jordan, with the seal and certificate of his office stowed in his pocket, saddled his horse, and rode off to comply with Cupid's demands. On one occasion the Squire's sense of propriety was outraged by the groom casually appearing in his shirt sleeves. Gruffly he ordered the man, "Put on your coat!"

At his home shy couples hesitated before knocking at the Jordan door, but once inside and their errand stated, they were soon at ease for Margaret was a gracious hostess. In the Jordan parlour the Squire, prayer book in hand, read the brief ceremony while Margaret and the servants stood as witnesses. There was an unseen audience too, for on the stairway, peering through the railings, were the Jordan youngsters. Quiet as mice they listened breathlessly to their father's voice booming out those mysterious words. Then, after a glimpse at the blushing bride, they'd scuttle off again to play.

For want of a school Squire Jordan taught his children as well as others in the neighbourhood. They'd gather each morning in the dining-room and while the young ones worked over the three "R's", the older ones struggled with the classics. Today, on a shelf in the old farmhouse in Loch Lomond lies a book of Latin verse, "Orestes and Electra", dated 1805. Its dog-eared and worn appearance would indicate that it gave those early students many a headache.

Though they lived in a little independent world of their own, they were not isolated. The boys found excitement at Mr. Cody's Inn down at the foot of the lake. Coaches rumbled daily along the old post road to St. Martin's, then a busy ship-building centre. Travellers stopped over at Ben Lomond House, "where could be had clean beds together with good stabling." Here they were privileged to sample Mr. Cody's "every delicacy in season".

Each summer the county militia trained at the Rifle Range a few miles away on the St. Martin's road. Small boys trailed the marchers and their fifes and drums for miles along the dusty roads to watch the Red Coats' sham battles.

For the girls the most exciting part of the year was when the dressmaker arrived. She stayed for weeks at the Jordan homestead making new dresses and thriftily remodelling old ones.

"Squire Jordan", as he was familiarly known, devoted fifty-seven years of his life to public affairs. Amongst other offices, he was coroner, Parish Court Commissioner and Supervisor of Government Highways and Bridges. For twenty-seven consecutive years the Honourable John Jordan attended sessions of the House of Assembly at Fredericton as a member of Parliament representing Saint John City and County.

In the Jordan household every busy day was closed by the family and servants gathering for prayers, for it was not until 1835 that a church was begun. Squire John donated land along with a generous contribution to the funds, and Mr. Cody provided for the adjoining burial ground. The bell of All Saints Church that sounded across the sparsely settled countryside in 1836 still echoes over the blue waters of Loch Lomond, calling to worship descendants of those pioneers who gathered when Bishop Inglis consecrated the edifice.

From the very beginning until today the Jordan family has participated in the church's affairs. A chair was presented in memory of Margaret's son John who was a lay reader when only nineteen years of age. Candlesticks that were in use in those early days are still to be found in the church. The original pulpit and reading desk are still in use and the altar prayer book dates back to 1824 and contains prayers for King George the Fourth.

When a part of the woodwork was removed to permit repairs to the roof, the name of George Cody, 1840, was discovered written on one of the beams.

In the Loyalist Galleries of the New Brunswick Museum is the quaint Dutch stove brought from New York in those far off days, an item of particular interest for it is doubtful if another exists in North America. Pewter plates dated 1763, mahogany furniture, books, swords and portraits are treasured by the descendants of Margaret and John Jordan.

Today Mr. Cody's Ben Lomond House is only a memory. All that remains of the Rifle Range, where Red Coats snapped to attention, is the Range Road, a dusty highway trailing between farms. But the Jordan homestead still stands on the shores of the Lake named by a homesick Scot.

BIBLIOGRAPHY

History of the Jordan Family, Courtesy of Mrs. E.F. (Juliet Jordan) Dickenson, Loch Lomond, N.B.; Miss Bessie Jordan, Loch Lomond, N.B.; Mr. Thomas Jordan, Loch Lomond, N.B.

City Ordinances, Chesapeake Negroes, Irish Colonists, from the files of the *Royal Gazette and New Brunswick Advertiser* 1812, 1823, Archives Department, New Brunswick Museum, Saint John, N.B.

Old Houses in Saint John, by A.H. Wetmore, Saint John, N.B.

Hannah Darling

Marblehead, in New England, was a bustling little port that day in early spring when Hannah Darling stepped briskly along the cobblestoned streets.

Stout little white houses, with shutters flung wide, revealed gleaming windows fresh from spring cleaning. Twin rows of conchshells edged near pathways up to the fan-lighted doorways as Hannah went about paying last-minute farewell calls on her friends. Cool sea breezes ruffled the waters of the bay and even now, as Hannah walked homeward, she could see the ketches, sloops, and fishing smacks riding at anchor, and the trim lines of her father's sloop anchored at the wharf below the house on the edge of the town in readiness for the summer journey to the North.

Hannah Darling was in her early teens and had been mistress of her father's home since the death of her mother, and this year she would sail with her father, Captain Benjamin Darling, to their summer house on the Island in the Kennebecasis River in the province of Nova Scotia. Even as far back as 1750, Captain Benjamin thought this was a summer haven, an ideal spot to escape the summer heat of New England, and also to trade with the Indians.

Hannah Darling's ancestors had come from England in 1617 and settled at Marblehead, where her father, Captain Benjamin, was born in 1730. From here the Captain, who was a pioneer trader and lumber merchant, sailed his sloop on an expedition up the Kennebecasis River exploring the beauties of the wild country. He was delighted with the scenery, the river broad as a lake with its little coves and sandy beaches — the miles of green forested hills reaching down the river's edge.

"Good hunting", he said, as he surveyed the place on the first trip. Here would be Indians, their paddles dipping silently in the stream, their canoes laden with glossy pelts waiting to be bartered for his cargo of pots and kettles and gunpowder and beads.

The Hammond River intrigued him, so he anchored and explored an island at the river's mouth. It wasn't very large, about four miles long, but he was delighted with the place and decided to stop for a while.

Along the hills of the mainland straggled the Indian village of Nauwigewauk, an important Malecite settlement. Here was a sandy beach for canoes, plenty of good spring water, good fishing in the Kennebecasis, and an abundance of game in the hills, and rich land where they could grow good corn.

The Indian Chief was friendly and after considerable dickering and pipe-smoking, Captain Darling persuaded him to sell the Island for "two bushels of corn, a barrel of flour, a grindstone, some gunpowder and shot and sundry knives and hatchets." Both the Chief and Benjamin were satisfied they had made a good trade.

Soon Captain Darling's men cut trees and built a comfortable two-storey log house. The upper flat was used as a storeroom for his trading supplies.

For several years Captain Darling sailed North each spring to his summer quarters bringing his family with him. Although he did not know it at the time, the Captain was the first English-speaking person to attempt a settlement in the Hammond River district of Nova Scotia, Canada.

So this spring, while Hannah's Father was busy collecting his axes and pots and bolts of cloth and gunpowder, Hannah packed featherbeds, blankets, flour and tea and spices. She even packed a medicine chest for she had to be prepared for every emergency in that isolated country place. When all was ready she closed the shutters and locked the doors of their Marblehead home. Then on board the sloop, with its sails filling out in the stiff breeze, Hannah sat on deck with her cousin for a companion and watched the little white houses, church spires and groups of chattering housewives blur in blue distance — and a lump came into Hannah Darling's throat at leaving it all behind. But she was a Captain's daughter; sailing was exhilarating, the days would pass quickly and she well knew that after her summer of splendid isolation she would catch up with all the urban gossip when she returned.

Hannah and her cousin were not lonesome on the Island, for there was plenty to keep them occupied on the long summer days. They cooked and mended and cleaned and sewed. There were candles to be moulded and soap to be made from the clean birch ashes of the logs burned in the huge fireplace. And when their work was done, the girls would stroll along the shore or sit working embroidery.

They had enough flower seeds from their Marblehead garden to make the place more homelike, but, when they began digging, the Indians appeared and objected to their disturbing the ground. Finally the Indians were pacified and Hannah's garden grew and prospered.

Often when Captain Darling had business with the Indian Chief, Hannah went along with him to the camp. Hannah was amazed at the clutter and confusion in the camp. Papooses, strapped in their cradles hung from tree branches, slept in the sun. Children and dogs ran around underfoot. Squaws, with their long matted hair tied with bright strips of cloth, squatted on the ground scraping deerskins.

She smelled the awful stew that bubbled in great pots over open fires and watched the braves eat with their fingers. It was all so indescribably dirty that Hannah's tidy New England soul rebelled. If she could only give those children a good scrubbing and tidy them up in civilized clothes! But Hannah was no reformer — she well knew that reform and trading didn't mix. So when the squaws reached out greasy, brown hands to touch the white girl's dress, and talked and laughed amongst themselves, Hannah just smiled, opened the little basket she carried and brought out beads and coloured ribbons. Shyly the children held out their grimy hands for the trinkets, then scuttled away from her like wild creatures.

But other eyes watched the lovely white girl one day. Silently a young brave slipped away from the group gathered around Captain Darling. Cautiously he slid amongst the trees as he circled the camp to get a better view. Eagerly he watched as Hannah distributed her gifts, and desire surged as he crept nearer watching her every movement. He never had seen so beautiful a woman before.

This young brave was ready to take his "he-pit". He had done his share of hunting and killing and had proved his ability to the elders of the camp. Soon the braves would gather for his courtship ceremony — for Indian marriages were community affairs of economic importance.

By Indian laws, both the suitor and the girl had to prove their suitability to set up a family; he as a hunter and canoe builder; she as a maker of moccasins and showshoes, and a tanner of skins for clothing.

The brave, watching Hannah that day, had earned his right to take his "he-pit". (Malecite word for wife, meaning "she who does her work sitting down".) He would have his courtship ceremony, feasting and talking around a council fire, while drums thudded softly far into the night. He would sit with other braves swaying to the rhythm of the drums while the "gi-naps" (big-men) of the tribe elected his proxy. Then his proxy would go to the chosen girl's parents and offer his gift — the "mutdegun", a soft, silky valuable fur robe. Quietly the circle of braves would watch as the proxy entered the tent. Eagerly they waited. Would the gift be returned? If the gift was accepted, the parents approved and the proxy approached the girl. Once, twice, she could refuse, but not a third time; for then the gi-nap came forward and held out a cross to her. She knew then that the whole village had approved and the choice was final.

Even as the bronzed young brave stood in the shadows watching Hannah distribute her gifts he pictured this marriage: The "Bu-o-win" in his ceremonial robes; the braves in paint and feathers and he, the central figure; the squaws at a respectful distance — their hands briefly idle. And while the Bu-o-win chanted the tribal rites, his chosen he-pit, in her best deerskin skirt and leggins would squat humbly behind him. Afterwards the fierce ceremonial dance and feasting, and the night in the forest under the stars.

But the brave, who stalked Hannah Darling that day, chose Hannah for his wife. There would be no proxy, no ceremonial courtship, no mutdegun, no he-pit grovelling at his feet. He had other ideas — modern ones.

When Captain Darling had finished his business with the Indians that day, he set out for the Island, and Hannah, in her gown the colour of the skies, went down the path between the trees to the river with her Father. The brave, watching Hannah, now trailed along behind the others. The boat was shoved off, men pulling strongly on the oars, and Hannah's blue dress faded to a bright dot on the wide Kennebecasis. After they were gone the brave stretched his sleek, bronzed body on the sands.

He knew it was the custom to invite Captain Darling and his men to join in the beaver hunt. Every year they saved a dam or two for the white man's sport and after they had built their 'barns' for the winter food all the Braves would go hunting. Slowly a look of cunning crept into his face. All the Braves? All?

For days after Captain Darling's visit there was great activity in the Indian camp. It was barn-building time. They dug large holes in the ground and lined the bottom and sides with birch bark. Here they stored fruits and fish and corn and meat. All summer long the squaws gathered berries, which were dried, wrapped in birch bark and deposited in the barn. Corn and beans were added as they ripened. Muskrat meat taken at the spring hunting had been smoked and dried along with moose meat and fish. And bear oil stored in bladders provided cooking fat for all good food for the long cold winter.

Nauwigewauk, meaning "place we have been coming to", had long been known to the Indians as an eel-fishing ground, and the Indians had a method of their own for catching them. They poisoned the deep pools with a mixture of crushed poke root and Jack-in-the-Pulpit and scooped up the eels in their nets. It was the squaws' work to skin and dry them. Wrapped up in birch bark they were added to the store, and when the barns were full they were covered with birch bark and moss for concealment and protection against animals.

When the barns were finished, the gi-nap spoke with the young brave of his courtship ceremony. "Another moon after the hunt", he answered, for he was in no hurry.

Back in the two-storey log house on the Island one morning Hannah Darling moved quickly about as she readied the candle moulds. A great pot of tallow bubbled on the hearth, and while her cousin swept and dusted, Hannah threaded wicks in the moulds. There would be no meals to prepare for the men that day, for Captain Darling had taken them all along to the beaver hunt.

Sunshine dappled the clearing in front of the house; it was too lovely a day to spend indoors; but after the candles were made the girls would idle away the long afternoon. Embroidery would grow beneath their skilful fingers as they rocked in their chairs out in the sunshine. It would be a lovely day.

It was Hannah who first saw the canoe with its bronze lithe figure. She watched the rhythmic stroking of the paddle as the craft sped across the glistening river.

Suddenly she turned from her work and went to the doorway. As she watched, the canoe turned towards their landing place. Evidently the Indian was starting out on a journey — there were bundles in the canoe. Did he come to make a trade? What would he want, a kettle, a grindstone, or a blanket?

Hannah had often watched her Father trading. Perhaps she could make a good bargain too — but, no, the Indian didn't bring anything from the bundle after he had beached his canoe. As he crossed the shore his hands were empty, and Hannah wondered, for Indians always brought something to trade. Something for something was their creed; never something for nothing. And the fellow was travelling alone. Usually they travelled in pairs when trading. Strange too, she thought, for him to come today, for all the Indians were supposed to be at the beaver hunt, and they knew her Father and the men were away.

Hannah's cousin joined her in the doorway. "Was it bad news?", she asked. No it couldn't be, for Captain Darling would send one of his men, not an Indian. The girls looked at each other anxiously, for even as the Indian came up the path and crossed the clearing there was arrogance in his bold measured stride. The Indian came straight up to Hannah and stood before her. "What do you want?", Hannah enquired politely. He looked at her steadily for a moment — his dark eyes cunning and sly. Then without any palaver he told Hannah he had chosen her for his squaw and had come to take her to the forest! They would go at once.

Hannah' ?art thumped and for a long moment she was breathless with astonishment. She, his squaw! Her thoughts raced. His Squaw! To paddle his canoe; to cook his food; to eat her meals of leftovers when he had finished! His squaw to make his moccasins and sleep in his tepee! Hannah almost laughed in that brown face — it was so absurd. But his determined look sobered her. She realized she would have to be careful. This was no bargaining visit. He meant to take her away with him — now — this very moment. Hannah shuddered as her awful helplessness confronted her. Hannah reached out and clung to her cousin for support, but she was even more terrified and began sobbing hysterically. But Hannah Darling stood there bravely, blocking the doorway and talked at random while sparring for time.

"You must have my Father's consent", she said, hoping to humour the Indian. "Come back when he is at home". The Indian watched her stolidly, but made no answer. "This is not the white man's custom", she couldn't go away without telling her Father; this was utter nonsense; come back tomorrow. Did he understand? "No", the Indian answered stubbornly, "you come now, we go to forest".

His determination was terrifying — the whole thing was unbelievable. This near-naked fellow daring to tell her such a thing!

"You wait here." Hannah's voice was sharp now. The two girls backed slowly into the room. Step by step the Indian followed, like an animal stalking its prey.

Her cousin collapsed in a chair sobbing hopelessly; but Hannah faced the Indian angrily. "Wait outside, I have dresses to pack", she ordered, but he made no move. Then she saw the shears on the table beside the candlewicks and her hand crept slowly towards them; but the Indian saw the movement. He reached out strong fingers and gripped her arm till it hurt. She pulled away from his grasp and dodged behind the table shouting at him to "get out!" He stood silently, menacingly. His fingers touched the knife at his waist — then Hannah knew there was no escape. For a long moment they stared angrily at each other and suddenly a wild hope flashed in Hannah's mind. Smiling at the Indian she offered to go with him of her own free will. Her cousin shrieked with astonishment and tried to hold her back, but Hannah shook off her clinging arms and kissed her cousin good-bye. Then she stepped out into the sunshine and started down the path, the Indian following her. Never once did she look back.

As they neared the waiting canoe she paused, turned, and spoke pleasantly to the Indian. She had forgotten something, something she must take with her. Would he wait until she went back for it. She would only be a moment. Slowly she walked, so as not to arouse his suspicions. Was he following her? She dared not run, she dared not look back, but at every step she expected to feel the steel grip of his hands.

Up the path from the beach, across the clearing, between the rows of flowers in the dooryard — if he was not behind her he couldn't reach her now. Hannah lifted her skirts and ran the last few steps across the threshold.

"Close the shutters, bar the windows", Hannah called to her cousin, while she swung the wide door shut, the Indian seeing he had been tricked, raced up to the house. He dashed over to the woodpile and seizing an axe began to batter down the door. Again Hannah Darling was too quick for him. She snatched her Father's loaded musket from above the fireplace, and when the Indian had smashed a hole in the door he saw Hannah and the loaded musket which was pointed directly at his head. Slowly the Indian lowered the axe and for a time that seemed endless he stood glaring angrily at her. Then recalling his defeat he swung the axe away and crept back to his canoe.

All that long summer day Hannah sat by the door, the musket beside her, watching and waiting; and when dusk had fallen it was with relief and thankfulness she heard her Father's voice echo across the water in a hearty goodnight to his Indian companions.

When Captain Darling reached his home, saw the shattered door and heard Hannah's story he was furious. He ordered his men into the boat and off they went to the Indian camp. What he told the Chief is not recorded, but council fires blazed on the hillside that night.

Next morning the Indian Chief, his Bu-o-win and gi-naps arrived at Darlings Island bringing the culprit with them. His hands were tied up to his neck; his arms pinioned behind him and he was unceremoniously dragged across the clearing to Captain Darling's house. Canoes full of warriors waited at the river, the whole tribe was in an uproar. Standing before the shattered doorway Captain Darling and Hannah waited for the Chief to speak. They explained that the tribesman had found the captive guilty of violating their Indian laws. Now it was for the white maiden to pronounce sentence on the transgressor.

"Shall we kill him?", demanded the Chief, speaking directly to Hannah. Hannah faced the crowd of Indians — she saw their knives and axes. Would it be death or torture? She had heard so many stories of Indian cruelty. She turned to the brave standing straight and silent in his bonds. There was no arrogance; no cunning; no ruthlessness now, only a calm stoical defiance. The eyes of the crowd behind him were fixed on Hannah. In spite of the bright morning sun her hands were like ice and her heart pounded like a drum. Why had they brought him back here she wondered. She never wanted to set eyes on him again. He could have killed her yesterday — would they have punished him for that?

There rose an angry muttering from the crowd, and, as if from a distance, Hannah heard her Father's voice speaking to the Chief.

Then to her bewildered mind there flashed, 'Do unto others' — 'thou shalt not kill'. Impatiently the Chief's voice broke in demanding again, "Shall we kill him?"

Hannah's voice struggled in her throat, but her glance never wavered as she looked directly into the red man's merciless eyes. "No", she said, "let him go, he has done no harm." Then she felt her Father's arm supporting her as the ground swayed beneath her feet. The Chief gave a signal and the captive's bonds were cut. Was that a flicker of gratitude she saw in the captive's dark eyes? Then the Bu-o-win spoke solemnly and ordered the prisoner banished from the tribe; never to return under penalty of death. Slowly the crowd parted and there was an uproar of voices as the culprit raced between the long lines of braves down to the river.

Plunging in, he swam across the swift Hammond River followed by the tribe in their canoes. Up the steep bank of the headland the outcast scrambled, the shrieking warriors streaming after him. Over the hill and down to the Kennebecasis he ran. While his tribesmen watched he swam across. Then he disappeared amongst the trees along the shore — never to be seen again.

When summer ended and Captain Darling sailed back with his cargo of furs to Marblehead, with its ships and its wharves and its little white houses, the story of Hannah's vacation experiences was much more exciting than those of her friends.

And although Hannah's Father, Captain Benjamin Darling, never settled permanently in New Brunswick, the Darling Family continued to come as summer residents.

In 1783, after the American Revolution, Captain Benjamin Darling, Junior, and other members of the family came directly to his Father's Island and made their home in the log summer house. But they did not own the entire Island. When Captain Darling bought it from the Indians he had neglected to get a title to the land from the British Crown. When the Loyalists came, the entire Island was laid out in lots, and Benjamin the second drew lot number eighteen on the west end of his Father's Island. Here the family lived until about 1812.

But life on a corner of an Island was too restricted for the adventurous son of the old trader; so Captain Benjamin the second built a "sloop-of-war" from the timber cut on Darlings Island. He had it rigged at Saint John, and securing a letter of marque from the British Government at Halifax he sailed as a Privateer during the War of 1812.

Luck did not smile on Benjamin this time, for altho' the seas were swarming with prizes, Benjamin and his ship were captured by the French. And because Benjamin had mortgaged his farm on the Island to meet the expenses of fitting out his sloop he lost his portion of his Father's Island in the transaction.

After some time, however, Benjamin escaped his captors and returned. This time he built a house and saw- and gristmill, instead of a ship. It was built on the mainland, about a mile above Nauwigewauk where the Indians had their encampment. Travellers on the road along the Kennebecasis River can today still see that sturdy old house built by Hannah Darling's brother. But of Benjamin's saw- and grist-mill, not a vestige remains. Even the stream that used to turn their wheels has disappeared. But behind the old house on the hillside the apple trees, planted by Benjamin's hands, still blossom every spring-time. Benjamin, being quite an adventurer, lost that house too; but the present homestead, also built by Benjamin, overlooks Darling's Lake. There is a big, open fireplace in what is now the cellar and there used to be old iron pots and pans lying about. Upstairs in the house there are fireplaces with long built-in cupboards on either side in nearly every room. In the attic, children of a later generation play on rainy days with two old spinning wheels.

And Hannah Darling always came to keep house for her Father on this Island every summer until she married Christopher Watson. Christopher Watson was a Loyalist, so what better could they do than set out for the Island when the loyal Britishers were driven from their homes. With bag and baggage the Watsons took over the old house, and here Hannah reared her family of eight children. Year after year Hannah watched wide fields of grain and hay and apple orchards replace the dense forest of the Island. And Hannah lived to be one hundred and eight years old. In the family cemetery at the west end of Darlings Island great, tall elm trees cast their graceful shade over the grave of that valiant Petticoat Pioneer.

Ever since 1750, seven generations of Darlings have lived in the Hammond River district and on the Island; and today members of the family come from distant parts of Canada and the United States to spend their summers there — keeping up the old family tradition in very earnest.

BIBLIOGRAPHY

The story of Hannah Darling, compiled from family history, courtesy of Mr. & Mrs. Winfred Darling, Hammond River, New Brunswick, and Mr. & Mrs. William E. Darling, Lancaster, New Brunswick.

Material from "The Darling Letters" 1869-1885, courtesy Lillian Moran Gill, Turtle Creek, Pennsylvania, U.S.A.

Other material from the Archives Department, New Brunswick Museum.

Indian customs were supplied from notes of Mr. Edwin Tappan Adney, Upper Woodstock, N.B., a noted authority on Indian Lore.

NOTES

NAUWIGEWAUK
Meaning "place we have been going to"

INDIAN BARNS
Large holes in the ground with bottom and sides lined with birch bark. The holes were filled with dried and smoked meat and fish. Oil stored in bladders: dried berries, corn and beans were stored in the same way.

HE-PIT (hay-pit)
"One who does her work sitting down" was the Malecite name for wife.

BU-O-WIN
Spiritual man, frequently called by the New Englanders 'Pow-Wow-Man'.

GI-NAPS
Big men, stressing mental bigness, power. Leaders of war parties were Gi-Naps.

MUTDEGUN
Skin of an animal or robe. A fur robe was frequently offered as a present to the Bride-to-be. Hence a fair exchange was made "A skin for a skin". The idea of something useful as a substantial present is an old Indian custom. The gift was not a bribe or auction to the highest bidder. The better qualified suitor was better qualified as a man. Indians always believe "Never something for nothing, always something for something!" Even in their prayers asking for something meant offering a sacrifice or gift of valuable property.

THE CROSS
Used in the courtship ceremony was of Norse origin and came to the Malecite mythology from the visits of Greenlanders to the shores of what is now the Maritime Provinces about the year 1000. The Indians had adopted this feature from the Norsemen long before Christian Missionaries came to these shores. The Cross was pre-Christian Norwegian, the Cross of Thor.

COURTSHIP CEREMONY
The actual courtship and marriage ceremonies were presided over by the Bu-O-Win.

This account of the Malecite ceremonies was given by a Passamaquoddy Chief, William Neptune of Saybec, an authority on old Malecite customs. William Neptune is a direct descendant of the old Neptune family of Malecite Chieftains.

Other Indian Customs were supplied from notes given to the author by Mr. Edwin Tappan Adney, Upper Woodstock, New Brunswick, a noted authority on Indian Lore.

Elizabeth Hazen Chipman

In the Loyalist Gallery at the New Brunswick Museum hangs a portrait of Elizabeth Chipman. Beneath her lace-frilled bonnet, dark brown hair curls about her face and there is a faint smile on her lips as she gazes serenely beyond the window, to where a modern highway bustles with traffic in a world she never knew.

For Elizabeth Chipman lived in the days of candlelight and crinolines and the white wings of her father's sailing ships in the Port of old Saint John.

Elizabeth's father, William Hazen, was a New England trader and lived at Newburyport. He was in Boston that 17th of June, 1775. Cannon rumbled through the heat. Smoke billowed over the spacious white homes of Charlestown, and British regulars toiled up Bunker Hill. William Hazen pocketed the dollars from the last sale he would make in the Colony, said good-bye to his Boston friends and turned his horse north on the great road towards Newburyport.

The Port of Boston was already closed. British frigates and sloops-of-war blockaded the Harbour. No ship could enter or leave, and Marblehead, some sixteen miles distant, was now the official Port of entry.

Even as Mr. Hazen urged his horse along, the road was crowded with waggons carrying supplies to the ships. Money was to be made here; privateers to be fitted out with guns and provisions; but, Mr. Hazen keen trader that he was, was not interested in cargoes at the moment. He had had enough of taxes and boycotts. The last vessel from his partners, Messrs. Simonds and White at the Saint John River, had been obliged to return with its cargo and Mr. Hazen was getting away from the horrors of the gathering Revolution.

Mr. Hazen had planned for this emergency as far back as 1771, when he arranged with his partners to build a house for him at the Saint John River, and James Simonds, his partner, had written: "We shall cut Mr. Hazen's frame in some place near the water where it may be rafted at any time. Have cleared roads and cut some small stuff out

194

of a large body of wood and timber, but a great part of it must remain on the spot until next winter."

Mr. Hazen's house had been 'cheerfully' raised by the workmen at the Trading Post, for in the firm's Day Book Mr. Hazen is charged "November 17th, 1773 for 4 gallons West India Rum, 3 lbs. Sugar, 3 quarts New England Rum, Dinner, etc., 25 shillings."

Elizabeth Chipman

Courtesy of The New Brunswick Museum

Strongly built, the original walls, laid up by those early workmen, still stand today at the corner of Simonds and Brooks Street in Saint John. Its original two storeys and hipped roof have been altered by the addition of another storey; but its two foot thick cellar walls and old-fashioned kitchen fireplace are still in good repair, and in the rear, partitioned off from the first floor, is what was apparently Mr. Hazen's wine cellar.

In the time-worn Day Book, a weekly bill of groceries includes "67 pounds of moose meet at a shilling a pound." For although the Hazen household, at the time of leaving Newburyport, consisted of "4 men, 3 boys and 3 women", the family increased until there were sixteen children.

Elizabeth could never have been lonely with so many brothers and sisters, and while some of her brothers were sent to school in Quebec, there is no record of where Elizabeth received her education. Probably they gathered in the large parlor where some older person taught them the A, B, C's.

Good manners were just as important as reading and writing and Elizabeth was coached in all of the courtesies of the day. There was a proper way to flutter a fan and how to step a minuet, and just how much ankle was considered nice to show beneath those frilled and embroidered petticoats.

Good housekeeping was essential in the Hazen household. Elizabeth spent hours before that immense fireplace learning to make fish chowders and savory meat pies, so popular with pioneer appetites. Even if she burned her fingers handling the heavy pots and skillets, Elizabeth learned the difference between a roast of beef and a saddle of mutton and she could do a haunch of venison to the King's taste.

Then came that day in May, 1785, when the Loyalist Fleet arrived in Saint John Harbour.

Men and boys from the Trading Post walked down the path through the woods to the Landing Place to greet those banished "King's subjects." (That path is called Main Street now.) The children gathered on the Trading Post wharf, wide-eyed with excitement. Never before had they seen so many ships, or so many people. Soldiers marched down from Fort Howe, bugles blaring, drums throbbing, and all over the green hills tents were going up. Tents to house those refugees, who, after so many years of nerve-wracking experiences, had found safe harbour in the new colony under the old flag.

In the comfortable Hazen house welcome hospitality was extended to recently arrived friends, and to this house later on came Ward Chipman.

Back in New York City, Ward Chipman had watched the

turmoil of those Loyalists, who, like himself, had fled from their New England homes. Ward Chipman was a brilliant young man. He had led his class at Harvard where he graduated in Law and delivered the first oration on "The Influence of Learning". He had been practising in Boston when the Revolution began and his home, its library walls lined with precious books, had been destroyed when the rabble sacked the place.

Ward Chipman's School Exercise Book, 1763
Courtesy of The New Brunswick Museum   *Photo by William Hart*

General Washington was in New York too, so was General Sir Guy Carleton, Commander-in-Chief of the British Forces in America. And General Carleton, having great faith in Ward Chipman's ability, appointed him secretary to the Commissariat for the settlement of the British refugees.

On November 29th, 1783, Ward Chipman wrote: "I have been a witness to the mortifying scene of giving up the City of New York to the American troops. Twelve o'clock, Friday the 25th, all the Loyalist troops paraded. The Americans marched in thru Wall Street and Broadway under General Washington and Sir Guy Carleton looked

197

unusually dejected."

And well he might. For here were thousands of refugees fearful of banishment to the West Indies, and having their estates confiscated while Edward Winslow, formerly Collector of Customs for the Port of Boston, who was in Nova Scotia, had not completed his arrangements for the refugees already arrived in Halifax and Saint John.

It was the following Spring before Ward Chipman completed his work as Secretary and sailed with Sir Guy Carleton for England.

In spite of his losses Ward Chipman remained a scholar and a gentleman. He wore lace-ruffled coats and powdered his hair and he prepared for his sojourn in the new Colony by shopping at the store of J. Bergen, Perfumer, in the Strand. Even if he had to live in a wigwam he was going to live like a gentleman. So he bought "Lavendar water, Pomade, Tooth Powder, Sticking Plaister, Windsor Soap, Hair Powder, Tooth and Shaving Brushes", and '100 Tooth Picks' at 6 penny."

But Ward Chipman didn't have to live in a wigwam when he reached Saint John, for he, with two other young gentlemen, kept "Bachelors quarters" in the old Peabody house; the first frame house erected at Portland Point and not far from the Hazen home.

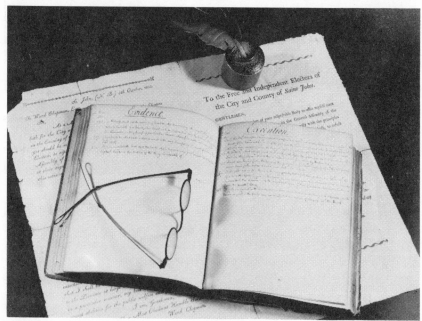

Manuscript of Legal Notes kept by Ward Chipman while studying law in Boston, 1774. Underneath the book is Chipman's Open Letter to the Citizens of Saint John giving notice of his intention to seek candidacy in the General Assembly of New Brunswick.

Courtesy of The New Brunswick Museum   *Photo by William Hart*

Perhaps on cold winter nights Ward Chipman found it convenient to wander over and toast his shins before Mr. Hazen's blazing fireplace. Very likely, after his own none too successful efforts at cooking, with a book of Virgil in one hand and a stirring spoon in the other, Mr. Hazen's well-set table with its good food and better sherry appealed to him. And the surroundings reminded him of his more luxurious days. To Ward Chipman, Greek and Latin were as familiar as French and English and the well-educated Hazen boys were good companions. There, too, was Elizabeth, sitting demurely with the toe of her slipper showing just so much beneath the flounces of her gown, while her busy fingers flew over and under her embroidery frame as she stitched intricate designs on a cushion. Evenings were spent in a game of cards, or they would talk of books and music, or walk a minuet if there was someone to play the violin.

In the new city there was plenty to occupy the young lawyer. Ward Chipman drew up the Charter for the City of Saint John, which included Parr Town and Carleton, the settlement across the Harbour, and on May 18th, 1785, Saint John became the first incorporated City in Canada. Ward Chipman also designed the official City Seal and proposed the City's Motto: "O fortunati quorum jam moenia surgunt" (O fortunate are ye whose walls are now rising). For Chipman loved his Virgil and compared the building of Saint John to the building of the ancient City of Carthage. When the Supreme Court was opened for the first time in New Brunswick, February 1st, 1785, Ward Chipman was appointed Attorney-General for the Province.

This clever and witty young man was much in demand socially as well as in business. But he still found time to pay his respects to Elizabeth Hazen. Even his friends were agreed that, "Elizabeth was perfect and calculated to make Chip very happy." So on the 24th of October, 1786, Elizabeth Hazen, wearing a prim white gown, white silk mittens and high-heeled slippers, stood beside Ward Chipman in the parlor of her Father's home while the Reverend George Bissett pronounced them man and wife.

For a time the Chipmans lived at the home of George Leonard and here their son was born. The quaint little walnut cradle that Elizabeth used to rock Ward Junior in may still be seen in the Loyalist Gallery at the New Brunswick Museum.

Then Ward Chipman built his famous mansion high on a hill in the fashionable part of the city. Of Georgian design with mansard roof and many stacks of chimneys it was surrounded by terraces and spacious lawns. Privet hedges edged the paths between formal flower gardens and the interior decorations were imported from England. In 1790, Ward Chipman writing to a friend in London asked him to select wallpaper for him, and because, "the rooms have wide cornices", he feared, "it might make a difference regarding borders."

To Elizabeth Chipman's "Tea-Routs" and "Gregories" flocked the fashionables of Saint John, their powdered hair piled high and tiny black beauty patches in the form of "coaches and four" or "King's men" decorating their faces. In Elizabeth's formal drawing room guests chatted of new fashions in bonnets and gowns "just arrived after seventy-five days passage from London." And the numerous gilt-framed concave and convex mirrors reflected the bare shoulders and brocaded gowns, frills and furbelows of her guests.

In the shaded glow of candlelight Elizabeth's silver gleamed on the polished mahogany dining table. Dudley plate and Crown Derby enhanced the delight of those dinner parties; and over the massive sideboard a portrait of a red-coated Tory looked down (perhaps longingly) at the glittering array of crystal decanters.

At the foot of the winding stairway, which led from a wide reception hall, guests retiring for the night would select a candle from the massive mahogany candle stand, light it from one glittering in its burnished sconce, and there would be a jingle of spurs and a rustling of ladies' gowns as they ascended the polished stairway.

It was a social, legal and political world Elizabeth shared with her husband. Governor Carleton dined with them. Statesmen and clergy fraternized in that hospitable home. Henry Goldsmith (Canada's first poet and nephew of Oliver Goldsmith) writes how he "enjoyed the comfort of one of Chipman's armchairs with both feet raised on a cushion."

On June 19th, 1794, the Duke of Kent (Father of Queen Victoria) was entertained at a Levee at Chipman House. His grandson, Albert Edward, Prince of Wales, (later King Edward VII) enjoyed the City's hospitality at the Mansion while visiting Saint John August 3rd and 4th, 1860. Two thousand school children, gathered on the spacious lawns under the arches of flowers and banners, greeted His Royal Highness with song.

General Benedict Arnold and his beautiful wife, the former Peggy Shippen of Philadelphia, were frequent guests of the Chipmans, while they made their home in Saint John. In 1787, Mr. S.S. Blowers, Attorney-General of Nova Scotia, had written to Ward Chipman, "Dear Chipman, will you believe General Arnold is here from England in a brig of his own, as he says reconnoitering the country. He is bound for your City, which he will of course prefer to Halifax, and settle with you. Give you joy of your acquisition." Ward Chipman and the Robinson brothers were on hand with others to greet the General, and for four years the Arnolds occupied a house on King Street and here their last son was born.

For Elizabeth there were morning rides with Peggy Arnold. No one could equal Peggy's light hand on the reins, and everyone paused to watch the General's lady in her smart London habit as she rode through the streets. Often they drove out together in the General's new carriage with his black "Punch" in gay livery on the box. And when Peggy wandered in the Chipman garden, often she would pick a bouquet of Heartease from Elizabeth's flower beds as a "breast knot" for her fashionable gown.

Letter written by Margaret Arnold
Courtesy of The New Brunswick Museum
Photo by Gordon Anderson

In September 1791 the General and his family returned to England. The *Intelligencer* of September 21st advertised: "For Sale:- Excellent feather beds; mahogany four poster bedsteads; elegant set of Wedgewood giltware; cabriole chairs covered with blue damask and a Lady's elegant saddle and bridle. John Chaloner, Auctioneer. If the weather be fine."

Ward Chipman purchased twelve dining room chairs and often his friends twitted him about having 'traitors chairs' in his home.

From Saint Anne's Street in London came lively letters from Peggy Arnold telling Elizabeth of new styles in bonnets and gowns and of theatres and receptions. But in politics Peggy admitted being a "miserable croaker." "I hear much of the gaiety of your little City", she writes, "but find that party spirit, especially among the ladies, still rages with violence. I shall always regret my separation from valuable friends among the first whom I recon Mrs. Chipman."

Peggy Arnold sends a bonnet "in the latest London fashion" for

Elizabeth and she "hoped the bonnet would please for it is very fashionable — a thing of great importance." To Mr. Chipman she sends a pair of gloves and flannel hose and begs him to accept them, "the latter being very proper to keep your feet warm at Church."

Trinity Church, where Elizabeth and her husband attended services, had been completed in 1791, and over the Governor's pew was installed the Royal Coat of Arms of the British Hanoverian Dynasty. This interesting relic of early colonial days had been removed from the Council Chamber of the Colony of Massachusetts Bay, where it had hung between the portraits of Charles II and James II. Edward Winslow had brought them to Halifax and Ward Chipman was instrumental in having them placed in Trinity Church. The age of the Coat of Arms is not definitely known, but it is thought it belongs to the reign of King George I, 1714, when Royal Arms were placed in all important colonial towns. After the Declaration of Independence they were publicly destroyed; six only are known to have survived the Revolution.

To Attorney-General Bliss, who purchased his house in Saint John, General Arnold writes: "Mrs. Arnold and myself sincerely congratulate you and Mrs. Bliss on the birth of another son, which we hope will prove a great blessing and comfort to you." Other letters from the General are mostly concerned with business matters. He asks Mr. Putnam his solicitor, "to sell the frame and materials for the Ship at Digby," which he had started to build before leaving Saint John, and wished he "could realize all the little property I have at or near Saint John," and he urged to have his debts collected. Though Arnold had many critics, they were in no hurry to pay their accounts.

For Mr. Chipman, legal business became almost overwhelming. There was much property being transferred, contracts had to be drawn up and he found it necessary to be absent from Saint John during the Legislature Sessions. The seat of Government had been transferred to Fredericton, because General Carleton considered it a safer place in case of enemy attack. Ward Chipman required a clerk to copy his briefs and Jonathan Sewall took up residence at Chipman House. And Jonathan was a talented young man.

Jonathan's father writes to Ward Chipman saying how pleased he was "with his son's drawings and his astounding proficiency on the violin, the best instrument in my opinion. It would raise your admiration greatly for he now plays overtures of the first masters with great correctness, and perhaps these accomplishments would serve as amusements to keep him out of mischief." But, the elder Sewall warns, "Jonathan is an impetuous individual; he cannot stop to look a second time at what he does not comprehend in one glance."

But life was not all music and drawing for young Sewall, for members of the Chipman household rose early. Ward Chipman and his young clerk took long walks before their seven o'clock breakfast. Office hours were from eight to three and Jonathan spent long hours copying legal documents in his beautiful script.

When the Putnam house at the foot of King Street was sold, Ward Chipman handled the transfer. It was a rather unusual transaction, for the purchaser was required to pay cash in hard cold silver dollars to the amount of two thousand pounds sterling, and every dollar had to be counted out to Mr. Chipman in person.

So Mr. Barlow, the purchaser, got a wheelbarrow and up the steep hill to Chipman house he trundled those silver dollars. Word got around about the time Mr. Barlow was ready to start up the hill. From McPherson's Coffee House sailors left their grog and came to watch this interesting spectacle. And by the time Mr. Barlow was half way to Chipman House his enthusiastic audience, now lining both sides of the street, was shouting encouragement and jokes and jibes to this gentleman who paid his bills the hard way. After two journeys up the hill, pushing his barrow of dollars and providing amusement for the onlookers, Mr. Barlow's philosophic comment was "Labor omnia vincit".

The lack of regular school facilities in Saint John was a matter of anxiety to Elizabeth and her husband, for Ward, Junior, was a bright little chap. Everyone called him "Little Chip". He was plump and jolly and fond of fun as any other lad. His best friend was Charlie Peters who lived not far away, and their favorite pastime was walking on stumps of trees from one end of the city to the other. If one of them stepped on the ground en route he had to pay a forfeit.

For a time Little Chip and Charlie were tutored by an old soldier, Jeremiah Pecker. But this proved rather unsatisfactory for Jeremiah was too fond of his bottle. So, when the Chipmans went on a visit to their relatives, the Grays, in Salem, Massachusetts, they took Little Chip along so he could remain to attend a school.

William Gray, who signed himself William Tertius Gray to distinguish him from the other William Grays, had married Ward Chipman's sister Elizabeth. He was one of the first New England merchants to trade with Russia, India and China and at one time he owned 113 vessels and employed over three thousand seamen.

Here in this old city of Salem, founded by Roger Conant in 1626 and famous for its witchcraft trials in 1692, Little Chip made his home with "Aunt Gray" and studied with the "best masters."

Although only ten years of age his progress at school was extraordinary. He writes to his father: "We study Virgil Mondays and Tuesdays and translate the Gospels of John and Matthew from the Greek. There is no corporal punishment, but anyone caught whispering has to stand in a box until he catches another whispering, who then replaces him."

Little Chip recalls school days spent in Saint John and "wishes to be remembered to Mr. Pecker, if he isn't too drunk when you see him."

February 18th, 1798 — Salem, he writes, "My dear Papa, Last Wednesday I received one letter from you dated 21st January and on another page one from Mama dated 24th. I was very sorry to find that you were so laid up with the gout, but I hope you have got over it by this time. I was very much disappointed in not seeing Mr. J. Sewall as I was at Haverhill when he arrived and departed from Boston, but I expect to make a journey to Canada pretty soon, at least when I come out of college.

"I suppose you have returned to Fredericton by this time and I hope you are well pleased with your jaunt. I received a letter from William last week in French with which I am very well pleased. I wish Sir you would tell Mama that I am afraid I shall leave my heart behind me when I return to St. John but I anticipate the time with pleasure when I shall again meet you and Mama. By the first vessel I shall answer Edwin's and Lebaron's letters which I received with yours. The Vauxhall gardens are to be on Mr. Jarvis' Farm in view of West Boston. Aunt says she promises herself great pleasure in rambling in some of the walks on a summer's evening with Mama. I have nothing else of consequence. My love and respects to all my friends and believe me Dear Papa that I still remain your most affectionate, Dutiful Son, Ward Chipman Junior.

"P.S. I employ some time every day in playing with my little namesake who can go alone and can read French as well as English. I wish I could say as much for myself. The 'Elizabeth' arrived at New York and we are in hourly expectation of Captain Ward, as he sailed from Calcutta 7th September 1797. Our relatives here are very well. Uncle and Aunt join in sending very affectionate greetings to Mama and you."

The following month Little Chip writes in French to prove his progress in that language.

Dancing lessons were also a part of Little Chip's education, but he despairs: "I never expect to be able to walk a minuet handsomely." But on the polished floor of the Gray's elegant drawing room Little Chip proved to be quite a master of those sweeping bows and intricate evolutions in the popular single couple Court Minuet.

The Grays even hoped he would become a citizen of the United States; but Ward Chipman, Senior, had other plans for his son. On his thirteenth birthday Little Chip had to decide what profession he would follow. He chose Law and graduated from Harvard, leading his class at the age of eighteen.

Elizabeth Chipman could not bear the separation from her son any longer, so in July 1804 she and her husband journeyed to Salem. Never a good sailor, Elizabeth was very ill during the voyage but was delighted to find Little Chip very well. After a few weeks of "amusements, idleness, fatigues and expense" they were glad to return to "our comparatively humble dwelling." And Little Chip went to England to complete his studies at The Temple in London.

On a wild, white, stormy morning in January 1806 the news of Nelson's Victory at Trafalgar the previous October was published in the *Saint John Gazette* and there was much rejoicing.

There were celebrations in Saint John, Norton and Kingston with much drinking to the King's Health. But on February 14th, 1806, Fredericton celebrated with a Ball at Province Hall unequalled in display and extravagance. Ward Chipman being in Fredericton, attending the Sessions of Legislature, Elizabeth joined him and together they attended the Ball.

All the rooms of the House of Assembly were used for that occasion. The flag-draped ballroom was decorated with arches of evergreens and artificial flowers crowned with Prince of Wales feathers. Paintings of the Nelson Arms filled every nook and corner. Even the floor was chalked with appropriate designs and mottoes. The guests assembled before nine o'clock and hundreds of candles shed their glow over the gay throng. And at midnight, after dancing to the music of the military band, the guests sat down to supper, speeches and toasts, which lasted far into the morning.

Evening concerts were becoming the fashion in the new colony and at Chipman House Jonathan Sewall's violin threaded a gay melody of overtures from the "best masters". Guests contributed the favourite romantic ballads with their "fa, la, las", and no evening was complete without Ward Chipman's "sprightly singing", as a part of the entertainment.

And when Ward Chipman, Junior, married Elizabeth Wright in 1817 there were receptions for the couple at Chipman House, and gay parties with dancing that set the walls of the old mansion ringing with rhythm and song.

Later the junior Chipmans made a tour of England and the Continent and were presented at Court. From the yellowed pages of the *Saint John Courier* of September 25th, 1830 we read: "His Honor, Judge Chipman, arrived in town on Thursday from London after an absence of nearly two years. His Honor and Lady came by land from Saint Andrews where they took the new Coach recently established between the City and the latter place, being the first passengers that travelled en route in a Stage Coach."

The cradle in which Elizabeth Chipman rocked her baby

Elizabeth Chipman continued to carry on her duties as Chatelaine of Chipman House, often tending herself those bright little beds of flowers in the formal gardens all bordered with privet and boxwood hedges, as well as her many household duties.

In February 1824, while attending a Session of Legislature, Ward Chipman, Sr., suddenly collapsed in his chair and died. When the news reached Saint John the bell of Trinity Church, where he and Elizabeth had worshipped so often, tolled all day long and the flag on Fort Howe flew at half-mast.

Ward Chipman, Jr., died November 26th, 1851 and Elizabeth survived him only six months.

Chipman House, with its gracious hospitality has disappeared, replaced by a modern building, the Y.M.C.A., on the Street called "Chipman Hill".

Today, over an old mahogany sideboard, in the Loyalist Gallery of the New Brunswick Museum, hangs the portrait of Elizabeth Chipman and nearby is the little walnut cradle in which she rocked her baby.

But portraits and ivory-tinted letters and cradles and candlestands are not just dusty records of by-gone days, for Elizabeth

206

Chipman was one of that proud procession of pioneer women who helped create a civilization out of a wilderness.

BIBLIOGRAPHY and NOTES

Letters by James Simonds, New Brunswick Historical Collections.
Letters from Winslow Papers — New Brunswick Museum.
Ward Chipman Jr. Letters — New Brunswick Museum.
Hazen House notes from A.H. Wetmore's "Old Houses in Saint John".
Royal Coat of Arms — Historical Guide to New Brunswick, J. Clarence Webster.
Royal Coat of Arms — History of Saint John, D.R. Jack.
General Benedict Arnold letters etc., from the notes by Mrs. A.E. Vesey, St. Stephen, N.B. and Archives Department, New Brunswick Museum.
(Benedict Arnold lived in a large frame house at the corner of King and Cross [now Canterbury] Streets in Saint John from 1787 to 1791. The house was purchased by Attorney-General Bliss, who lived there until he moved to Fredericton as Chief Justice of New Brunswick. About 1870 the house was torn down to make room for a brick building later to be known as 'Cheape Corner', because it housed the first cut-rate grocery store in Saint John. Today, that corner, 32 King Street is occupied by a broker's office.)

Ann Mott

It was January 1815. Snow blocked the streets of Saint John and frost screened the windows of a small two-storey building on Prince William Street when Ann Mott left her comfortable living quarters to go downstairs to the Print Shop.

Candles flickered in the dark shop; the place smelled of fresh ink and stale paper. Over the doorway hung a huge sign, a Bible surmounted by a crown and underneath the lettering "Jacob Mott King's Printer", indicating that here was the official Government Printer authorized by His Majesty to print all the official proclamations for the King's forces in this new country of New Brunswick.

Ann Mott, widow of Jacob Mott, had a busy day ahead of her. She had taken over the newspaper established by her husband, an unprecedented thing for a woman to do in those early days, and she was the first woman in New Brunswick to own and operate a printing business.

But Ann was no stranger to printer's ink. Printing had been a family affair; for back in the days when they had lived in New York her husband had carried on a printing business. Then came John Ryan from Boston by way of Newport, Rhode Island, just one jump ahead of the Revolutionary forces; he joined Jacob Mott in his business and married Amelia, Jacob's sister.

Ann and Amelia had much in common in those anxious days, including a hurried exit from New York when their husbands had to leave their precious type and presses behind. But the tenacious Irishman managed to recover most of their property after landing with the Loyalists at Parr Town, and on December 18, 1783, seven months after the Loyalists had clambered ashore from the ships, Ryan published the *Royal Gazette and Nova Scotia Intelligencer*, the first newspaper established in the new colony.

John Ryan had done so much travelling, even though it was more from necessity than choice, that he could not settle long in one place. So in 1797 when he went to Newfoundland to try his luck there, his brother-in-law, Jacob Mott, took over the *Royal Gazette*, which he published at his own printing shop, "The Sign of the Bible and

Crown", until his death in 1814.

Now any other widow with a young son to care for would have sold out and retired. But Ann was different; for at the age of thirty-seven, when other women had retired from active management of their homes and had their memories as consolation in advancing years, Ann Mott began a career for herself. For her in reality, "Life began at forty".

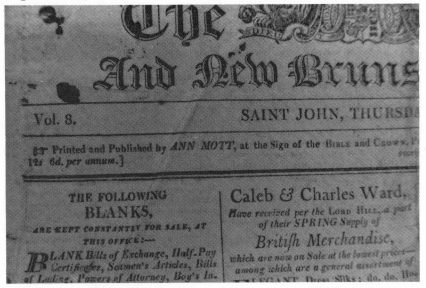

Masthead of Ann Mott's newspaper, *The Gazette and New Brunswick Advertiser*   Courtesy of The New Brunswick Museum ·   Photo by Gordon Anderson

Time and again Ann had been told that no woman could run a newspaper successfully, but obstacles only proved incentives to her. She was obliged to change the name of her newspaper however, for no woman could be a "King's Printer" and use the word "Royal". But, although she changed the name to *The Gazette and New Brunswick Advertiser*, she still used the Royal Coat of Arms on the masthead of her paper. The wooden sign of the "Bible and Crown" continued to swing out over the doorway of her Print Shop, and she charged the same price for her paper: "6 penny single, 12 shillings 6 pence per annum." Her business prospered, in spite of the fact that the duties of printer to "The King's Most Excellent Majesty" was transferred to Christopher Sower, another Saint John printer.

Ann had a nose for news and considerable journalistic ability. And she wasn't afraid of work. For, while other ladies of the new city were entertaining at "receiving dinner parties", so popular in those days, and chatting about newly arrived gowns from London, and Paris bonnets, Ann was deep in the pages of the recently arrived newspapers. Editing current news with her quill pen, Ann had a gift for condensing long and tiresome reports. Scissors and paste were part of her stock-in-trade too. Many were the clippings from the *London Gazette Extraordinay, The Boston Repertory* and New York papers that found their way into the columns of Ann's *Gazette and New Brunswick Advertiser.*

In her first newspaper of January 11th, 1815, Ann notified her readers that "The subscriber begs leave to inform the Public that she has now the sole conduct and management of this paper aided only by the exertions of her son. Under these circumstances she ventures to throw herself on their protection with a grateful sense of their past kindness. And while she assures them that no pains shall be spared on her part to render the Paper worthy of a continuance of their support, she cherishes a hope that she still may be favored with that indulgent encouragement, which cannot fail to animate her exertions in their service and which it is ever grateful to generous Patrons to bestow. As their smiles will in this instance tend to relieve the necessities of the widow and to foster the industry of the fatherless she feels a just confidence that these considerations will not lessen her claim to the Public favor."

Evidently Ann's exertions in the service of her patrons favored their "indulgent encouragement" for Saint John merchants continued to advertise in her paper. Whole columns of advertisements appear on every page, and on February 9, 1815, a supplement, printed on one side only, is devoted entirely to advertising.

Ann's little four columned weekly is a striking contrast to newspaper styles of today. Printed on dull gray or cream coloured paper, resembling ordinary wrapping paper, the small "pica type, with the old-fashioned long "s" (like an f) is difficult reading. But newspapers were precious in those days and respectfully read; then folded carefully, they were put away safely for further perusal.

And printing was done the hard way. Line after line of type set laboriously by hand and columns packed firmly in the forms. And when the forms were set, Ann pinned a sheet of paper to the frame of the press, pulled a long handle, which worked a lever and 'Bang' went the paper against the type, striking off one sheet at a time. If Ann worked steadily and had no interruptions she printed about one hundred sheets in an hour.

Carried over from a previous issue and dated Dec. 18, 1814, "John Droust, Courier, Informs the Public that he has commenced driving his sleigh for the winter season as usual on his route between here and Fredericton. He intends changing horses at Mr. Gouldings, Long Island going and returning. The stage will leave this city every

Saturday at noon and Fredericton on Tuesday. Application to be made for freight or passage to Mr. Gabriel Van Horne at Fredericton and at his house in this city opposite Mr. Wade's Taylor Shop."

Evidently John Droust found that advertising paid, for he had many passengers in spite of the long and cold journey.

Headlined in great primer type we read:

"TEN GUINEAS REWARD"

Escaped by breaking Goal on the night between the 6th and 7th inst., an American Prisoner of War from Augusta, district of Maine, detained in my custody as a Debtor under mesne process.

GERSHOM NORTH

Nearly six feet high, stout made, but thin habit, brown grey hair very short, a large scar on his forehead and bold look, supposed to be drest in dark brown and blue pantaloons with boots.

Any person who will apprehend the said prisoner, or give such information as shall lead to his apprehension and safe conduct to His Majesty's Goal for this City and County shall receive the above reward with necessary expenses. All mariners and others will avoid giving countenance or assistance to the said North in his escape as they would avoid the heavy penalties of the Law.

WILLIAM HAZEN, Sheriff.

Sheriff's Office, St. John, 7th February 1815."

Another advertisement of interest to Saint John's thirsty citizens ran a "great primer" headline:

"Rum and Shrub"
92 Puncheons) Rum
11 Hogsheads)
2 Puncheons Shrub
Superior Quality for sale on Reasonable Terms.
Nehemiah Merritt."

May 18th, 1815.

John Burns, Clock Maker, advertised that he had "opened his shop in the house of Mr. Burtis, opposite the Market where he intends carrying on his business in all its branches. Making and repairing clocks, cleaning and repairing duplex horizontal and vertical watches." And he hoped that "his long experience in Britain would entitle him to a share of the public patronage."

Ezekiel Barlow's supply of spring merchandise came by the Brig PEGGY from London and included the "best coniac brandy, muscovada sugar by the hogshead and fourteen thousand barrels of Liverpool salt."

The Brig ALEXANDER from Glasgow brought a large assortment of "fashionable and other goods" for John Knutton's store on Prince William Street, which by the way, was next door to Ann's Printing Shop. John offered a variety of "elegant muslins and printed calicos, parasols, morocco slippers, bombazeen, black crepe and mattresses."

Thomas Nisbet, Cabinet Maker and Upholsterer, offered to make "bed and window curtains" and advises that "a quantity of baked hair had arrived and he was now prepared to supply sofas and mattresses." He also had "considerable mahogany on hand and would be happy to execute orders for furniture." Then he adds a footnote: "Wanted eight to ten thousand feet of good quality birch boards." Perhaps those cherished heirloom sofas are more birch than mahogany.

Cargoes of "Boots and Shoes" were offered for sale. Tenders to build sawmills and churches were "invited."

John Robinson, merchant, advertised "A few boxes of Muscatel Raisins", a "Case of Straw Bonnets", and a "Genuine Remedy for Toothache."

There was a "Lost and Found" column in Ann's newspaper: "Lost on the night of the 13th inst. a six oared Boat, clincher-built. Black top and white bottom. Whoever may have found the same by returning her to the "Theodore", Robert Wilson, Master, will be rewarded for their trouble.
St. John, June 15, 1815.

"Wanted", runs another advertisement, "One hundred head of Good Stall Fed Oxen. None under five years old to be furnished as wanted between the first day of January and the first day of April next; a generous price will be given for the same. Any person wishing to contract for the whole or part will call on John Toole, Butcher, St. John, where the cattle are to be delivered."

One advertisement, set upside down, in the July 13th issue, states: "Mr. Mitchell acquaints his friends and the public that he has opened an Evening School in consequence of his intention to leave this City for Nova Scotia. Every favor from the Public will be thankfully received."

Stephen Humbert, a bookseller, advises the musical world: "Union Harmony or British American Sacred Vocal Music. The second edition comprising three hundred pages of Select English, American and original music adapted to Devotional and Schoolastic exercises will be ready for Delivery September next. The subscriber respectfully informs the Amateurs of the Science of Sacred Music, that no pains have been spared in selecting approved music suited to the various meters used in the respective worshipping assemblies in the British Provinces, and altho' this Edition will be much improved and enlarged, it will be sold much cheaper than Music Books introduced from the United States. 21st June 1815."

"The Last Day but Two" runs another headline, "The Public are respectfully informed that the Museum of Wax Figure Paintings etc., which are now exhibiting at Mrs. Cox's in King Street will close in this Town with the Present Week and the Proprietor is induced to fix the price of Admission at 1 shilling 3 pence for those who shall visit the Museum during the Daytime and 2s 6d for those who shall attend in the Evening. No person will be admitted without paying for each time of admittance. Profiles neatly Cut, Shaded and Framed. St. John, July 27th, 1815."

Social doings of Saint John were recorded in Ann's newspaper and ladies gowns were faithfully described down to the last hand-painted ruffle.

Ann Mott was up-to-date — the 1815 date — with fashion hints and beauty recipes. "To make the Hair Curl", she advises, "Rub it with the yolk of egg and then wash off with clean water and put on a little pomade." And she kept a little corner for household hints, where "Bears Grease" was recommended for rubbing painful rheumatic joints and "Sand and Ashes" suggested for cleaning copper pots.

At the bottom of nearly every column Ann kept a space for brief advertisements:

"For sale at this office,— Blank bills of Exchange, Half Pay Certificates, Seamen's Articles, Bills of Lading, Powers of Attorney, Boys Indentures, Deeds, Subpoenas, Etc."

"Rags! Rags!" "Cash will be given at this office for clean Linen and Cotton Rags."

"Wanted, an Apprentice for the Tin Plate working Business. Inquire at this Office."

"Wanted, a steady woman that can be well recommended to take care of two children on a passage to England and Ireland. Liberal wages will be given. Enquire of the Printer."

"Wanted, as an apprentice to the Printing Business a Lad from 12 to 14 years of age. Apply at this Office."

Ann's business was expanding!

Murder was not front page headline news in Ann's time, but news was news, and down in a corner at the end of a column two lines tell: "On Saturday last a Soldier belonging to the 102nd Regiment was committed to Jail for the murder of his wife, the particulars of which we have not learned."

Of European news Ann writes that, "In many parts of Germany the robbers are so numerous that detachments of the Military have been sent out to guard the great roads."

From France she reports, "It is said the French Government has suspended the payment of Bonaparte's pension" and that "Marseilles has been made a free Port by the French Chamber of Deputies by a majority of 127 to 21."

"Accounts from Spain," Ann says, "Report that everything goes on there with the same consumate stupidity as ever, and arrests continue daily."

From a Glasgow paper Ann copies a Marriage Notice: "Married in Glasgow, Mr. Henry Cain age 34 to Mrs. Maxwell of Clark's Bridge, age 66. It is the sixth time of the Bridegroom and the ninth time of the Bride's being joined in wedlock."

With dry humor Ann aptly quotes below the Notice: "If Love's a flame that's kindled by desire; an old stick is surely best, because it's drier."

Captioned "Uncle Sam's Pay", Ann reports that, "The Plattsburg Gazette of the 9th inst. states that the Militia, who had been in Public service for these months had been discharged; but without receiving a cent of pay. The poor fellows were obliged to beg their way home, from whence the writer guesses they will not return, unless they have some better evidence of the public faith than they have experienced."

"By the late arrivals from Castine we have received Boston papers; they contain a variety of statements relative to the New Orleans Expedition from which we have selected what appears to be most important."

"General Jackson commenced the attack about eight o'clock in the morning; the engagement lasting about an hour and the killed and wounded amounting to about two hundred men."

"Our late Boston advices, though brought down to the 7th Inst., do not furnish any extraordinary event," Ann writes, "But Mr. Madison is said to be ill of a Typhus Fever."

"It is said that the Honorable William Gray of Salem is become a bankrupt. This gentleman was supposed to be the wealthiest individual in the United States and as mad a Democrat as Madison himself, he took a considerable portion of the late loan; his failure will be a heavy blow to the reigning faction. Mr. Gray had embarked most extensively in the trade to China and the East Indies. In the first year of the War [1812] he lost several of his most valuable vessels by capture; one of which was worth 400,000 dollars. These losses and the destruction of the fisheries must have operated to his ruin, as Mr. Gray owned so many vessels as induced him to be his own under-writer."

Then with the War over and everyone remembering how the British had chased the American "Constitution" into Marblehead; the fight between the "Chesapeake" and the "Shannon"; and how the

British had laid the Capitol in Washington in ashes, Ann copies the report from the *Boston Repertory* describing the rejoicings of peace there.

"The news of Peace between this country and Great Britain has been received here with every demonstration of Joy. By order of the Selectmen the Bells were rung through the day. All the mercantile streets and wharves were profusely ornamented with flags; and all business was suspended, and nothing was heard but rejoicing and acclamation. In the evening the Exchange Coffee House, all the Printing Offices and many other buildings in Congress Street and many houses in different parts of the town were splendidly illuminated. The day was one of more general and enthusiastic rejoicing than has ever before occurred within the memory of the inhabitants of the town."

Later in the month, Boston celebrated with a "Peace Ball" when the belles of Boston in their best party gowns, their hair arranged in braids, bandeaux and curls, danced and flirted with the beaux of the town, celebrating Peace in their own manner.

"Similar rejoicings have taken place in New York and many other towns," Ann continues, "in celebrating the happy tidings of the return of Peace."

And with Peace, inflation must have been just around the corner, for after reading the stock reports Ann comments shrewdly, "Almost all kinds of stock has already been raised 10 or 12 per cent."

Even in those days there was some effort at price control, for landlords were ordered to charge lodgers for the night "sixpence to sleep in a feather bed, no more."

From the British papers Ann informs her readers that "Admiral Cochrane has made an application for some three deckers to be built for the American service", and that "much damage has been done to the shipping on the English coast by gales beginning in December."

"We have received the Halifax papers to the 6th inst.," Ann writes, "and from them have copied the Prince Regent's speech and other interesting articles."

Dated, House of Lords, November 8, 1814, George, Prince of Wales, addressed the Members: "My Lords and Gentlemen, It is with deep regret that I am obliged to announce the continueance of His Majesty's lamented indisposition." He continues to speak on other matters in a two column report, but neglects to mention that, while George III was both blind and insane, he, the Regent, and his brothers were constantly quarrelling with each other and piling up debts for the harassed country to pay.

But if the Prince Regent was busy in England, the Princess went visiting. "Dec. 6, Naples. The Princess of Wales was met by King

Murat at the outside of the City of Naples and entered it in the King's carriage. She was received with great accclamations and a guard of honor was placed before her residence. A few days after her arrival the Princess went on board a Neapolitan Frigate and while on this excursion visited the Admiral's Ship of the English Squadron, where Her Royal Highness was received with all the honors due her rank."

From the London papers came the Monthly Report of the King's health. "Windsor Castle, Dec. 3, 1814. His Majesty has been uniformly composed throughout the last month, but without any alteration in the state of his disorder."

In her *Saint John Gazette and New Brunswick Advertiser*, Ann Mott condenses news from other parts of the country: "Accounts from Canada mention that the British are sending immense quantities of ordnance from Montreal to Kingston; no doubt intended for their new ships in the Spring. A contract for 100,000 dollars has been entered into for the transportation."

Referring to the project of a "Grand Canal" she edits the story: "The Canadian Papers say a Grand Canal of 80 miles is contemplated to be cut between Montreal and Kingston to avoid the rapids and currents of the River."

Under the heading "Saint John News" local happenings gave added zest to Ann's newspaper:

"We stop the press at half past twelve to announce the arrival of His Majesty's Brig Thistle in three days from Halifax with one hundred and twenty volunteer seamen for the Lakes in Canada, who are to proceed with all possible expedition, and are to be followed by another division of volunteers in His Majesty's Brig Manly, which is hourly expected."

"Sir George Prevost and his suite arrived from Quebec via Fredericton", and "A salute of nineteen guns greeted His Excellency. At Indian House he was received by a number of the principal inhabitants and was escorted to the house of John Robinson, Esquire, by a detachment of Militia. Next morning His Excellency embarked on His Majesty's Ship Cossac, the Honourable Captain Rodney, for England."

During and after the Revolutionary War, Privateers of all nations swarmed the seas and stories of those wild old days have been handed down for generations. The losses were heavy, but Saint John's seafaring citizens were determined to cope with this outlawry, so they organized a convoy system to protect their shipping. They crowded into Ann Mott's little press room for their meetings and finally this notice appeared in her newspaper:

"All Merchants and Shipowners now in this Town, whether subscribers to this News Room or not are requested to call there this

Evening at five o'clock, when the Memorial to be sent to England on the subject of Convoys will be read, and to secure the object of forwarding it by the Mail this Evening; the Committee hope that every person intending to sign it will punctually attend for that purpose at the above hour."

The petition was successful and soon a staunch armed vessel, the BRUNSWICKER was providing safe convoy to all vessels sailing from the Port of Saint John.

Marine news in Ann's newspaper included arrivals and departures of ships and their passengers and often the story of shipwreck.

"For Liverpool, England", runs one advertisement, "The fine copper bottomed Ship, Theodocia, James Unsworth, Master, having superior accommodations; two or three gentlemen can be accommodated by applying to Messrs. H. Johnston and Son or the Master on board."

The perils of the sea were brought out sharply in these stories. "The Brig Mary Ann, Captain Richards from Bermuda for this Port was unfortunately wrecked on Murr Ledges, near Grand Manan. Captain Richards and his crew arrived here Friday last in a very distressed situation from being severely frost bitten."

"The Schooner Neptune, Captain Magee, has also met a similar fate. She sailed from this Port on the 15th inst. and was driven ashore the same evening on Grand Manan; through stress of weather; fortunately no lives were lost."

Amusements were not overlooked in Ann's newspaper. A Theatre located at Mallard's Inn on King Street offered the Play "The Cure for the Heartache."

Down in Drury Lane, off Prince William Street, another theatre with the high sounding name "Theatre Royal" offered competition with "The Cure for the Heartache", by presenting the "Tragedy of Douglas".

"*THEATRE DRURY LANE*"

"On Tuesday evening of the 15th of August will be performed by Gentlemen of this City, the Tragedy of

DOUGLAS

Men		Women	
Lord Randolph,	Mr. Allan	Lady Randolph,	Mr. Randall
Glenalvon,	Mr. I. Lyster	Anna,	Mr. Ketchum
Norval,	Mr. M'Duff		
Douglas,	Mr. N. Parker		
Officer)	Mr. Watkins		
Servant)			

To conclude with the much admired farce of

Men		Women	
Jeremy Diddler,	Mr. W. Lyster	Miss L. Durable,	Mr. I. Johnson
Sam,	Mr. M'Duff	Peggy,	Mr. Randall
Plainway,	Mr. Watkins		
Fairwould,	Mr. Kerr		
Richard)	Mr. Sutherland		
Walter)			

Tickets may be had at the Bar of the Coffee House on Tuesday at 12 o'clock.
Doors open at ½ past 7, Performance to commence at 8 o'clock.

There was a "Poets Corner" in Ann's *Gazette and New Brunswick Advertiser* and in the August issue she prints the lively rhyme "Lines written by a brewer's daughter on her father's discharging his coachman for getting liquor." With this brief title the verses ramble down the full length of the column with the sorry tale, and conclude with the coachman grumbling:

"'Tis soakers like me whom you load with reproaches,
That enable you Brewers to ride in your coaches."

J. Allen, a Surgeon with the troops of Fort Howe, set up in private practice after the troops were withdrawn from the Fort and broadcast his wares in Ann's paper:

"FRESH DRUGS and MEDICINES,
J. Allen, Surgeon.

Respectfully informs the Public that he has commenced Business in the line of his Profession, and hopes by care and attention to merit a share of the Public patronage. He has received by the late arrivals, now opening at the house of Captain Kennedy fronting on Market Square, a general assortment of Fresh Drugs and Medicines, simple and compound. Also a quantity of the most approved patent medicines in use. Surgical Instruments, viz: Amputating and Trepanning; best and second Lancets; cases pocket Instruments; a large variety of Trusses for Adults and Children, among which are a few on an improved Principle, well worth the attention of Invalids. Scales and Weights. Likewise a quantity of Cinnamon; Nutmegs, Arrow Root; Honey by lb. or bottle; Oil Peppermint; Essence Lemon; Salt Petre in ¼ cwt. boxes; Spices of all kinds and Perfumery. All of which he offers wholesale or retail as low as can be procured here.

Medicine Chests for Sea or Family use, with printed directions, put up or repaired on shortest notice and most reasonable terms.

St. John, 3rd June 1815."

Week after week news of the world of 1815 clattered off Ann

Mott's press in that stuffy little room on Prince William Street. Over the doorway the old wooden sign of the Bible and Crown creaked in the wind. The same wind that brought sailing ships from all over the world to nuzzle their bows against the wharves of the Market Slip just across the street from Ann's shop.

But Ann didn't let the creaking old sign bother her and she was much too busy to watch the ships from the small paned windows of her pressroom. She enjoyed her work and had good reason to be proud of it; with reporting, editing, setting her type and interviewing prospective employees for her subscribers, Ann had few dull moments.

Then came a day when this advertisement appeared in her paper: "Rooms to let. A Genteel Parlour, Two Bedrooms and the use of a Kitchen. For particulars apply at this office."

Ann had decided to sell her newspaper. Later on she went to New York where she lived to celebrate her eighty-seventh birthday. An active little old lady with a keen mind, long memory and grand sense of humor, she must have been an interesting companion to all who knew her.

Closely packed brick buildings edge Prince William Street in Saint John today, and Ann's little Print Shop and the huge "Bible and Crown" sign have long since disappeared. Gone too are the colorful windjammers and their hardy crews that anchored in the Market Slip.

But there remains ample evidence of one woman's enterprise and a link with the past that is only half remembered in the *Gazette and New Brunswick Advertiser* for 1815. Printed on durable greyish-white paper by Ann Mott, pioneer newspaper woman of New Brunswick, they are as legible today as when they first came off the press in Ann's little shop at the sign of the "Bible and Crown" on Prince William Street in Saint John, New Brunswick.

BIBLIOGRAPHY

"Newspapers of New Brunswick" in *Footprints* by J.W. Lawrence.
The Gazette and New Brunswick Advertiser, 1815 Ann Mott.
News, advertisements etc. from the files of *The Gazette and New Brunswick Advertiser*.
Archives Department, New Brunswick Museum, Saint John, N.B.

ABOUT THE AUTHOR

Charlotte Gourlay Robinson was born in 1890 at Saint John, New Brunswick, a busy seaport and rail terminus on the Bay of Fundy that had been populated a hundred years earlier, in 1783, by the arrival of thousands of refugees of the Colonial Revolution — the British Loyalists.

At an early age she became interested in the tales of the people who had come to the Canadian wilderness to establish a new life. She too developed a pioneer spirit and with a practical dedication apprenticed in Pharmacy completing her qualifications at Montreal to become the first New Brunswick woman to do so.

In World War I she served briefly with the RCAMC, but it was mutually concluded that they weren't yet organized to accommodate women Pharmacists in the field, so she returned to Hospital work in Montreal and New York.

Soon after her marriage in 1919 she returned to Saint John and, with her husband established a Pharmacy there which closed following a disastrous fire. The family then moved to the suburbs on the Kennebecasis River where her interests centered primarily on homemaking, along with gardening, church activities, and the Red Cross. She also started to write and had articles and poems published in magazines of the day.

Her interest in historical matters led to many pleasant years of association with the New Brunswick Museum and to active participation in historical and writing societies.

The series of articles contained in this publication were originally prepared in the early 1940's and were broadcast by the CBC. Hopefully the content of perseverance by the pioneer women may have encouraged those of a later generation in World War II days.

Following her husband's death she travelled extensively continually writing and gathering data of historical and current interest.

In many ways Mother was similar to those she had recorded here — intelligent, determined — yes, strong willed, but tender and gracious.

Should a dedication still be in order, and while the book is really about women, I am sure she would have wanted it to be to Dad — "Guy Thomas Robinson".

Undoubtedly, Mother was somewhat ahead of her times as she was both liberated and a lady, so I trust those who read this book will enjoy and appreciate its content.

John F.H. Robinson

Charlotte Gourlay Robinson

Photo by Climo, Saint John, N.B.

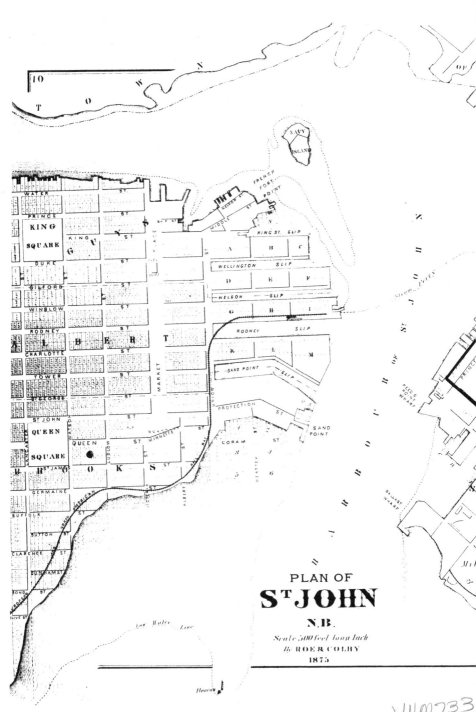

PLAN OF
St JOHN
N.B.
Scale 500 feet to an Inch
By ROE & COLBY
1875